CASTLES AND
STRONGHOLDS OF
NORTHUMBERLAND
A HISTORY · AND GAZETTEER

BRIAN LONG

CASTLES AND
STRONGHOLDS OF
NORTHUMBERLAND
A HISTORY AND GAZETTEER

BRIAN LONG

First published 1967
This edition published 2024

The History Press
97 St George's Place, Cheltenham,
Gloucestershire, GL50 3QB
www.thehistorypress.co.uk

British Library Cataloguing in Publication Data.
A catalogue record for this book is available from the British Library.

ISBN 978 0 7509 9409 5

Typesetting and origination by The History Press.
Printed and bound in Great Britain by TJ Books Limited, Padstow, Cornwall.

MIX
Paper | Supporting
responsible forestry
FSC
www.fsc.org   FSC® C013056

Trees for LYfe

Dedicated to Laura Gatling
Without you this would not have been complete

Alnwick Castle viewed from Robert Adam's Lion Bridge with the famous Percy Lion in the foreground.

Contents

Preface to the Second, Revised and Enlarged Edition

Castles of Northumberland was first published in 1967, to be followed in 1970 by *Shielings and Bastles* by Ramm, McDowall and Mercer. Twenty years later (1990), Peter F. Ryder produced his excellent report *Bastles and Towers* for the Northumberland National Park, all increasing our knowledge and understanding.

Over the years the number of recognisable remains and sites of peles and bastles has grown. My own interest in this field led to many visits and surveys while working for the Forestry Commission in the vast forests of Kielder, Redesdale, Tarset and Wark. I recorded everything from shielings to deserted villages as well as my main interest: the many peles and bastles of the county.

This new edition, *Castles and Strongholds of Northumberland*, is the result of my continuing quest and the accumulated knowledge of numerous historians and archaeologists, to whom we should be grateful.

Brian Long

Chapter I

Being Introductory

Northumberland has more castles, fortalices, towers, peles, bastles and barmkins than any other county in the British Isles. Castles of all periods were the private residences and fortresses of kings and noblemen. The fact that they were private residences was the principal difference between them and their predecessors, the Anglo-Saxon burghs, which were fortified towns, etc., such as were at Heddon, Yeavering and Bamburgh. Their private nature is again the distinguishing factor between them and forts erected at a later date by kings and governments for national defence. The towers, peles, bastles and barmkins were also private residences fortified by small, not so powerful lords, or by rich farmers and land-owners as a means of defending themselves from raiding parties and securing their cattle in times of such raids.

Motte-and-Bailey Castles

Many castle sites are either not known or can only be traced as names on a map or a few green mounds in a field. Indeed, many of these green mounds never had fortifications of stone erected on them and only existed as the motte-and-bailey castles of the Norman invaders, our first castle builders. Whatever the precise plan of a motte-and-bailey castle, the earthworks in themselves were a formidable defence crowned with timber stockades. The outer fringes of these castles, the counter-scarp, on the outside of the ditches of both motte and bailey, also had their bristling defences of pointed stakes set at angles and interwoven brambles.

Motte-and-Bailey Castles with Map References (see Figure 1, p.12)

D.35	Alnwick	F.20	Morpeth
B.18	Bamburgh	H.12	Newcastle
B.1	Berwick	A.2	Norham
E.38	Bellingham	H.8	Prudhoe
G.23	Bellister	D.56	Rothbury
F.40	Bolam	E.55	Simonburn
F.19	Bothal	D.13	South Middleton
H.6	Bywell	H.19	Styford
D.42	Callaly	?	Tiefort[1]
A.12	Carham	D.32	Titlington
E.18	Elsdon	A.1	Tweedmouth
B.2	Fenham	H.14	Tynemouth
D.4	Fowberry	G.53	Warden
E.50	Gunnerton	A.16	Wark on Tweed
G.13	Haltwhistle	E.53	Wark on Tyne
C.15	Harbottle	D.46	Warkworth
D.15	Ilderton	C.5	Wooler
F.21	Mitford		

---

1   *Tiefort:* This castle is mentioned in the *Histoire des Ducs de Normandie*, and has been translated as being either Styford, Tynemouth or Tweedmouth. The only other clue is the date of 1216 when the *Histoire* was written.

Opposite: Four images showing the development of motte-and-bailey castles with the motte at Dinan, the motte-and-bailey at Elsdon, a reconstruction of a motte-and-bailey castle and Warkworth Castle with the later stonework following the original earthworks.

The sketch of the motte at Dinan is based on the Bayeux Tapestry and shows a timber keep surmounting an earthen mound with a moat. Elsdon Castle is shown in this old drawing with a bold motte and a larger but lower bailey with no trace of the timber castle that must have capped them. A complete motte-and-bailey castle with moated motte-and-bailey is shown with a shell keep on the motte and great hall and other offices in the bailey, all of timber construction.

ELSDON CASTLE AND TOWER

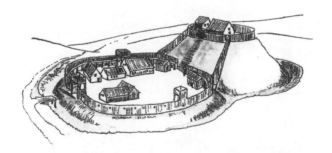

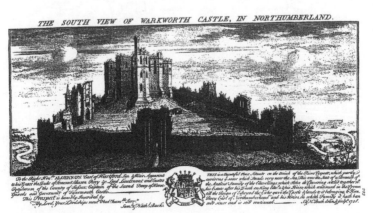

THE SOUTH VIEW OF WARKWORTH CASTLE, IN NORTHUMBERLAND.

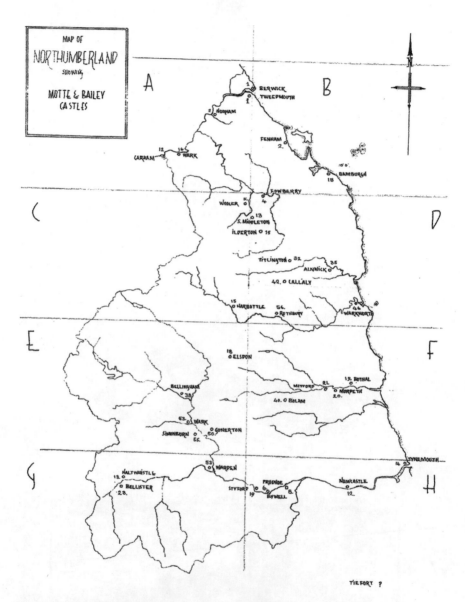

Figure 1: Map of Northumberland showing the distribution of motte-and-bailey castles in the county.

Castles of Northumberland

Upon the summit of the motte or mound, within the stockade, usually rose a wooden tower, which was the residence of the lord and the ultimate stronghold and vantage point of the castle by reason of its superior height.

The exact time and place or origin of this type of fortification is unknown. A castle of this type was mentioned for the first time in AD 1010 and stood on the banks of the Loire in France. It was built by a man skilled in military affairs whose name was Fulk Nerra. He was also the first man to employ mercenary soldiers. It cannot be denied that a motte is a fortress for a man who wishes to defend his family and close friends from all would-be enemies, whether other lords or his own rebellious retainers. Whatever its origin, the motte was in wide use in Normandy before William conquered England.

The tower on the motte was not always a crude and uncomfortable lodging on stilts as stood at Durham in the castle of Prior Laurence: 'Four posts are plain, on which it rests, one post at each strong corner.' Many were comfortable tower houses, as described by Lambert of Ardres in 1117:

> Arnold, Lord of Ardres, built on the motte of Ardres a wooden house, excelling all the houses of Flanders of that period both in material and in carpenters' work. The first storey was on the surface of the ground, where were cellars and granaries, and great boxes, tubs, casks and other domestic utensils. In the storey above were the dwelling and common living rooms of the residents, in which were the larders, the rooms of the bakers and butlers, and the great chamber in which the lord and his wife slept.
>
> Adjoining this was the private room, the dormitory of the waiting maids and children. In the inner part of the great chamber was a certain private room, where at early dawn, or in the evening, or during sickness, or at time of bloodletting, or for warming the maids and weaned children, they used to have a fire … In the upper storey of the house were garret rooms, in which on the one side the sons (when they wished it) and on the other side, the daughters (because they were obliged) of the lord of the house used to sleep. In this storey the watchmen and servants appointed to keep the house also took their sleep at some time or other. High up on the east side of the house in a convenient place was the chapel, which was designed to resemble the tabernacle of Solomon in its ceiling and painting. There were stairs and passages from storey to storey, from the house into the kitchen, from room to room and again from the house into the loggia, where they used to sit in conversation for recreation, and again from the loggia into the oratory.

It may be noted that neither the Bayeux Tapestry, nor indeed many of the contemporary accounts, mention or show the bailey. It should not be deduced from these facts that in most castles the bailey did not exist, but it should be taken as an implication of the immense importance of the motte both militarily and socially. The bailey must have been essential for stables, barns, smithies and affording shelter for the garrison and its supplies in most, if not all, of the early Norman strongholds.

As mentioned above, the Bayeux Tapestry shows several of these castles with their towers on the motte and bridges in position. The pictures of the siege of the castle at Dinan shows just how vulnerable they were when fire was used. There can be little doubt that the walls were hung with wet hides to prevent them catching fire. One of the many tragedies that must have overtaken these houses and their besieged occupants happened in 1190 when the Jews of York were attacked by a mob and had taken refuge in the motte, and many of them perished when it was fired.

Motte-and-bailey castles were cheap and quick to build but a castle of importance required more permanent defences, and as timber in contact with damp soil rots quickly, the second build of such a castle would at least be on stone sleeper walls if not entirely rebuilt in stone when circumstances allowed. It was at this time that many sites were abandoned in favour of stronger and healthier sites. Elsdon Castle, the best motte-and-bailey in Northumberland, never had stonework built on it as the occupants moved out when the timber decayed. The remaining mounds, known as the Moat Hills, are worthy of inspection.

The next step in castle building came about by a change of materials rather than tactics, and the keep-and-bailey castle came into being. The keep, normally, was a large square stone structure taking the place of the motte, or incorporating it in its own defences, as at Warkworth. The plans of these castles were the same as those of timber, though as the first urgency of the conquest declined and the lords began to seek the comfort and safety of stone, quite a number of the original sites were abandoned, as was Elsdon, for safer and more suitable ones.

The main gate, the most vulnerable point of the bailey, was the first to be strengthened by a stone tower. A strong square tower, beneath which ran the entrance passage, would be built. Then came the bailey walls enclosing the site; this enabled the occupants to work in safety on the keep and other offices. Norman ramparts can still be seen under the successive layers of stonework of nearly every period at Alnwick, Warkworth, Morpeth, Mitford and Norham. As mentioned above, keeps were normally large square structures, as at Newcastle, Norham, Bamburgh and Prudhoe. The normal arrangements in these large towers or keeps can be seen to advantage at Newcastle. It is obvious that much in the way of comfort was sacrificed, but in days of peace there would be other more comfortable lodgings in the bailey. Because of their weight, great towers and keeps were seldom placed on the earlier mounds as at Warkworth. To replace the security offered by the height of the motte, the entrance to the later stone keeps was often on the first- or even the second-floor level and housed by a forebuilding.

Bamburgh, built on its rock, was so inaccessible as to be safe with its entrance on the ground floor, or so the builders thought. No two keeps are exactly the same, but all are similar in many respects, internally and externally. They have shallow but- tresses in the centre of each side and at the corners. The corner ones often terminate in small angle turrets, but the bases of all of them are splayed. The walls were of great height so as to protect the high-pitched roof from fire arrows. In some castles, such as Warkworth, the keep was so large and of such excellent design that it may have been in general use and at least would have been much more comfortable than most.

Shell Keeps

The keep was the strongest point of the castle and had to be a self-sufficient unit capable of separate and successful defence. The simplest form of keep, placed upon the motte, its stonework following the line of the timber stockade, was known as a shell keep. Within this strong enclosure, the timber tower house was replaced by strong buildings either for the residence of the lord or the defence of the keep. Like the buildings in the bailey, they were ranged against the inside of the wall so that the centre of the enclosure was left free. Castles in Northumberland with a shell keep include Alnwick, Mitford and Wark on Tweed.

There are traces of the buildings that once lined the walls of the keep at Mitford but in the thirteenth century they were removed to make way for a five- sided tower that stood in the centre of it, almost filling it.

Sieges

Few methods of siege warfare could be used against the massive keeps but keeps and bailey walls were all vulnerable to mining. A passage or sap would be driven under the walls or across the corner of a keep and the walls supported by timber frames. When the passage was complete, a fire would be lit in it to destroy the supports and so bring down the wall, exposing the defenders. A sap of this kind was found at Bungay in Suffolk but seems to have been built or engineered by the occupants so as to destroy the castle in case of surrender.

To counter this threat, as previously mentioned, the corners of keeps had but- tresses that projected from the wall almost like small towers. In some cases, as at Warkworth, towers were built projecting from the centre of each face so as to cover the walls. The bases of square keeps were splayed to prevent the sappers

ALNWICK CASTLE
SHELL KEEP Brian Long 75

The shell keep at Alnwick Castle with a small central courtyard and building of many periods and styles forming the outer wall (the shell).

from coming into contact with the actual wall. This also had the advantage that missiles dropped from above would bounce off its surface at unpredictable angles into the shelters used by the sappers. The keep at Newcastle has a widely splayed base. During the religious wars (First Crusade, 1096) in the Near East, the knights noticed how walls were protected by projecting towers at intervals along their outer face, and they had to turn to such weapons as the ballista, trebuchet and belfry. When they came home, they in turn defended their castles against these weapons.

To break into such a castle, the moat first had to be filled in under the cover of bows and stone-throwing machines to enable the sappers to reach the base of the wall; once at the foot of the wall, this had to be breached by one of a number of methods such as sapping, or crossed by the use of the belfry (a high wooden mobile tower), which was pushed up to the wall. To combat this problem, the defenders built higher walls to prevent the use of scaling ladders and the belfry. Now all that remained was to protect the berm, or space immediately in front of the wall, since this was the spot attacked by sappers. One device was the brattice or hoarding, a covered wooden gallery built out from the top of the wall supported on horizontal wooden brackets. The holes for these timber supports can be seen in the south wall at Warkworth. These galleries had holes in their floors, through which missiles could be dropped on to attackers.

The gatehouses of Newcastle and Warkworth are other results of these observations during the Crusades. The towers on the gatehouse at Warkworth are polygonal, while those at Newcastle are semicircular. Of the older, Norman gates, the only ones remaining are those to the shell keep at Alnwick, and the gates of the outer baileys of Prudhoe and Norham.

Gatehouses

The castles of Edward I in Wales, with no keeps but large gate towers, were never completely copied by the Northumbrians of the time, and the greatest achievement in that field was Dunstanburgh. Work at Dunstanburgh began in 1314 and it had no other keep except the gatehouse. Other examples of the gatehouse keeps are Bothal, Tynemouth and Bywell of a later date. The disadvantage of this arrangement was that the gatehouse was the first line of attack and the last resort of the holders who must live in the midst of the battle because there was no other lodging strong enough included with the castle walls. John of Gaunt closed the gate at Dunstanburgh and built a complicated barbican at the side leading to a gate a little distance away. Other castles with barbicans added to their gates were Tynemouth, Prudhoe and Alnwick, which also had a barbican to the shell keep. With the uniting of the crowns, peace came to the border and castles were abandoned for the more comfortable houses of the type that the south of England had enjoyed for the past two centuries.

Houses

The plans of the houses of the period were remarkably uniform, whether large or small, castle or hall. The main feature was the hall. Halls could be on the ground floor or raised on a cellar and approached by steps and open to the rafters. At one end was the dais where the lord and his family ate. Others ate and slept in the marsh, the area of the hall below the dais. In the early days an open hearth would blaze in the centre of the floor, the smoke escaping where it could. At the other end of the hall was a screen, behind which were the entrance doors and the doors leading to the buttery and pantry. Above the screen was a gallery or room.

The solar, or private room, was at the same end as the dais and was reached through a door behind the dais. Other rooms and a chapel were added where the site would permit. Hall houses were built in the thirteenth century but they had to be strengthened and fortified at a later, not quite so peaceful, date. Of outstanding interest is Haughton Castle, which under fourteenth-century fortifications hides a large hall house of the 'palas' type. Remains of a smaller house can be seen at Heaton and are known as King John's Palace. Another house forms part of Featherstone Castle.

Of fortified manor houses, by then becoming very popular in the south, Northumberland can boast one of the earliest examples: Aydon Castle, a very extensive house in a well-defended position above the Cor Burn, which winds round three sides, with very steep banks up to the house. The castle, or house, had no keep or even strong towers to protect its curtain wall. Edlingham consisted of a rather fine hall house but unlike Aydon had a keep attached at a later date.

The *OED* on Peles, Peels or Vicars' Peles

If you can't find 'pele' in your edition of the *Oxford English Dictionary*, just move on to 'peel', where they say that in early usage it was a pale or stake. Later it was a palisade formed using pales or stakes, or even a moated enclosure or small castle.

They go on to say that modern writers use 'peel' to describe a massive square tower or fortified dwelling occupied by sixteenth-century borderers as a defence against forays. The result is a tendency to call all towers large or small pele towers, be they the houses of local headsmen, the mansion of the vicarage or home to other person of standing. Hidden in this changing interpretation is the present belief that early peles consisted of moated sites with a timber palisade and houses set within their own small island enclosure.

The *OED* does not mention vicars' peles but I read into the above that the later peles or towers were built using stone, with some having a barmkin or stockade of stone built around them.

This resulted in what I consider correct: that only towers with an enclosure in which they stood can correctly be termed as pele towers; that is, a tower within a palisade, a stockade or a barmkin.

Towers

Such houses as Aydon were not to be the rule, however, as strife was almost continuous in the border counties during the fourteenth and fifteenth centuries, and towers were still being erected in the late sixteenth or early seventeenth century. Most of these towers were of the same design as the square keeps of the Normans, regardless of the period in which they were built, and observers may find them difficult to date. Many churches had towers either built for defence or as places of refuge in time of war. Churches with such towers are Ancroft and Edlingham. Towers were also built at Carham and Farne.

List of Towers (see Figure 2, p.22)

Abberwick	D	Burnbank (Bought Hill)	E
Acton	D	Burradon (Coquetdale)	C
Adderstone	B	Burradon (N. Tyneside)	F
Akeld	C		
Alnham Vic	C	Callaly	D
Alnwick (St Mary's)	D	Caraw	E
Alwinton Vic	C	Carham	A
Ancroft Vic	B	Causey Park	F
Antichester	C	Charlton (South) Vic	D
		Chatton	D
Bamburgh Vic	B	Chatton Vic	D
Barrow Bavington	E	Cheswick	B
Beadnell	D	Chipchase	E
Beaufront	G	Chollerton	E
Bebside	F	Choppington	F
Bedlington	F	Clennell	C
Belford	B	Cocklaw	E
Belsay	F	Cocklepark	F
Benwell	H	Coldmartin	D
Berrington	B	Corbridge Vic	H
Bewick	D	Cornhill	A
Biddlestone	C	Cotewalls	C
Birks	E	Coquet Island	D
Birtley	E	Coupland	A
Bitchfield	F	Craster	D
Blanchland	G	Crawley	D
Blenkinsop	G	Cresswell	F
Bolam	F		
Bolt House Vic	F	Dally	E
Branxton	A	Darques	E
Buckton	B	Detchant	B
		Dilston	G

Downham	A	Hedgeley	D
Duddo	A	Hefferlaw	D
Dunstan	D	Hepple	C
		Hepscott	F
East Shaftoe Hall (Belso)	F	Hesleyside	E
Earle	C	Hethpool	C
East Ditchburn	D	Heton	B
East Woodburn	E	Hobberlaw	D
Edlingham Vic	D	Holburn	B
Elliburn	F	Hoppen	B
Ellishaw	E	Howick	D
Elsdon Vic	E	Howtel	A
Elswick	H	Hulne Abbey	D
Elwick	B	Humbleton	C
Embleton Vic	D		
Eslington	D	Ilderton	D
		Ingram	D
Fairnley	F		
Fallowlees	F	Kilham	A
Falstone	E	Kirkharle	F
Farnham	C	Kirkley	F
Farne Island	B	Kirknewton	C
Featherstone	G	Kirkwhelpington Vic	F
Fenham	B	Kyloe	B
Fenton	A		
Fenwick	F	Lanton	A
Ford Vic	A	Lemington	D
Fowberry	D	Little Bavington	E
		Little Harle	F
Goswick	B	Little Haughton	D
Great Ryal	D	Little Swinburn	E
Great Swinburn	E	Long Haughton Vic	D
Great Tosson	D	Longhorsley	F
Green Leighton	F	Lowick	B
Grindon Rigg	A	Low Trewitt	D
Gunnerton	E		
		Meldon	F
Halton	H	Middleton (Bamburgh)	B
Haltwhistle	G	Middleton Hall	D
Harnham	F	Mindrum	A
Harterburn	F	Morpeth	F
Hartington	F		
Hazelrigg	B	Nafferton	H
Healey	H	Nesbit	A
Heaton	H	Nether Trewhyt (Low Trewitt)	D
Heaton (Old Heaton) Castle	A	Netherwitton (High Bush)	F
Hebburn (Hepburn)	D	Newbiggin	A

Newbrough	G	Simonburn Vic	E
Newburn	H	South Charlton Vic	D
Newlands	B	Stamfordham	F
Newstead	D	Stanton	F
Newton Hall	H	Starward	G
Newton Underwood	F	Swinburn	E
Newtown	D		
Ninebanks	G	Thirlwall	G
North Middleton	F	Thornton (Newbrough)	G
North Sunderland	B	Thornton (Thornebie)	A
Nunnykirk	F	Thropton	D
		Tillmouth	A
Old Bewick (Bewick)	D	Titlington	D
Otterburn	E	Togstone	D
Overgrass	D	Tosson	D
		Troughend	E
Paston	A	Tweedmouth	A
Ponteland Vic	F	Twizell	A
Portgate	G		
Preston	D	Wallington	F
Prendwick	D	Walltown	G
		Walwick	E
Ritton White House	F	Weetslade	F
Rock Hall	D	Weetwood	D
Roddam	D	Welton	H
Roseden (Ilderton)	D	West Lilburn	D
Rothley	F	West Thornton	F
Ryal	F	West Whelpington	
		(Kirkwhelpinton)	F
Saint Margarets (Alnwick)	D	Whalton Vic (Rothbury)	F
Scremerston	B	Whitlow	G
Seaton Delaval	F	Whitton Vic	D
Seghill	F	Whittingham Vic	D
Settlingstones	G	Widdrington	F
Sewingshields	E	Witton Shield	F
Shawdon	D	Wooler	C
Shield Hall	G	Wylam	H
Shilbottle Vic	D		
Shoreswood	A	Yeavering	A
Shortflat	F		

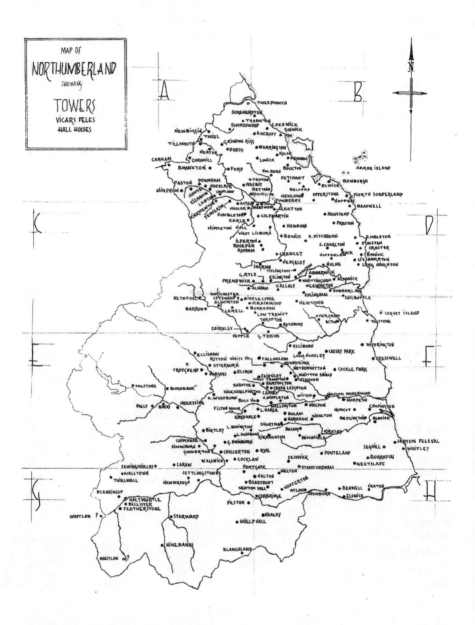

Figure 2: Map of Northumberland showing the distribution of towers, vicars' peles and hall houses. Towers were the most numerous type of fortified house in the county.

Chapter II

Definitions

If the development of any one building is to be fully understood, it is important that the terms fortalice, tower, pele, bastle and barmkin are interpreted correctly.

Fortalice

A fortalice is a small castle or large tower or group of towers. Horton, by the sea, was described as a fortalice in 1415 and had double moats, but at Detchant and Swinburn no moat can be traced. These are not easy buildings to identify and documentary evidence is the only accurate method of classifying them. The list of 1415 mentions the castles of 'Horton, Blenkensope, Swinburne, Dichant and Kippitheton', but in the margin their status was corrected to that of 'Fortalicium'. 'Fflotwayton, Harnhamhall and Shortflate' were the only buildings termed 'Fortalicium' prior to the marginal corrections. In 1541 Horton and Swinburn were called 'great towers' and held a garrison of 100, while 'good towers' held only fifty. Could it be that fortalice was a 'great' or large tower or group of towers, such as Etal and Ford, being capable of holding 100 men?

Buildings Listed as a 'Fortalice' in the Survey of 1415

Horten Iuxta Mare – licence to crenellate 1292
Shortflate – licence to crenellate 1305
Blenkensop – licence to crenellate 1340
Swinburn
Dichant
Kippitheten
Harnhamhall

At least three of these houses listed as being a fortalice in the 1415 survey are known to have a licence to crenellate. The others, also listed as fortalices, have no known licence but the surveyors evidently saw them as being of the same status.

Tower

There are more towers in Northumberland than any other form of fortification and they vary a great deal, more in size and plan than the peles and bastles. As a rule, the main block of a tower was rectangular, but this could be changed to an L or T shape by entrance towers or other offices. Entrance towers were often carried above the battlements, which all towers had, and gave access to them as well as giving the entrance the cover of crossfire. Just like the Norman square keeps, many towers had their entrances on the first floor. Most towers and some peles and bastles had vaulted basements, which were used as byres or store rooms. Some towers even had vaults on the first and second floors. For extra protection many towers and bastles stood within a barmkin.

When the crowns united, some towers were made into houses and halls such as had been in the south of England for more than 200 years. Comfortable apartments were built, as a wing, on to many, and it was at this stage that some were wrongly termed castles, the wings in some cases being built as sham castles. The barmkins were made into pleasure gardens. See p.19 for a note on pele towers.

Barmkin

A barmkin is a yard or open space girt by a high wall that could be used to protect livestock and owners alike in time of strife. Towers and bastles often stood within a barmkin, but it was also a perfectly independent fortification, as can be seen from the following:

Acts of Parliament for Scotland 1535

> … every landed man dwelling on or near the border having land worth £100 a year shall build a barmkin upon his land in a place most convenient and of stone and lime. The area of the barmkin should be three score square feet and the wall should be one ell thick and six ells high [one ell = 34½ft] and it should be used by the tenants and their goods in time of strife. If he wishes, the owner can build a tower within the barmkin for his own safety.

All other landed gentry of smaller income should build peles and great strengths as they please for the safety and protection of themselves, their tenants and their goods …

The survey of 1541 uses the term in the same way: 'The descripc'on of the p'sent state of all the castells towers Barmekyns and other fortresses standinge and scytuate nere unto the utter border.' The same document gives plans for the building of:

Barmekyns aboute every towre … Avoydinge of xcessyve costs such towers and fortresses as be in the same precyncte begonne to be buylded may be finished and lykewyse where there remayneth standyne a parte of anye fortresse which hath bene before tyme rased or decayed the same to be newly reedified and repared wth Barmekyns about every towre.

In 1544 a report from the English Wardens of the Marches to Henry VIII gave an account of 'forrays' into the counties of Berwick and Roxburgh.

Sir Robert Bowes, writing on the 'State of the frontiers and marches' in 1550, informs us that:

If there were there made a stronge towre wth stables bynethe and lodgings above after the fashion of Roclyf [Carlisle] My Lord Dacres house upon the west borders able to conteigne many men and horses and in circuyte about it a large barmekyn or fortylage for save garde of cattle whiche might easely in that place have water in a ditche rownde aboute.

Barmkin, Barmekyn, Barnekyn

The small traditional pele, the home of poor farmers. These farmers, or the 'landed gentry of smaller income' were permitted to 'build peles and great strengths as they please for the safety and protection of themselves, their tenants and their goods.' Men with land worth £100 a year were to build a barmkin of stone and lime. This hints at the fact that barmkins could be constructed using stout timbers. In 1541 Ilderton had a 'strong barmkin of stone' as against other material. Pele owners could not afford an expensive barmkin and what stock they had would be secured in night folds or, with smaller animals, in the basement of their pele. The Carnaby drawing of Haughton shows and gives the dimensions of the barmkin there.

The following barmkins are mentioned in the survey of 1541, which reported that a ward within the ruinous Wark Castle 'serveth as a barmkin', while it was noted that Carham, Paston, Akeld, Earle, Branxton, Ruddam and Chatton were, to

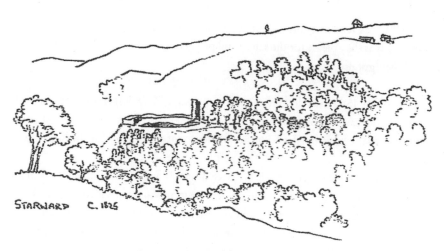

STARWARD C. 1825

STARWARD WITH REMAINS OF BARMKIN - 1825

This image is a copy from an old sketch showing the remains of a ruined barmkin at Starward Pele as in 1825.

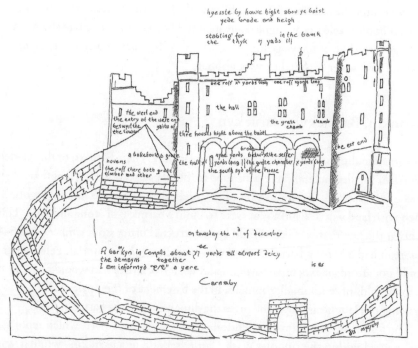

Haughton Castle from a drawing of 1595 shows the barmkin wall in poor condition. The original sketch was annotated and the little I could decipher is shown.

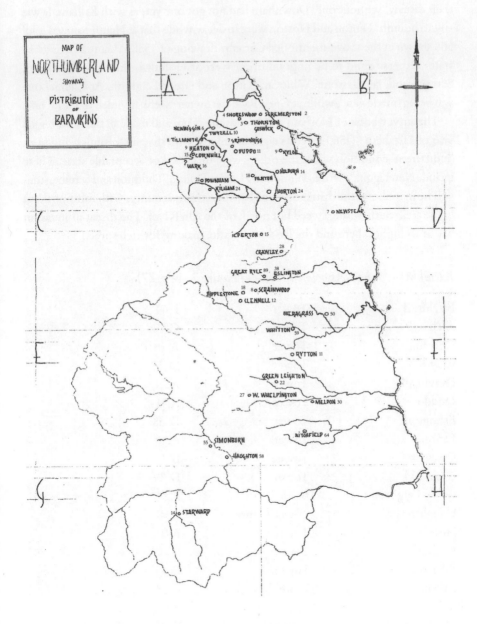

Figure 3: Map of Northumberland showing the distribution of barmkins, with most being on the most fertile land to the north of the county.

their dismay, without one. Downham had not got one yet; as with Kilham, it was still to be built. Fenton and Horton were in decay while that at Haughton was 'old' and shown in the above-mentioned Carnaby drawing of 1538 as being in a reduced state. Others found to be in good order were at Holburn, Ilderton, Eslington, Screenwood, Biddlestone, Whitton, Ritton and Green Leighton. At Clennel one was being 'made new', while at Great Ryle the owners were 'mynded to build' one.

The survey book of Norham and Islandshire taken and made in the third regnal year of Elizabeth I (1560–61) lists eight barmkins, with that at Cornhill being in an 'indifferent' condition while the others were in a good or acceptable state. These include Newbiggin, Twizel, Tillmouth, Heaton, Duddo, Thornton and Scremerston.

The map shows the distribution of barmkins in the county, with most of them in the area south of the Tweed but north of the Aln River. The threat of invasion was at its highest here and the land was fertile, making for rich spoils.

Barmkins and their Associated Houses (Figure 3, see p.27)

Bitchfield	Tower	F.64
Clennell	Tower	C.12
Cornhill	Tower	A.15
Crawley	Tower	D.28
Downham	Tower	A.21
Duddo	Tower	A.11
Eslington	Tower	D.38
Fenton	Tower	A.18
Goswick	Tower	B.4
Great Ryle	Tower	D.39
Green Leighton	Bastle	F.24
Haughton	Tower House	E.58
Heaton	Tower	A.9
Holburn	Tower	B.14
Ilderton	Tower	D.15
Kilham	Tower	A.24
Kyloe	Tower	B.9
Meldon	Tower	F.30
Newstead	Tower	D.7
Overgrass	Tower	D.50
Ritton (Rytton)	Tower House	F.11
Scrainwood	Tower	C.8
Scremerston	Tower	B.2

Shoreswood	Tower	A.4
Simonburn	Tower	E.55
Starward	Tower	G.14
Thornton (Thornbye)	Tower	A.3
Tillmouth	Tower	A.8
West Whelpington	Tower	E.27
Whitton (Rothbury)	Tower	D.59

Barmkins, Barmekyns, Barnekyns as Listed in Contemporary Surveys

1. Wark Castle – the utter most ward s'veth for a barmekyn
2. Kilham – a new tower and barmekyn be made
3. Fenton – a great tower wth a barmekyn
4. Horton – a great tower wth a barmekyn
5. Holburne – a tower and a barmekyn
6. Ilderton – a great tower wth a strong barmekyn
7. Roddome – a little tower wthout a barmekyn
8. Eslyngton – a tower wth a barmekyn
9. Great Ryle – mynded to buylde likewise a barmekyn
10. Screnwood – a tower and a barmekyn
11. Byttylsden – a tower and a barmekyn
12. Clennel – making a newe barmekyn
13. Whytton – a tower and a lytle barmekyn
14. Rytton – a stone house and a lytle barmekyn
15. Greenlighton – a lytle stone house wth a barmekyn
16. Haughton – an olde barmekyn p'tely decayed
17. Newbiging – a good barnkin
18. Twizell – a barnkin
19. Tilmouth – A little tower or pile – a little barnekin
20. Cornhyle – one tore, or pile with a barnekin about the same
21. Heton – a barnek
22. Duddo – one barnekin
23. Thorton – a barnkin
24. Scremerston – good towre with a barnekin
25. West Whelpington

Barmkins were not as numerous as the surveyors wished: they noted that Carrame, Downham, Pawston, Akeld, Yerdle, Brankstone, Chatton and Roddome were without.

Haughton 'castle' in the drawing of 1538 shows the front elevation of the house and gives dimensions not only of the house but the barmkin as well, showing it to be 'olde' and 'p'tely decayed'. First mentioned in 1327, the site is stunning and impregnable, being a tongue of rock protected by a gatehouse in the barmkin wall, then at the far side of the yard the remains of the house or 'pele' of rather fine masonry for a house classified as a pele.

The small traditional pele, the home of lowly hill farmers, did not include an expensive barmkin as what stock they had would be housed in the basement 'byre' in troubled times. A number of peles had night folds associated with them to shield their cattle. There is a school of thought that cattle were turned loose in the deep, wooded cleughs, the thinking being that they would be more difficult to round up and drive off than animals in a fold.

What the map shows is that barmekins were built in areas where the land was more productive, with most being on the richer land to the north of the county. The surveys used to plot these barmkins are that of 1541 and that of Norham and Islandshire of the third year of Elizabeth I, 1560–61.

The *OED* on Barmkins

The *OED* says that 'barmkine' or 'barmekin' is a corruption of 'barbican', an outer fortification of a castle. This may help us to understand the pele and barmkin that stands between the double moats around Prudhoe Castle. The term is to be found applied to earthworks topping prominent hills up the eastern side of Scotland, as in the case of the barmkin at Easter Culfosie, Aberdeenshire. Other similar earthworks are known as peles, with a good example to be found at Lumphanan, also in Aberdeenshire.

Vicars' Peles

Old surveys describe them all as being the 'mansion of the vyccaredge' or 'the mansion house of the p'sonage', be they large or small. This group of houses ranges from the basic small, free-standing tower or a 'panic room' built on to one end of the church at one end of the scale, to much more comfortable, more complicated, houses – even mansions – at the other.

Those at Ancroft, South Charlton and Edlingham saved the vicar considerable expense by using stout walls of the church as the basement of a small tower.

Alwinton's 'mansions of the vycaredge' were strongly described as a 'lytle bastell' house of stone (as against one of wooden construction), then at another time it was 'a pile builded to the end of the church'. Another surveyor described it as a 'lytle fortresse'.

The 'mansion of the vycaredge' at Whitton, Rothbury, is a rather fine tower and even had a 'lytle barmekin', an unusual feature for this group of houses. While not built on the scale of Whitton or Elsdon, perhaps the finest for its time was the vicar's pele at Corbridge. It had some interesting domestic detail of this period, being built around 1300. The most comfortable abodes were the houses at Ponteland, Whalton and Embleton, which consisted of a rather fine domestic range with a more secure bolt hole in the form of a secure solar tower incorporated in the layout. Embleton is a gem of a house, being mostly the work of John Dobson (1828). The tower started life in the fourteenth century as a wing of a larger building but towards the end of the century it was made more secure with the addition of corbelled out battlements and a simple cap-house to cover the top of the stair that gave access to the parapet walk.

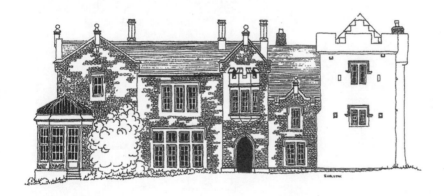

Embleton (*above*): The fine house by John Dobson was built in 1828 and hides or replaces a much older vicarage with the only ancient part left being the small solar tower. These small towers were built on the end of the church and we can imagine the parishoners with their valuables and even livestock huddled in the body of the church. Just to emphasise that all vicarages were not fine houses, that at Ancroft (*left*) was built on top of the west end of the church.

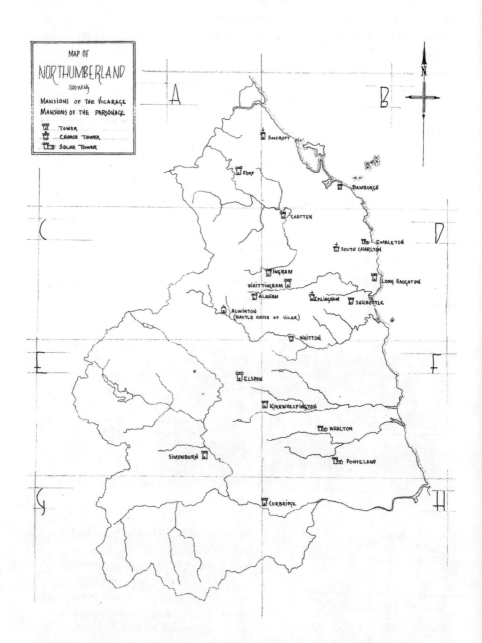

Figure 4: Map of Northumberland showing the distribution of towers designated 'Mansion of the Vicarage', 'Mansions of the Parsonage' (vicars' peles) and solar towers.

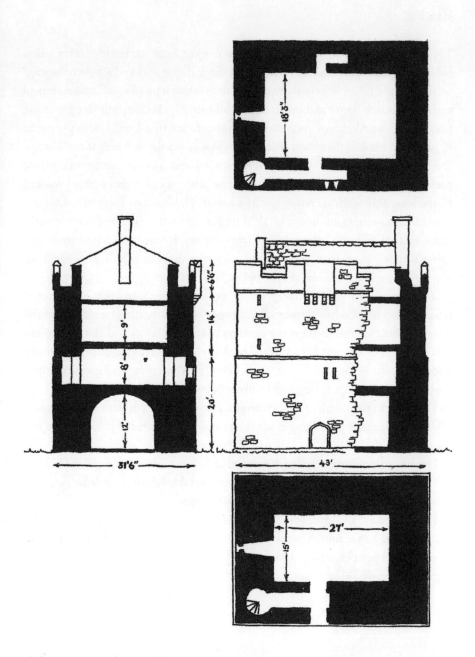

Elsdon Tower was home of the vicars and once the heart of the largest parish in the county, described by a poet as 'the world's 'unfinished neuwk'. The Rev. C. Dodgson recorded how he endured a three-year stint living in the tower.

Bastles

This group of houses for the most part are what some authorities term peles, both being small stone houses with a first-floor living area and a byre or storage on the ground floor. Where there is a problem is that a number of houses termed bastles are much larger and much more comfortable. Included in this group are houses such as Akeld, of such size and importance that Lord Dacre proposed to place ten men in the tower under John Wallis for the defence of the border. Doddington was a later building built in 1584 and incorporated much of the prevailing domestic architecture of the time with an embattled parapet walling to the long side walls. Starting life as a tower, Hebburn or Hepburn was later converted to a mansion house in 1564 with extensions. Bellister was termed a bastle in 1541 and, while remains are fragmentary, it was a hall house with later tower situated on an artificially scarped hill with a moat or a ditch, once again not a bastle of the Black Middings type (see p. 143).

These houses are either 'strong houses' or hall houses, a group much removed from the home of a hill farmer of the type we term bastle or pele. From the outside, this type of house is the same as Black Middings and Gatehouse but this hides the fact that it has a vaulted roof to the basement, resulting in a much stronger house. This vaulted basement belongs to one of a small group of similar houses, being much larger than most peles/bastles in the county and only to be found in the north. Even without a vaulted basement, this style of house offers greater comfort, having three floors and a battlemented gable on one end for security.

Hebburn (Hepburn) bastle is recorded as a tower in the surveys of 1415 and 1541, it was converted into a much more comfortable house, a bastle far removed from the houses at Gatehouse and Black Middings.

Even in ruins, Doddington bastle exhibits a departure from the basic pele/bastle and the larger towers in the greater comfort of its plan. Built in 1584, it had an embattled parapet, a ridged roof and a projecting turret housing the staircase. Bart Milburn would be so envious.

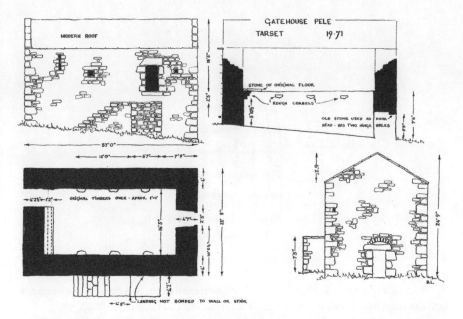

Gatehouse Pele or Bastle is shown here by a plan, section and elevations to be typical of the type found in the upland areas to the west of the county such as the North Tyne, Redesdale and Coquetdale. My drawing was made at the time when the roof was intact and the stumps of the original roof timbers still existed. Along with Black Middings (*below*), these are the most usual type of pele/bastle to be found in the county.

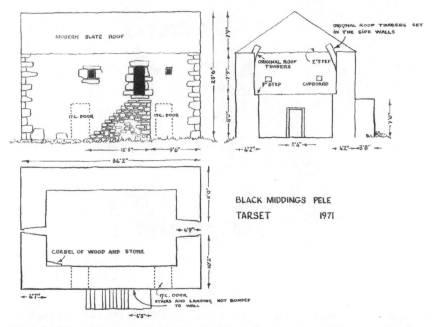

Black Middings Pele or Bastle is shown here by a plan, section and elevation. Similar in design to that of Gatehouse Pele or Bastle (*top*).

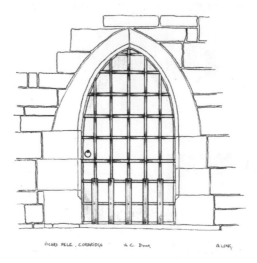

The best example of a vicar's pele of the late fourteenth century is the small tower built into the churchyard wall at Corbridge. It was restored and reroofed in 1910.

'Hirst Castle' or Low Hirst, Ashington, was a comfortable house known by the locals as 'the castle' but actually it was a strong house far superior to any pele.

Pele or Bastle? A Problem of Nomenclature

> There is no clear warrant from ancient usage for the choice of the term bastle
> to describe buildings known as peles.
>
> H.G. Ramm, R.N. McDowall and E. Mercer, *Shielings and Bastles*, 1970

Or vice versa. These are the most used and misused of terms. The medieval use
of the term 'pele' meant a position or place of great strength, made of timber
and earth. These houses must have looked like the circular huts of past ages,
and indeed the Celtic name for a fort was a pill. Some houses that later became
towers and even castles were once peles.

Peles

The ground floor of a typical pele consisted of a large store room or byre 23ft by
36ft externally on average, with walls 4ft to 5ft thick. In most cases, the entrance
was in one of the 23ft gable ends and was never very large. Some were only 2ft
3in wide and so low that one had to stoop to enter, which begs the question as
to how large the animals were that they kept there. The door was bolted on the
inside with stout oak timbers as much as 5in to 6in thick, which could slide back-
wards and forwards in the thickness of the wall. Some owners did not trust the
strength of one stout bolt and so incorporated two in their plan. Others even had
two doors, one behind the other, each secured by the above bolts.

Once safe behind locked doors you were anything but comfortable, and
usually the only light came from a small slit or window in the wall at the opposite
end of the room from the door, although some peles had other windows or vents.
It is possible that a small glimmer of light came from the trapdoor in the ceiling
above but this is doubtful. This dark, dank room was used to store the essential
supplies to survive a harsh winter. In some houses the height of the room could
be divided into two floors by the insertion of a temporary floor or shelf on which
dry goods could be stored. The put holes for the stout beams that carried this
floor are still to be found in a few houses.

Above this storage area were the living quarters of the owner, which could
be reached by a trapdoor and ladder from the basement or an outside stair. The
upper room was only a little larger than the basement but had more and larger
windows, especially in one of the long side walls and the side that incorporated
the upper door and external stair. This stair is a prominent feature in a few
remaining peles and is interesting in that it seems to have been a later refinement. A gatehouse was built over a ground-floor window. I do not know of

any remaining stair of this type that is bonded to the main wall and therefore contemporary with the original building. This would suggest that originally a retractable wooden ladder would be used and only dispensed with at a later date. This later date was not necessarily a much safer one, as an interesting and strange thing is that the landings or stair heads are always lower than the threshold of the entrance they serve. This meant that any would-be aggressor was at a disadvantage if the occupant came to the door, standing at a more advantageous elevation for the defence of his home. If it was decided that a fire would open the door then the low landing again meant that a lot of combustible material had to be carried in several trips up and down the stairs to build a fire large enough to burn even the threshold. Adding to the difficulties, the windows of the upper apartments were so arranged that at least one window was over the foot of the stair, enabling the defence of the same from within.

This large room was the all-purpose living area of the pele, perhaps being subdivided by wooden-framed partitions into kitchen, work area and a bedroom. No fireplace was included in the early houses and therefore no chimney was provided in the thickness of any of the walls. One rather fine pele, the Hole, has remains of wattle and daub partitions on the first floor and a delightful simple stair to a group of small rooms in a loft but this was by no means general practice, being for the most part an afterthought, and even the first-floor fireplace was a later insertion. Some peles had vaulted basements but most had a floor of wooden planks or large slabs of stone resting on hewn beams set in the wall or resting on corbels or a small ledge that ran the full length of the building. The roofs could be of stone, slates or as in some reports thatch that would have a thick coat of mud. However, there is little evidence of roofing materials left for us to see.

In my opinion, the best existing example of a pele is Gatehouse North on the Tarset Burn, a tributary of the North Tyne. This was built around 1560, being of the normal stout construction and having a basement with the living area above it. Resting on rough-hewn beams were large slabs of stone, being replaced in part by stout planking. This room has an external stone stair of great interest. The basement door is, as is most common, in one of the gables and was bolted from within. Access to the living area from the basement room was gained by a small trapdoor and a ladder. This trapdoor could be so situated as to form a murder hole just above the basement entrance to be used if anyone should break in. The first floor consisted of one large room that may have been subdivided. It is possible that a loft was built into the roof space. All the windows in this house are in the side that incorporates the external stair to the upper door. As in some other houses, the other, back wall was plain.

Most peles had the basement entrance in a gable wall and this helps us to read ruins where little remains but low walls and rubble. If you stand and face the end of the gatehouse that has the basement door in it, the blank wall is to your right and the external stair and first-floor windows are to your left. This holds true for peles in the Tyne and Rede valleys at least. Once you find the basement entrance in its gable you can place the stair to the left and importantly the highest point, the landing, is nearer to the basement entrance, the foot of the stair being towards the end with the small window or vent. Once more, this is true of most buildings of this type in the Tyne and Rede valleys and the hills between the Rede and Coquet.

There are houses that break the rule, having both doors in one long wall, one above the other, or even both doors in the same gable wall. John Hodgson tells us:

> The peel house called the Bolt House consists of a byre or cow house below and the family apartments above, viz.: an upper room with a boarded floor and a garret, both approached by stone stairs on the house, and the whole covered with thatch. The door to the cow house is under the landing of the stairs and the door of it is fastened with a strong bolt in the inside, for which purpose the byre and the upper room had a communication by a trap hole, that is by a horizontal door in a corner of the floor, and a trap or ladder.

I believe houses where the external stair incorporates the basement entrance point to a later date if we believe that originally a retractable wooden ladder was used, followed by unbonded stone stairs. A good example of a later house was Melkridge pele, now demolished but recorded in detail by the National Monuments Record in superb drawings dated 1954.

Houses Designated Peles and/or Bastles by Surveyors and Auditors of the Crown

The gentlemen who produced the various surveys of fortified and strong houses in Northumberland were confused by the designations they thought applicable to the particular building they were recording. It is not unusual for the designation being applied to a house to be at odds with what we know to be the situation based on existing remains.

Bellister is recorded as a 'Bastell house', when we know it to be a rather fine fortified house or hall with at least two towers attached. Akeld was recorded as a 'Lytle Fortelett or bastle house', when it was one of a superior group of houses, which includes Pressen and Castle Heaton, that stand out by reason of their greater proportions. Akeld's vaulted basement is 63ft long, Pressen is 65ft long and Castle Heaton is 68ft long, giving us a type of house not found in any other part of the county, where bastles/peles are well under 50ft long. The chart on p.73 gives the dimensions of fifty bastles/peles for comparison.

'Stone houses' range from simple 'stone houses built by villagers for their own good safeguard', as at Beal where the security of a tower and barmkin did not exist. Other listings recorded 'stone houses, little stone houses, strong stone houses' or 'little stone house or pile'. A few of these are now known to have been towers with a barmkin, as at Green Leighton, or simply towers, as at Hethpool and Ritton.

The survey of 1560–61 produced by Anthony Roone Esq., one of the auditors of Queen Elizabeth I, and Thomas Baytes, 'surveyor of her Majesties lands in the county of Northumberland', lists a number of 'towers or piles', including in their number Tillmouth, Cornhill, Duddo, Goswick, Heathpool and Yerdle. All are now known to be towers so is this an early, contemporary use of the designation pele tower? Use of the terms pile, pele or bastell are just as confusing, including in their number vicars' peles as at Alwinton and a rather fine fortified mansion or hall house with two towers attached as at Bellister, but most we now know to have been towers.

At least on the northern side of the border we have evidence that men having land worth £100 a year had to build a barmkin for use by their tenants and their goods in times of strife. All other landed gentry of smaller income had to build peles for protection (Acts of Parliament for Scotland, 1535). This would point to any listing including a barmkin being a tower, or, as above, is this a contemporary use of the designation pele tower?

I was born into a world when the Ordance Survey called the small barn-like houses of hill farmers 'peles' but designated the larger, finer, much more comfortable houses of richer farmers 'bastles', and I believed them. This has coloured my opinion to this day but I accept that there are other opinions held by other respected authorities.

The whole subject of nomenclature relating to peles and bastles abounds with controversy and as pointed out by Peter Ryder in his *Towers and Bastles*, respected authorities hold diverse opinions as to the correct usage. Two noted historians, John Hodgson and David D. Dixon, held opposing views with Hodgson favouring the term pele while Dixon firmly favoured bastle. These diverse opinions were and still are held by respected authorities. *Shielings and Bastles*, published in 1970, tells us that 'there is no clear warrant from ancient usage for the choice of the term bastle to describe buildings known as peles'.

While there is architectural variation, what I see as more important is that the larger 'bastles' were built by relatively wealthy landowners farming land that was much more productive than the marginal ground 'pele' owners worked.

DIAGRAMS SHOWING THE DEVELOPMENT OF PELES/BASTLES

1. BASIC PELE WITH RETRACTABLE LADDER TO FIRST FLOOR.

2. BASIC PELE WITH A STONE LANDING TO FIRST FLOOR ENTRANCE.

3. FLIGHT OF STONE STEPS TO FIRST FLOOR. LADDER NO LONGER REQUIRED.

4. MUCH MORE COMFORTABLE WITH INTERNAL FIREPLACE AND LOOKOUT ON GABLE.

5. PELE WITH ENTRANCE TO FIRST FLOOR AND BASEMENT IN GABLE.

6. ENTRANCE TO FIRST FLOOR AND BASEMENT IN LONG SIDE WALL.

7. PELE WITH 2½ FLOORS WITH INTERNAL FIRE, LOOKOUT AND ENTRANCE TO FIRST FLOOR AND BASEMENT IN SIDE WALL.

8. NO EXTERNAL ENTRANCE TO FIRST FLOOR HOUSE HAVING AN INTERNAL STAIR OF SOME KIND

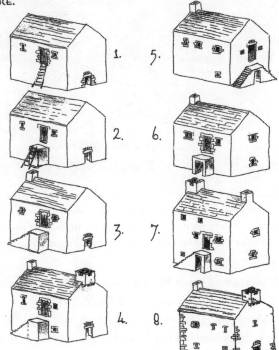

9. TWO HOUSES ATTACHED FORMING A MUCH LARGER UNIT EXAMPLES AT LOWSTEAD, GATEHOUSE, OTTERCOPS AND BARREN KNOW.

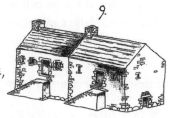

Diagram showing the development of peles/bastles in nine stages.

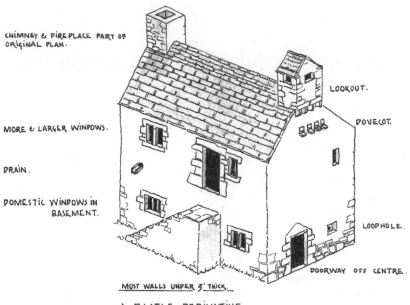

CHIMNEY & FIREPLACE PART OF
ORIGINAL PLAN.

LOOKOUT.

MORE & LARGER WINDOWS.

DOVECOT.

DRAIN.

DOMESTIC WINDOWS IN
BASEMENT.

LOOPHOLE.

DOORWAY OFF CENTRE.

MOST WALLS UNDER 3' THICK.

A BASTLE DERIVATIVE

This house has many more features of a domestic nature but is not quite as robust as the earlier peles/bastles. The walls for the most part are not as thick as in peles and the stair landing can be on the same level as the threshold of the first-floor entrance. There is evidence that the landing at the head of the stairs had some form of parapet.

The resulting better harvest is reflected in the larger size of bastles and their larger storage areas in houses such as Akeld, Doddington and Hirst (Ashington). Hirst, (Ashington), Hebburn, Doddington, and Akeld all display a more polite form of architecture, be they bastles or even strong houses. Black Middings, the Raw and the Gatehouse are simple vernacular buildings with little or no architectural refinement I know as peles.

Personally, I use, or prefer, the term pele to describe the many small, barn-like houses, and bastle for the larger and more varied homes of more wealthy land owners or farmers, with examples shown in my choice of graphics.

Houses Recorded as Bastles in Evidence (Figure 5, see p.44)

While the survey of 1415 covers the county as a whole, it only lists the more important houses known as castrum, fortalicium and turris. The survey of 1509 is more interested in the 'Garnysons' and gives a total for 'Thys men' of M^{LE}CCLXX, excluding Norham and Berwick.

The best survey is that of 1541 giving details of the East March and Middle Marches. Later, the *Survey Book of Norham and Islandshire* dated 1560–61 also lists a bastle or bastall at Felkington:

1. Aykeld – A lyttle fortelett or bastle house, C.3
2. Yerdle – A bastell house, C.6
3. Mydleton Hall – Two stone houses or bastells, D.13
4. Newebygginge – A strong stone house or bastell, A.6
5. Allaynton – Lyttle bastell house of stone, C.13
6. Lynne Brigge – A newe bastell house to be built, C.9
7. Harterburn – A strong bastell house, F.61
8. Sawnes – Pele house or bastell, F.27
9. Hawyke – A bastell house, E.42
10. Swetehope – Another bastell house, E.43
11. Fylton More – A bastell house, E.44
12. Carre Cottes – Another bastell house, E.45
13. Hall Barnes – A bastell house, E.55
14. Bellister – A bastell house, G.23
15. Felkington – One bastell house, A.5

Perhaps these surveys were carried out by a number of people, each given an area to cover. Their returns would have been combined to give the official return. The question is, did they all use the same terminology in recording their findings? All we can do is look at the existing remains of the buildings and compare them to other known examples.

Houses Listed as Peles in Old Surveys

1. Newebygging (gret henghe) – Strong stone house, A.6
2. Hethepol – Lyttle stone house or pyle, 1541, C.23
3. Hare Clengh – A strong pele house of stone, 1541, C.20
4. Elyburne – A strong pele house, 1541, F.66
5. Sannes – A lytle pele house or bastell, 1541, F.27
6. Twizell – Tower or pile, 1560, A.10
7. Tilouth – Little tower or pile, 1560, A.8
8. Cornehylle – Tower or pile, 1560, A.15
9. Dudoo – One pile or tower, 1560, A.11
10. Ancroft – One pile, built to the end of the church, 1560, B.7
11. Gosewick – One good pile, 1560, B.4

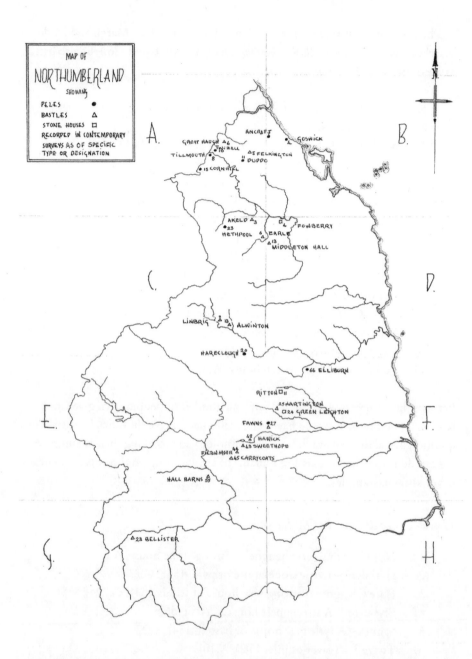

Figure 5: Map of Northumberland using the surveys 1541 and 1560–61 showing houses designated peles or bastles.

The survey of Islandshire was made in the third year of the reign of Elizabeth I, 1560–61, and the 'peles' mentioned are what I would regard as towers. The surveys of 1415 and 1541, along with the survey of Norham (1560), all refer to Twizell as much more than a simple pele, rather as an old fortress or castell. Tilmouth comes across as an old tower in a poor condition. Cornhill was a tower destroyed in 1385 but by 1541 it had been rebuilt and its barmkin was being built. The remains of the tower of Duddo are from the early seventeenth century but replace one destroyed earlier, while that at Ancroft is a vicar's tower being built on top of the west end of the church. Goswick was a late build, between 1550 and 1560, and as it had a yard or barmkin attached to a tower it was clearly not a pele.

While the 1970 publication *Shielings and Bastles* says 'there is no clear warrant from ancient usage for the choice of the term bastle to describe buildings known as peles', the reverse is also true, with few peles being listed in the official surveys or returns.

Houses Designated Peles or Bastles in Contemporary Surveys (Figure 5, see p.44)

NORHAM AND ISLANDSHIRE 1560–61

A.10 Twizell – Tower or pile with barmkin

A.8 Tillmouth – Little tower or pile and barmkin

A.15 Cornhill – Tower or pile with barmkin

A.11 Duddo – Pile or tower and barmkin

A.5 Felkington – A bastle house of small strength

B.7 Ancroft – Pile built on end of church

B.4 Goswick – One good pile

A.6 Groat Haugh – Great stone house or bastle (Shares a field with Newbiggin).

EAST MARCH 1541

C.23 Hethpool – Little stone house or pyle

C.3 Akeld – Little fortlet or bastle house

C.6 Earle – A bastle house

D.13 Middleton Hall – Two stone houses or bastles

D.4 Fowberry – Tower or stone house

MIDDLE MARCH 1541

C.13 Alwinton – Little bastle house of stone
C.9 Linbrig – Bastle house to be built
C.20 Harecleugh – Strong pele house of stone
F.66 Elliburn – Strong pele
F.11 Ritton – Stone house and barmkin
F.24 Green Leighton – Little stone house and barmkin
F.25 Hartington – A strong bastle house
F.27 Fawns – Little pele house or bastle
E.42 Hawick – Bastle house
E.43 Sweethope – Bastle house
E.44 Filton Moor – Bastle house called Whyte House
E.45 Carrycoats – Bastle house
E.55 Hall Barns – Bastle house
G.23 Bellister – Bastle house

Alphabetical List of Peles/Bastles

Alton side
Alwinton
Anick

Barrasford
Barren Know
Barrow
Bartys (Boghead)
Beltingham
Bellister
Bewclay (see Portgate)
Bickerton
Black Cleugh (Unthank)
Black Middings
Bog Hall (Rothbury)
Bog Head (see Bartys)
Bolton Pila
Boughthill (Burnbank)
Bower
Bowershield
Bowes Hill
Bradley
Branshaw

Branton
Brig (Corsenside)
Brinkheugh
Brockley Hall
Butter Knowes

Cambo
Camp Cottage
Carrshield
Catherside (Knowesgate)
Catcleugh
Charlton
Cherry Tree Cottage
Chesterwood
Chirdon
Coldtown
Combe
Combhill
Crag

Dale House
Darden Lough (High Rigg)
Dargues

Doddington
Dunns Cottage
Donkley Wood

Earle
East Woodburn (Hall Yards)
Eglingham
Elliburn
Errington
Evistones

Falston – Falstone Farm, Hawkhope,
    Stannersburn, Yarrow Shilling Pot
Fawns (Sawnes)
Felkington

Gastehouse
Girsonfield
Golf House
Grandys Knowe
Grasslees
Great Haugh
Greenhead
Green Leighton

Hall Yard (East Woodburn)
Halton Le Gate
Harecleugh
Harewalls
Hartington
Hartley Cleugh (Carrshield)
Hawkhope (Falstone)
Hayrake
Hebburn (Hepburn)
Henshaw
Hesleywell
High Bower Shield
High Callerton (Rebellion House)
High Cromer or Croner
Highfarnlaw
High Field
High Leam
High Shaw
Hill House (Wark Forest)
Hirst (Ashington)
Hole

Hole Head
Holm House
Hope
Housesteads
Humshaugh
Hurst Bastle

Iron House
Ivy Cottage (Ridley)

Kershope Castle
Kirkhaugh (Underbank)
Knowesgate

Lambley Farm
Leaplish
Lee (The) (see Elliburn)
Linbrigg
Lindenhouse (Humshaugh)
Little Ryal
Long Haughton Hall
Low Ardley
Low Buston
Low Cleugh
Low Farinley
Low Leam
Low Old Shield
Low Row (Kirkhaugh)
Low Stead (Melkridge)

Melkridge
Middleton Hall
Monk
Moorhouses
Mortley

Newton
Newtown
Nine Dargue

Ottercops

Pee House
Peel Crag
Pench Ford
Prudhoe Castle Pele

Ratten Raw
Ratten Row
Raw Pele
Ray Demesne
Rebellion House (High Callerton)
Redheugh
Ridge or Rig End
Riding (The)
Ridley (Ivy Cottage)
Rochester
Roses Bower
Rowan Tree
Rowan Tree Stob (Sinderhope)

Sawnes (see Fawn)
Sharperton
Shilburnhaugh
Shilla Hill
Shilling Pot
Shitlehaugh
Sills
Sinderhope
Smalesmouth
Snabdough
Snitter
South Healey (Nunnykirk)
Spartylea
Starsley
Starward
Steel

Stobby Lea
Stokoe Crags
Sweethope
Tecket
Thropton
Todburn Steel
Tone Hall
Tower House (Hole Head)
Tow House (Henshaw)
Town Foot (Elsdon)

Underbank (Kirk Haugh)
Unthank (Black Cleugh)

Wainhope
Wall
Warton
Waterhead
West Ealingham
Westside (Monk)
West Wharmley
White Hall (Whitley Chapel)
White Heather Cot.
White Lea (Kirkhaugh)
Whiteley Shield
Woodhouse
Woodhouses
Wooley (Allendale)

Yarrow Shilling Pot (Falstone)

Map of Northumberland (Figure 6)

Thie map shows the locations of buildings described as peles or bastles by respected authorities holding diverse opinions as to the correct term to use to describe, for the most part, the same buildings. There is no clear warrant for the use of either term from ancient usage and it is with this in mind that I show these buildings in whatever term you may favour under the same umbrella symbol.

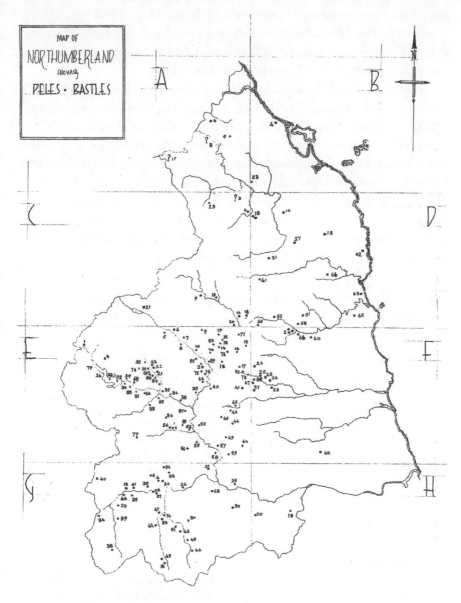

Figure 6: Map of Northumberland showing peles and bastles.

Notes on the Map Showing the Distribution of Peles/Bastles (*Figure 6*)
Respective authorities differ in the term they use, disagreeing as to what is the
correct term for what is essentially the same building. The map indicates, without favour, the distribution of what are variously regarded as bastles or peles.

It is obvious at first glance that the highest concentration of these houses
is in the west of the county; that is, in Upper Coquetdale, Redesdale, North
Tynedale, Allendale and South Tyne. All these areas have vast areas of poor, marginal upland producing little return for the effort involved. Breaking this 'rule'
is South Charlton, which has the remnants of a pele/bastle incorporated into the
walls of the one-time school and is the most easterly of this type of house, being
just on the western side of the A1 north of Alnwick.

Allendale and South Tynedale have a group of houses worthy of special study,
they being of a later date, yet with elements commonly found in bastles/peles but
with far less robust walls. These have become known as 'bastle derivatives' by and
large, a much more comfortable form of farmhouse than the earlier peles/bastles.
Three houses, having come down to use as bastles, are marked on the map with
a '?' as they are much larger than other peles/bastles and would at least be better
grouped along with 'strong houses'. Akeld has a vaulted basement 63ft long,
Pressen's vault is 65ft long, and that at Castle Heaton is 68ft long. Compare these
with the chart on p.73 giving the dimensions of fifty houses for comparison,
where their superior status will become obvious.

*Map Showing the Location of Houses Designated Peles or Bastles
(Figure 6, see p.49)*

A.5	Felkington	D.41	Little Ryal
A.6	Groat Haugh	D.51	Hope
		D.55	Thropton
B.23	Doddington	D.58	Newton
		D.60	Bickerton
C.6	Earle	D.62	Newton
C.9	Linbrig	D.63	Low Buston
C.16	Sharperton	D.65	Acton Hall
C.18	Snitter	D.66	Bolton
C.20	Hareclough Woodhouses		
C.21	Catcleugh	E.1	Kershope Castle
		E.4	Wainhope
D.10	Hebburn	E.5	Evistones
D.13	Middleton Hall	E.6	Sills
D.27	Edlingham	E.7	Rochester
D.31	Branton	E.8	Ratten Raw

G.34 Halton Lea Gate
G.35 Henshaw
G.36 Housesteads
G.37 Humshaugh
G.38 Kirkhaugh
G.39 Lambley Farm
G.40 Low Old Sheld (Greenhead)
G.41 Melkridge
G.42 Monk
G.43 Nine Dargue (Allendale)
G.44 Plenmeller

G.45 Sinderhope
G.46 Spartylen
G.47 Wester Old Town
G.48 West Wharmley
G.49 Whiteley Shield
G.50 Whitely Chapel
G.51 Wooley
G.53 Burnlaw

H.20 Todburn Steel
H.18 Healey

The map is broken into areas A to H, showing the relative densities of peles/bastles as below:

Area –
A.2 Norham and River Tweed
B.1 Islandshire and Bamburgh
C.7 Glendale and Upper Coquetdale
D.14 Alnwick and Lower Coquetdale
E.66 North Tyne and Redesdale
F.14 Rivers Wawsbeck and Blyth
G.17 Hexham, South Tyne and Allendale
H.2 Prudhoe, Newcastle

These densities vary over the years but percentages hold true.

Resident Reivers

If Jesus Christ were emongst them they would deceave him.

Richard Fenwick, 1597

While the 'heidsmen' of reiving groups lived in stone houses such as are to be found at Gatehouse and Black Middens, on the Tarset Burn, ordinary or lesser reivers' homes were much more basic structures, little able to keep out the wind and the rain. Bishop Leslie said they were little more than 'sheep houses and lodges … of whose burning they are not solaced'. But then it was not his home being destroyed, probably along with those of the neighbours, in a swift and merciless raid. Such was the existence of these poor country people that life and limb was ventured by the man of the house for his 'good wife and bairn' else they would starve and die, as the most part of his livelihood came from the enemy.

Among the reiving names were people of high and low degree living on the English side of the border: Anderson, Bell, Carleton, Charlton, Carnaby, Collingwood, Dodd, Dunne, Fenwick, Forster, Gray, Hedley, Heron, Jamieson, Lilburn, Milburn, Ogle, Potts, Read, Ridley, Robson, Selby, Shafto, Stokoe and Storey.

It is well known that the city Guilds of Newcastle upon Tyne forbade any guildsman from taking as an apprentice any member of the reiving families emanating from the North Tyne and Redesdale areas. It would even be punishable to go to the Hay market, north of the city, to take on a labourer from this group of people to do menial jobs by the hour or by the day.

While Bishop John Leslie of Ross was based far from the misty border hills, he must have lived or at least had an extended stay on the borders, which is shown in his insight into the people and their way of life. His history of Scotland (1572–76) gives further evidence of this insight into the ways of reiving, saying:

They sally out of their own borders, in the night, in troops, through unfrequented by-ways and their horse, in lurking holes they had pitched upon before, till they arrive at the dark in those places they have designed upon. As soon as they have seized upon the booty, they, in like manner return home in the night, through blind ways and fetching a compass.

The calendar of border papers of 1597 tells us just how brutal these forays were, no matter which side of the border the reivers came from: 'The commissioners charge Sir Walter Scott Laird of Buccleuch, keeper of Liddesdale, with a hostile invasion of Tynedale on the 17th instant, where he cruelly murdered 35 of the Queen's subjects, sparing neither age nor sex, cutting some in pieces with his own hand, burning others and drowning others.' As part of the foray he was accused of 'also burning 10 houses and dividing the goods of the country among his own men in reward for service'.

It would seem that the churches of England and Scotland were, in their exasperation, joined together in condemnation of this border warfare, with the Bishops of Durham and Glasgow calling down public curses, as vitriolic as anything emanating from the reivers, on the heads of the sinners. Gavin Dunbar, Archbishop of Glasgow was first off the mark in response to 'how men, wives and bairns are murdered, slain, burnt, spoilt and reft openly in daylight and under silence of the night and their farms and lands laid waste by common traitors, reivers, thieves, dwelling in the south part of the Scottish realm' with his 'great cursing'.

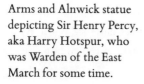

Arms and Alnwick statue
depicting Sir Henry Percy,
aka Harry Hotspur, who
was Warden of the East
March for some time.

The present-day assemblages of ancient border surnames have in some instances formed themselves into groups or societies such as clan Elliot or clan Armstrong, yet the reiving families were not Gaelic speaking, nor were they living under the same social structure that the Highlanders did. A big difference was that Highlanders of the same name were attached, even tied to the place, the area, of their birth and tore into battle roaring this place name. Border chiefs' headsmen who did not even understand Gaelic, never mind speak it, were not averse to a takeover of land, resulting in estates, if that is not too polite a word, with various named residents, so when they entered an affray they did it calling out their names, resulting in cries much like a short roll call of notorious brigands ringing out over the bloodied heather.

To assist in finding some of the reiver strongholds, the Ordance Survey published a map, 'In search of the border reivers', featuring over 800 reiver sites on the border lands of England and Scotland.

'Dressed to kill' from a painting by Angus McBride showing a group of reivers of high and low status, being from left to right a 'border lowne', border heidsman's son, 'border heidman' and a reiver *c.* 1585. (Image copyright of Osprey Publishing)

The reiver depicted here wears a steel bonnet, a quilted jack and long leather boots. His lance was at least 8ft long. Not visible are his broadsword and dagger. Hanging from his high-backed saddle is a small crossbow, while his rolled blanket would be slung diagonally across his back while on the field of battle. (Model by Keith Durham for his border miniatures)

Reivers' Attire

Headsman	Foot Soldier
Quilted Jak or Jack with plates of bone or iron sewn into layers of quilted canvas, fustian or leather worn over a shirt, under which was a shirt of chain mail.	Quilted Jack with plates of bone sewn into layers of cloth, worn over a shirt, under which was a shirt of chain mail.
A few had back and breastplates.	Bonnets picked up on the battlefield or a bonnet of cloth and leather in layers.
Steel bonnets of various designs.	Kercher or scarf.
Kercher or scarf wound around the neck.	Brogues of simple design with holes to let out water, held on and in shape by leather thongs.
Thigh-length riding boots of stout leather worn with spurs worn over Tudor hose.	Brass chains round legs and arms.
Brass chains wound round the legs to ward off sword blows.	<u>Dressed to kill</u> Short sword 30–33in. Dirk or dagger.
Gauntlets of steel and leather.	16ft pole or lance with on the English side a bill attached.
<u>Dressed to kill</u> Short sword 30–33in. A few had long broadswords. Dirk or dagger and rapier. Buckler or round shield. 8–12ft pole or lance. Single-shot pistols (up to three). Small crossbow or latch. Blanket roll on his back much like cattle drovers in nineteenth-century USA. High-backed war saddle giving a secure seat.	Longbow. Blanket roll. Small leather pouch for refreshments.

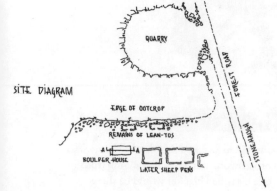

A REIVERS ABODE, WARK FOREST.

DIAGRAMS NOT TO SCALE

SITE DIAGRAM

QUARRY

EDGE OF OUTCROP

REMAINS OF LEAN-TOS

BOULDER HOUSE

LATER SHEEP PENS

FOREST ROAD

STONEHAUGH

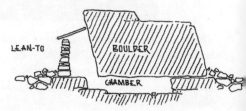

DIAGRAM OF BOULDER HOUSE.
(SECTION AA)

LEAN-TO

BOULDER

CHAMBER

While working in the vast forests on the borders, I recorded many monuments large and small, ranging from deserted villages to wayside crosses. One group of interest here are the remains of simple, primitive habitations – shiels – probably home to the majority of upland residents, with examples including lean-to shelters set against a cliff face and natural caves. An outstanding discovery was under a massive rock that had, centuries ago, peeled off from a crag and ended up some distance from the base of the outcrop. The resulting boulder is rectangular and has traces of a lean-to built up against it. Hidden inside this is a narrow entrance in the floor, to a small chamber situated beneath the boulder, it being to sleep in or to hide securely during any affray. Many reivers' houses were small rectangular structures with walls of mud and stone and a simple heather or turf thatch lying on birch poles to form a roof, an age-old method of construction.

These shiels, the homes of the less-affluent borderers, were usually permanently occupied, but as the borders pacified they were abandoned to be later used as shielings, the seasonal, temporary huts used by shepherds.

EMBLETON VICARAGE, NORTHUMBERLAND, ENGLAND

These are the goods left in 1431 by William Waede, the Vicar of Embleton, who lived in a small fortified house of which only the solar, known as Embleton Tower, survives.

Note that there is only one chair and the table or board stood on trestles.

VI	Oxen	13s. 4d	each
II	Horses	12s. 0d	each
1	Cart	8s. 0d	
1	Cart	5s. 0d	
1	Plough	3s. 8d	
2	Large brewing leades	£1 4s. 0d	each
1	Large brass pots	13s. 4d	each
1	Small	6s. 4d	
1	Boardcloth and two bowls (high board)	3s. 8d	
1	Boardcloth (sideboard)	1s. 6d	
6	Silver spoons	13s. 4d	
1	Great table for highboard	2s. 8d	

1	Great table for sideboard	1s. 6d	
2	Forms	1s.	
2	Pr trestles	1s.	
6	Cushions	3s. 6d	
1	Tapestry to ye Hall	11s. 0d	
	Bankers to ye Hall	1s. 8d	
1	Chair	1s. 6d	
6	Garnish vessels	6s. 0d	
2	Iron spits 1 @ 1s. 6d plus 10d		
2	Candlesticks	1s. 8d	
1	Basin and ewer	5s. 0d	
2	Pans 1 @ 5s. 8d 1 at 1s. 10d		
1	Pr tongs	8d	
1	Long brand iron	4s. 8d	
1	Bed with apparell	£1 0s. 0d	
1	Bed (single)	10s. 0d	
2	Bolsters	2s. 6d	
1	Yetling	6s. 10d	
1	Woorte tub	2s. 0d	
1	Gylletyng tub	2s. 6d	
2	Bowls	1s. 4d	

It is evident from the lack of documents like this that it was only the richer, more educated who produced this evidence. Even the pele/bastle owners did not fit into this category, so have not left us any wills, etc. to peruse. It follows that the lowly inhabitants of shiels, the largest group of upland residents, who could not read or write were not party to this legal nicety.

Higher up the social scale were the stout pyramid-shaped houses built using sturdy oak logs, with the site moated. These were followed by the small robustly built stone houses we know as peles or bastles, the most numerous types of secure houses on the borders.

Towers were much stronger houses of at least three floors and had a parapet walk, often with battlements, and while in good quantities they are not to be found in the wilder upland areas where peles/bastles are located. It was the goods and chattels of peles, bastles and tower owners that we recorded as insight gear when they were looted following a border raid, only to be distributed among the victorious enemy.

Records are few and fragmentary, being written by the victors and/or losers of any border affray, with few people having drawn up a will and inventory of their property. One such document is that drawn up by William Ward, the vicar of Embleton, whose superior house had a small tower attached, an early panic room, yet the furnishings he left were surprisingly few and simple.

A Reiver's Wardrobe

Never mentioned in inventories left by local gentlemen were the articles of clothing that constituted the obligatory uniform of a fighting man. Reivers aspired to a quilted Jack like those exhibited in interpretive centres all along the borders. This is an ancient term and form of dress with a much-disputed origin; it is thought to have been inspired by Arab nations but was found as distant as ancient China. I can't envisage many of the poorer inhabitants of our upland border areas being able to afford such a garment as part of their wardrobe unless it was picked up on a field of battle, being no longer required by a dead combatant. The garment was made using quilted leather or a stout canvas type of cloth, with each quadrant of the quilt having rectangular pieces of iron or bone mounted in them. Originally worn by foot soldiers, a shorter version of the coat was used by those on horseback and in time became known as a jacket.

Also boasted of were high-length boots and a steel bonnet. The foot soldiers at Flodden field are recorded as having kicked off their footwear to gain better purchase on the muddy battlefield. Known as brogues, these shoes were simple pieces of foot-shaped leather tied on using leather thongs wound around their ankles. These shoes had holes in them to allow water to escape. Present-day Highland dress includes brogues laced up to the calf, while smartly dressed country men wear brogues, now stout shoes with a pattern of holes punched into their uppers.

Peles and Bastles: A History

'Pele' is the most misused of all the terms. The medieval use of the word meant a position or place of great strength made of timber and earth. These houses must have looked like the circular huts of past ages, and indeed the Celtic name for a fort was a pill. Some houses that later became known as towers and even castles were once peles. Three of these were Bolton, Horton and Whittingham.

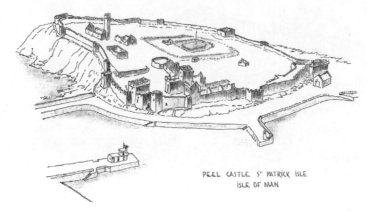

Peel Castle, Isle of Man.

A postcard view of Peel Castle, Isle of Man, with the earthworks of the original pele built by Magnus Barefoot, who died in 1103. This timber pele gave the castle and the town their name.

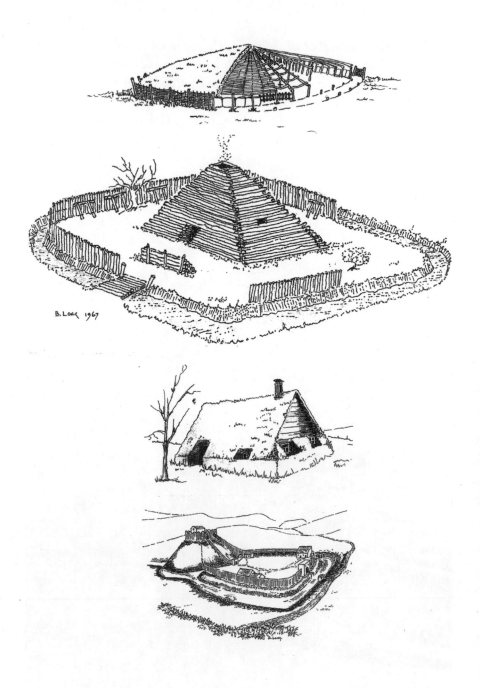

These four drawings show the relationship between a Celtic pill, an early timber pele, a Dutch plaggenhut and an early motte-and-bailey castle.

It would seem that the main features of the early peles were moats, ditches and palisades of wood and earth, and the dwelling. Peel, on the Isle of Man, was granted to the Earl of Northumberland in 1400 and traces of the 'pelam', from which the site takes its name, still remain in the bailey of the castle.

Magnus Barefoot, who died in 1103, built the original pele with wood imported from Galloway, since trees of the required size for the work were not to be found on Man. Richard Coeur-de-Lion built many peles while in Palestine during the religious wars, and Robert de Brunne, writing between 1327 and 1338, tells us, 'Richarde did make a pele on kestelle-wise allwais wrought of tre full wele'. Hare Cleugh was 'a strong pele house of stone' in 1541, and Heathpool was 'a lytle stone house or pele'. This would suggest that *c.* 1190 Richard's peles were made of wood but in 1541 they were either stone or wood.

Stone Peles and How They Evolved

While we accept that early peles were constructed using stout timber and at a later date they were built using stone, they continued to evolve, as shown in these sketches. While most basement doorways were in a gable end, we can't be sure about first-floor entrances as few peles of sufficient height survive. We tend to think that they were in one of the longer side walls but there is evidence that at least some were in the gable end above the basement entrance.

Quite a few basement entrances were in the same long side wall and positioned below the first-floor doorway. Some of these later houses had gun ports, even lookout turrets, and some had an extra attic floor. We assume that at first heating was from a brazier with built-in fireplaces and their chimneys were introduced later. Cooking may even have taken place outside.

The *Northumberland County History* hints at the possibility that ancient 'pils', the round houses of our forebears, were still being used by hill farmers of the North Pennines and the Cheviot Hills well into the late fifteenth century. Indeed, houses of similar construction were being used as late as the nineteenth century.

In 1578 a Scots bishop said that the more powerful among the poorer borderers constructed pyramidal towers made of earth and that they called them pailes. Earlier, in 1541, the commissioners, writing about residents of the English middle marchers, recorded that:

The headsmen of them have very stronge houses where of the most p'te the utter sydes or walls be made of great swarer oke trees strongly boonce and joined together wth great tenons of the same so thycke mortressed that yt wylbe very harde wthoute great force and laboore to break or cast downe any of the said houses'.

My sketches show a Dutch 'plaggenhut' reconstructed in the open-air museum at Arnhem and possible variations of early peles based on this and the contemporary sixteenth-century records.

The *Northumberland County History*, Vol. XV mentions that many of the ancient camps and hut circles in the county are post-Roman and implies they were in use up to the time of Elizabeth I. The survey of 1541 says of the peles in Tynedale:

> ... they are built in naturally strong positions and consist of walls and roofs of squared oak trees bound together and morticed. The whole is covered with earth and turves so that they may not be set on fire and they are so strong that only with great force and numbers could they be cast down.

Also mentioned in the same survey are strong pele houses of stone, but the sparing use of the word 'pele' is remarkable. It is quite clear, however, that it did not apply to the larger and stronger bastles and towers. Other gentry of smaller income had to 'build peles or other strengths'.

In Robertson's *History of Scotland*, Vol. I, p.109, are copies of two reports sent to Henry VIII from his 'Wardens of the Marches' and the mention of peles as distinct from towers suggests a difference. One of the reports, an account of an inroad by the Earl of Hertford between 8 and 23 September 1545, reads as follows:

Monasteries and Friar-houses	7
Castles, towers and piles	16
Market towns	5
Villages	243
Milns	13
Hospitals	3

All there were cast down or burnt.

A Scots bishop writing in 1578 of the people living on the border, states that 'their houses were cottages and huts ... the more powerful among them constructed pyramidal towers made of earth only ... and that to these they gave the name pailes'. In the present day, the word is employed to describe a small, simply made house with a high-pitched roof. The drawings of Raw and Gatehouse show them to be characteristic of peles all over the north.

While the lords lived in castles and fortalices, and the lesser gentry in fortalices, towers or bastles, the common people lived in peles. It probably was that in seeking the comfort of stone the poorer people first built the humble houses we know today. In this way, the name 'pele tower' or 'pele house' was transferred to buildings having a basement that would be used as a byre, with the family quarters above. These could consist of an upper room with boarded floor and a garret. The entrance would be reached by a stone stair or ladder on the outside. The basement entrance would be below this and the door to it would be fastened with a strong wooden bolt on the inside, for which purpose the byre and the upper room had communication by a trapdoor in the corner of the floor.

This would be a very uncomfortable house with rushes on the floor, no glass in the windows – just oak shutters – and no fireplace, the smoke having to find its way out through cracks in the ceiling and windows. To add to the general discomfort there would be the noise and smell of the cattle in the basement.

Other European areas, such as France, Denmark and Holland, had peles. In Holland they were known as 'plaggenhuts', and are described by the museum at Arnhem as follows:

Turf cabins formerly were numerous in the north-eastern part of Holland, and in a region of moorland and bogs. Like the hovel exhibited here, they were built of turf piled on top of each other to form the walls. The roof composed of fir-tree trunks joined by crossbeams and wooden boards, was also covered with turf. Such damp, unhealthy dwellings provided living accommodation for the poorest inhabitants and their domestic animals. The plan of these cabins resembles that of prehistoric dwellings excavated in the ground. Not before we have seen a turf cabin can we understand how Vincent Van Gogh, the famous Dutch painter, could write in 1883, that in the turf cabin, in which he was painting, two sheep and a goat were grazing on the roof. The goat climbed upon the ridge of the roof and looked into the chimney. The woman, who heard something on the roof, climbed up and flung her broom to the aforesaid animal, which jumped down like a chamois ...

We all accept the early motte-and-bailey castles constructed using stout timbers were for the most part rebuilt using stone as soon as it was safe to do so or when the timbers decayed. Crowned heads and lesser nobles also built peles for use during grand tournaments or as a temporary hunting lodges, being used only once then dismantled or left to rot. There are also records of peles – that is sections of stout wooden walls – being moved considerable distances to stone castles that had a breach in a wall and being used to form a barbican-like structure in front of the gap, only to be removed when a repair to the masonry was completed.

Much later, poor hill farmers are recorded as building houses of wood and turf known as peles. A few earthworks are known that may be the remains of these houses, but these are not numerous even though we are told that such peles were

Hole Head? Henshaw.

Hole Head, Henshaw, is an example of an early stone pele, now much altered. The original basement entrance is in the right-hand gable end. The original retractable wooden stair has been replaced by a stone one, the windows enlarged, and a sleeping loft inserted under the thatch roof. Drawing from *The Authentic Tudor and Stuart Dolls House* by Brian Long.

still being built as late as 1578. The stone houses we know as peles or bastles were by this time numerous in the marginal pastures of the Northumbrian uplands, so it is obvious that the poor farmers desired and built more secure and comfortable houses when they could, in the same way that the residents of motte-and-bailey castles did centuries earlier.

It has long been held that the basements were used as byres but I tend to question this. Farmers I have spoken to tell me they are too hot to keep cattle in for any length of time and that later openings knocked through the thick walls don't help much. I suggest they were only used in this way in troublesome times when greater security was required. There would be no problem in the housing of sheep but the large horned cattle of the period would have problems negotiating the narrow entrance. A few basements show signs of sockets in their side walls to take the timber supports of a loft or mezzanine flor to store dry goods and other winter supplies.

In most peles the first floor was supported on rough transverse beams carrying large stone slabs. Few of these survive but Gatehouse North has some at one end of the large first-floor room, the rest of the floor consisting of later planking. Vaulted basements are much fewer in number and may point to the wealth of the builder or just the fact that suitable timbers were not available in the area.

While in the areas of the North Tyne, Rede and Coquet doorheads tend to be simple monolithic slabs of roughly hewn stone giving a square head, south of the Tyne and in the Allendales doorheads are round, constructed using one or two large stones. A few examples of a triangular shape are to be found, again formed using one or two large stones.

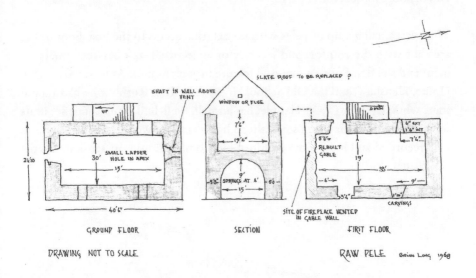

The early timber peles, like motte-and-bailey castles, were not intended to last, being for the most part temporary, to be replaced and even abandoned in favour of stone structures at a later date. The temporary nature of timbers meant that works constructed this way were at the bottom of the scale for longevity, security and defence, even status.

The term pele was throughout history applied to the poorest structures of their type and came to rest on what were the simple, defensive homes: the peles of hill farmers earning a living out of the marginal land they worked. I see this development as a rich pedigree and one to celebrate and cherish. Its use to describe these houses can only serve to highlight the higher social status of bastles, with their greater architectural pretensions and more varied plan and elevations resulting in greater comfort and security.

Peles/Bastles with Internal Stair (No First-Floor Doorway)

Shilla Hill, Tarset
Woodhouse, Harbottle
Falstone Farm
Crag (Craig), Hepple/Elsdon
Iron House, Hepple
Tow House, Henshaw
Hebburn, Chillingham
Henshaw
Old School House, Snitter

There is a small group of peles with no external access to the first-floor living area but with the comfort and security of an internal stair between the basement and the first floor, an unusual feature in such houses. At least two – Tow House, Henshaw, and the Old School House at Snitter, Rothbury – had a spiral stair, while Crag or Craig, Hepple, has a small, well-built mural stair set in its south-east corner, having a small slit to light its foot. Woodhouses, Hepple, is well recorded and has a more comfortable, commodious stair set in its south-east corner.

MELKRIDGE BASTLE (c.1642) AFTER GIBSON

Melkridge Bastle.

All these houses have vaulted basements. Henshaw 'Tower House' belongs to that group, having internal stairs to the first floor but no vault to the basement.

Variations in Design of Peles/Bastles

There is a problem area where some peles have greater architectural pretensions, starting with the byre door being in a long side wall with the first-floor door not quite directly above it. The ground-floor entrance is protected by a porch that forms the landing of the external stair. Some have an internal stair so an external entrance to the first floor is not required.

Windows were basic, giving little in the way of lighting to the living quarter but in some, especially those with side wall entrances, superior mullioned windows can be found. Stone sinks and spouts to carry water through the wall are a refined feature. Houses such as Melkridge and Ivy Cottage, Ridley, had small lookout turrets/gunloop holes mounted on corbels on their gable ends. Melkridge even had gun ports in the basement walls, a most unusual feature.

Attics at first would have been little more than a few planks but some were original to the plan, examples are found at Woodhouses, The Hole and Melkridge giving three floors to the house. The question is, are these superior houses bastles? If so that puts them in a class superior to the basic pele architecture, yet the owners were still farmers of marginal land giving a poor harvest.

Vaulted Basements

A small number of peles have vaulted basements, while most first floors were carried on rough, heavy beams that carried flagstones forming an uneven floor.

The diagrams show that most vaults were much the same, no matter what size. The examples chosen range from 31ft × 15ft to 24ft 3in × 15ft 2in, with most being in the valleys of North Tynedale and Redesdale. Examples include Boghead, Branshaw, Crag, Evistones, Falstone, Highshaw, Hole, Hornestead, Raw, Thropton, Woodhouses, Akeld, Presson, Castle Heaton, Hebburn Chillingham, Simonburn, Biddlestone and Swabdough.

Such a refinement as a vaulted basement not only made the house stronger and more secure but must have raised the status of the building and its proud owners within the community. Access to the first floor from within the vault was in most instances by a ladder and through a small ladder hole. Persons of a stout nature could not pass through such an aperture. At Akeld the hole is 11in × 14in, which is normal, with few having one as large as the one at High Shaw, at 1ft 10in × 1ft 10in.

Bastles

The infamous Bastille in Paris was one of two built just outside and protecting gates into the city because of the threat from the English in the Hundred Years' War. Built in stages from 1357 onwards, the result was a royal fortress with eight massive projecting towers overlooking the gateway of the Porte Saint-Antoine on the eastern edge of the city.

Under Louis XV and XVI it was partly used to detain prisoners from varied backgrounds but mainly as a base for the Parisian police charged with enforcing government censorship. Most prisoners were kept in relatively good conditions but criticism grew during the eighteenth century fuelled by autobiographies written by former prisoners with a political axe to grind.

In 1789, when the mob consisting in great part of dissatisfied soldiers broke through the walls, they found seven cells containing four forgers, two lunatics and a young nobleman. The prisoners were not the reason for the storming, but it was to bring down the single most important symbol of the king's power. At the end, eighty-three attackers were dead with seventy-three injured. The governor had his head cut off, while one guard was killed and three wounded.

A lack of knowledge about the Bastille created a mystique of terror at how information was coerced out of prisoners, while in reality all the prison rooms until the year 1701 could be furnished by the occupants. Wealthy prisoners brought in their own items, even their own servants. Food was good but luxurious meals were to be had if you had money. Hence, the infamous

The French term '*bastile*' relates to defensible farmhouses up to royal castles.

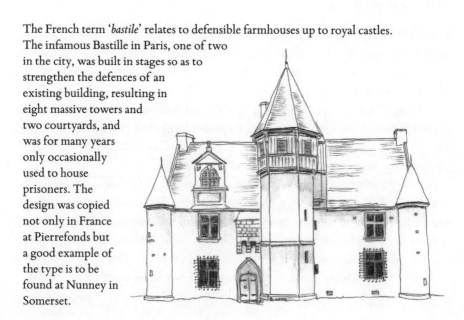

The infamous Bastille in Paris, one of two in the city, was built in stages so as to strengthen the defences of an existing building, resulting in eight massive towers and two courtyards, and was for many years only occasionally used to house prisoners. The design was copied not only in France at Pierrefonds but a good example of the type is to be found at Nunney in Somerset.

building was in no way representative of the houses of the same name found in much of rural France.

In 1523 a *'bastide'* was a fortlet or a country house and by 1655 *'bastel'* referred to a fortified house, then later in 1549 a *'bastillion'* was a small fortress or tower. Like our word pele, bastille was even used to describe wooden structures defended by palisaded entrenchments and a moat. The only thing they all had in common was a position beyond the limits of towns, in the countryside, and a wish for some security.

In Northumberland, bastles were built in similar situations but differ from the basic Black Middens type of house, a pele, in one important aspect in that they mostly have greater storage areas in their basements to secure the results of a superior harvest gained from the superior land on which they were built. Examples of bastles in Northumberland include Low Hirst, Ashington; Akeld on the lower slopes of the Cheviots and by the River Glen; Hebburn in Chillingham Park; Doddington on the Till; Presson on the Tweed and Castle Heaton, west of Etal in the Till Valley.

Houses such as Snabdough and Melkridge are far superior to the normal run of peles but is this architectural superiority enough to lift them up to what must be the highest social status enjoyed by the owners of the examples above? For a balanced view of life in 'the bastle' see Schama, Simon, *Citizens: A Chronicle of the French Revolution* (London: Penguin, 2004) ISBN 978.0.14.101727.

An example of an entrance to a pele or bastle.

The *OED* and Bastles

The *OED* tells us that a bastel house was in 1544 a variant of the French bastile, a fortified house. In 1523 a bastide was a country house or fortlet in southern France, while a bastille was a tower or bastion of a castle, even one of a series of huts defended by entrenchments for the accommodation of besieging troops. Perhaps the term was introduced by educated officers of the Crown (civil servants) who produced official documents in French?

Bastle Derivatives

This group of houses consists of a seventeenth-century style of building to be found in the south of the county along the River South Tyne and Allendales. It is thought they are later in date than the peles and bastles found in number in that part of the county north of the 'Tyne Solway Gap'.

Looking more comfortable than their northern neighbours, they exhibit more and larger windows, not only to the first floor but to the basement as well. The basement entrance can be off-centre and could have had a loophole for a gun to protect it. Built-in fireplaces are thought to have been the norm from the outset. Some had lookout turrets sitting on a gable, and even dovecots are found.

Where they differ most is in the thickness of their walls, being for the most part only 2ft thick with perhaps the gable containing the entrance being 3ft thick. It was only in the mid- to late-seventeenth century that the Northumbrian hill farmer could consider rebuilding or converting his pele to a more conventional farmhouse. There are examples of later cottages being built close to the earlier pele, which was now used for storage, then later the cottage and pele were abandoned in favour of a conventional farmstead.

Peles/Bastles Built in Groups

Chesterwood, South Tyne
Evistones, Redesdale
Wall
Haltwhistle
Wooley, Allendale Town
Stokoe Crag

PELES/BASTLES WITH GUNLOOPS

High Shaw, Redesdale
Black Cleugh, Unthank
Melkridge
Rebellion House, High Callerton

PELES/BASTLES WITH LOOKOUT TURRETS

Hirst, Ashington (strong house)
Melkridge
Whiton Shield
Healey Hall
Harnham

PELES/BASTLES WITH BOTH DOORS IN SIDE WALL

Westside, Allendale
Low Cleughs, Redesdale
Melkridge
Hirst, Ashington
The Riding, Bellingham
Anick, Hexham
Black Cleugh, Unthank
Bolt House, Kirkwhelpington
Low Leam (Jointure Cleugh)
Starsley, Falstone
Hawkhope, Falstone
Shittleheugh, Otterburn
Holme House, Whitley Chapel
Hesleywell, Whitley Chapel

Variations of Basement Doors in Peles

These diagrams show how harr-hung doors were set in post holes in the top and bottom of the doorway. While most houses had only one door, others had two, all being secured by stout wooden bolts set in the thick stone walls.

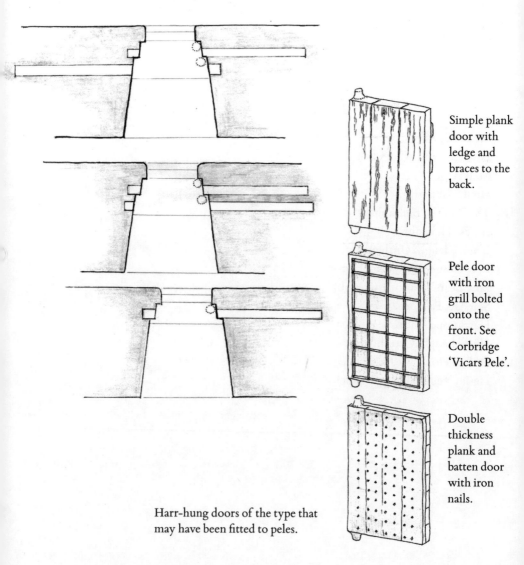

VARIATIONS OF BASEMENT DOORS

TWO DOORS, BOLTS BOTH SIDES
TWO DOORS, BOLTS ONE SIDE ONLY
ONE DOOR AND ONE BOLT ONLY

Simple plank door with ledge and braces to the back.

Pele door with iron grill bolted onto the front. See Corbridge 'Vicars Pele'.

Double thickness plank and batten door with iron nails.

Harr-hung doors of the type that may have been fitted to peles.

While looking for Crusader castles in the Jordanian Desert I found this example of a harr-hung door still in position. No original wooden doors remain in Northumberland but they would have been just like this one, although made of stout timber.

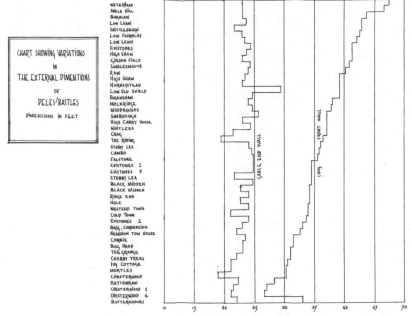

This chart shows the variation in external dimensions of houses designated as peles or bastles. Duplicated and numbered entries on this chart represent addtional buildings within the site which have also been measured. For example, Evistones has at least 3 peles onsite.

DIMENSIONS OF PELES AND BASTLES

'V' denotes a vaulted basement

Castle Heaton	68ft × 26ft	V
Pressen	65ft × 26ft	V
Akeld	63ft × 24ft	V
Little Ryle	55ft 6in × 26ft 6in	V
Waterhead	47ft 3in × 23ft	
Low Hirst	47ft × 25ft	
Shilla Hill	46ft 6in × 23ft	
Burnlaw	43ft 6in × 23ft	
Low Leam	42ft 8in × 23ft 8in	
Shittleheugh	42ft 8in × 21ft 8in	
Low Fairnley	42ft 6in × 23ft	
Low Leam	42in × 23ft 6in	
Shittleheugh	42ft × 21ft 3in	
Evistones	41ft 4in × 24ft 4in	
High Shaw	41ft 4in × 23ft 8in	V
Girson Field	41ft 4in × 22ft	
Smalesmouth	40ft 8in × 24ft 4in	
Raw	40ft 4in × 24ft	
High Shaw	39ft 3in × 23ft 6in	
Horneystead	39ft × 23ft	
Low Old Shield	39ft 5in × 29ft 6in	
Branshaw	39ft 5in × 24ft 8in	V
Melkridge	38ft × 24ft	
Woodhouses	37ft 8in × 24ft 8in	
Snabdough	37ft × 25ft 7in	V
High Carry House	37ft × 23ft	
Whitlees	37ft × 24ft 4in	
Crag	37ft × 21ft 6in	V
The Riding	36ft 6in × 19ft 6in	
Stobby Lea	36ft × 24ft	
Cambo	35ft 9in × 24ft 6in	
Falstone	35ft 6in × 24ft 6in	V
Evistones 1	34ft 6in × 24ft 8in	V
Evistones 3	34ft 6in × 24ft 8in	
Stobby Lea	34ft 6in × 21ft 6in	
Black Midden	34ft 6in × 24ft 8in	

Black Midden	34ft 2in × 23ft 8in	
Ridge End	34ft × 24ft	
Hole	34ft 2in × 22ft 7in	V
Westend Town	34ft × 24ft	
Coldtown	34ft × 21ft	
Evistones 2	33ft 9in × 24ft	
Brig Corsenside	33ft × 23ft	
Butterknowes	33ft × 22ft	
Henshaw Tow House	32ft 6in × 23ft 6in	
Corbie	31ft 6in × 22ft–24ft	
Bog Head	31ft 6in × 23ft	V
The Grange	31ft × 22ft	
Cherry Trees	31ft × 21ft	
Ivy Cottage	30ft 6in × 21ft	
Mortley	30ft 3in × 19ft	
Chesterwood	29ft × 22ft 4in	
Rattenraw	28ft 3in × 23ft	
Chesterwood 1	27ft × 21ft 8in	
Chesterwood 4	26ft 9in × 21ft	

Fifty-five houses were measured but the four superior houses of Castle Heaton, Pressen, Akeld and Little Ryle fall outside the typical pele group of houses. Being of a much higher status, they are not included in the calculation to find an average size of the basic pele. The dimensions of the other fifty-one houses were used to give an average of 35ft 11in × 22ft 6in. P. Ryder, in his *Bastles and Towers in the Northumberland National Park*, gives an average of 39ft × 26in for houses within the park.

A glance at the figures would tend to suggest that peles in the South Tyne and Alendale area are smaller than those to the north. As a rough guide, the gable end walls tend to be 60 per cent of the length of the longer side walls.

Basement Plans and Dimensions

The chart gives the dimensions of fifty peles and bastles but there is no mention of Akeld, Pressen, Castle Heaton and Little Ryle as, due to their superior dimensions, they fall into a special group with storage within their vaults more befitting a monastic establishment or the home of a wealthy person.

The Hole, Bellingham, is a more average size for a pele or bastle, if of superior build than most, while Ray is one of the smallest with little room in its basement and cramped accommodation upstairs for the farmer and his family.

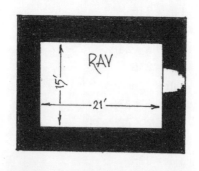

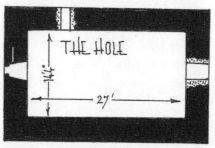

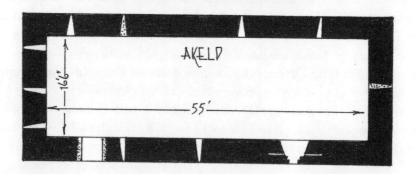

BASEMENT PLANS & DIMENTIONS   10' - 1"

WALLS ALL 3'6" - 4'0"   BRIAN LONG.

The large variation in the dimensions of houses termed peles or bastles is shown in this group of three basement plans, viz. Ray, Hole and Akeld.

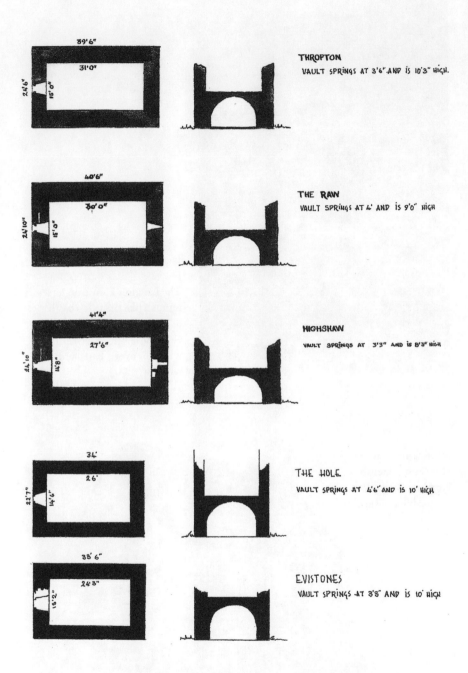

THROPTON
VAULT SPRINGS AT 3'6" AND IS 10'3" HIGH.

THE RAW
VAULT SPRINGS AT 4' AND IS 9'0" HIGH

HIGHSHAW
VAULT SPRINGS AT 3'3" AND IS 8'3" HIGH

THE HOLE
VAULT SPRINGS AT 4'6" AND IS 10' HIGH

EVISTONES
VAULT SPRINGS AT 3'3" AND IS 10' HIGH

Shown here are some variations of basement doorways and doors. No original doors exist and as shown, some houses had a single door while others could have two doors and would require multiple bolts.

The Langlois House on Jersey is much like the peles/bastles of Northumberland. As at Gatehouse, the external stair was built over a basement window.

A hill farmer's house at Hole Head, Henshaw, Northumberland, started life as a small pele or bastle.

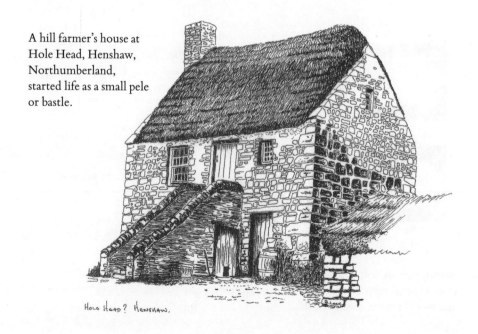

HOLE HEAD? HENSHAW.

Gatehouse Pele/Bastle:
These images demonstrate the development of the first-floor entrance, as can be seen in the non-bonded masonry of different periods.

1. The house was built with a retractable ladder required to gain the door and security of the first floor. A stone plinth has been built against the wall but a retractable ladder would still be required to gain access.

2. Note the 'landing' formed by this plinth is well below the level of the threshold, perhaps as protection against fire.

The existing flights of steps have been built leaning against the wall of the house and the pedestal or landing.

3. In building this, the landing has extended and a ground-floor window or vent was enveloped and partly obscured. The window through the masonry of the steps and landing was blocked at some unknown time, only to be reopened in recent years.

The doorhead to the basement has post holes for two doors, while at the bottom there is a hole for only one door.

GATEHOUSE NORTH PELE/BASTLE
SHOWING DEVELOPMENT OF FIRST FLOOR ENTRANCE AS SEEN
IN THE NON BONDED MASONRY OF DIFFERENT PERIODS

Gatehouse North pele, a rather dour farmer's abode.

First-Floor Living

The numerous peles and bastles of the border counties are well known as having their main domestic apartments on the first floor above a basement used as a storage area and or/a byre. This tradition also exists in other areas of Britain such as Jersey, as well as in northern France. Later variations can be found in the fishermen's cottages of south-west England and on the east coast of Scotland in the East Neuk of Fife and beyond.

The town of Conway in north Wales had many merchants' houses built this way, while Haltwhistle still has the remains of many peles incorporated in its houses. No. 2 Holy Island, Hexham, once known as 'Toad Hall', is dated 1657 and had stout oak shutters to the windows of its low basement store to secure the trade goods within. Evidence would suggest that the smaller window to the left of the door had shutters hung in such a way that when opened they formed a sheltered display area for retail trade, with one shutter falling forward to form a bench and the other being pulled up to shelter the goods from the elements. To the rear of the house was an external stair to the first-floor living area. The examples shown on pages 78–9 are:

The 'Langlois House', Jersey
Hole Head, Henshaw, Northumberland
Gatehouse Pele/Bastle, Northumberland

While on the richer lowlands fine houses were being built, in the marginal areas of the Pennines the yeoman farmer lived in a much smaller house. The ground-floor doors are modern insertions, the original entrance being in the right-hand gable. Once numerous in the town, not many of the type remain now. Other examples can be found in places such as Chester, Shrewsbury and York.

Toad Hall, Hexham

This 'Tudor' house was built as late as 1657 but the pintels or hooks used to secure the shutters to the basement windows are evidence of its original use as a merchant's house, having a low ground floor to store his stock. The small window to the left of the door has its pintels at the top and bottom, not either side as in all the others. Here one shutter fell forward to make a shelf for the display of the retail goods. The other shutter was raised, forming a canopy protecting the goods on display from the elements.

The first floor is much higher and was the main living area. At the rear of the house there was a stone stair that gave access to the first-floor living area.

Chapter III

Evidences

As most towers in the county are of the same plan and type, they cannot without documentary evidence be attributed with certainty to any particular date. The castles, due to border strife and constant use, were not as well advanced architecturally as castles of the same period in the more peaceful south, and here again only documents can date them and record their development for us.

Parts of the documents used to establish the foundation and development of the buildings in the county are printed below with notes.

Licences to Crenellate (Figure 7, see p.82)

Before building a castle or erecting battlements on an existing house, sanction of the Crown had to be obtained. This was known as 'licence to crenellate' and was in fact permission to build or erect crenels or embrasures and merlons, the square structures on the walls. The licence not only gave the owner permission to fortify and crenellate his house, but also gave official sanction for him and his heirs to 'hold it, thus fortified and crenelated for ever without let or hinderence', from the Crown or any of its officials. The following is a list of all the known licences to crenellate in Northumberland:

Tarset	5 December 1267	Henry III
Horton	28 December 1292	Edward I
Tynemouth	5 September 1296	Edward I
Shortflat	5 April 1305	Edward I
Aydon	5 April 1305	Edward I
Newlands	22 July 1310	Edward II
Eshot	22 July 1310	Edward II
Dunstanburgh	21 August 1315	Edward II
Eslington	20 February 1335	Edward III

Ford	16 July 1338	Edward III
Blenkinsop	6 May 1340	Edward III
Etal	3 May 1341	Edward III
Ogle	11 May 1341	Edward III
Barmoor	17 May 1341	Edward III
Widdrington	10 September 1341	Edward III
Bothal	15 May 1343	Edward III
Crawley	20 November 1343	Edward III
Chillingham	27 January 1344	Edward III
Whitley	9 April 1345	Edward III
Haggerston	4 June 1345	Edward III
West Swinburne	16 March 1346	Edward III
Fenwick	26 November 1378	Richard II

Figure 7: Map showing licences to crenellate.

The Survey of 1415 (Figure 8)

This is the only survey to cover all of the county showing castles and towers, then a group of buildings known to surveyors as 'fortalices'. The part of the survey showing castles has marginal notes reducing castles such as Horton iuxta Mare, Blekensope, Swinburn, Dichant and Kippitheton to the rank of a fortalicium.

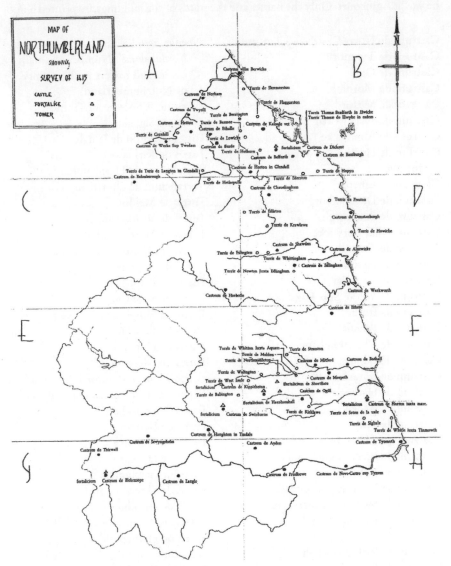

Figure 8: A survey of the county made in 1415 is thought to have been composed to inform King Henry V in whose hands his border with Scotland would be while he was at Agincourt. This survey is the only one to cover the county as a whole; the results are shown here in map form.

The part listing towers upgrades them to fortalicium, they being Harnamhall and Shortflate, indicating that the surveyor thought there was a class that was superior to a tower but not quite up to the standards of a castle (see p.23).

The proprietors or custodians were also listed, and it is thought that it was composed to inform Henry V in whose hands his border with Scotland would be while he was at Agincourt. Only the names and the status of the buildings are printed here:

Castrum de Novo-Castro sup Tynam
Castrum de Tynmoth
Castrum de Ogil
Castrum de Morpeth
Castrum de Mitford
Castrum de Warkworth
Castrum de Alnewicke
Castrum de Horton ixuta mare
  fortalicium
Castrum de Eshete
Castrum de Dunstanburgh
Castrum de Bamburgh
Castrum villae Berwicke
Castrum de Twysill
Castrum de Hetton
Castrum de Norham
Castrum de Werke Sup Twedam
Castrum de ffurde
Castrum de Ethalle
Castrum de Chauelingham
Castrum de Edlingham
Castrum de Kaloule vet
Castrum de Harbotle
Castrum de Ayden
Castrum de Langle
Castrum de Thirwall
Castrum de Blekensope fortalicium
Castrum de Prudhowe
Castrum de Horton in Glendall
Castrum de Swinburne fortalicium
Castrum de Haughton in Tindale
Castrum de Sewyngsheles
Castrum de Rokesborough
Castrum de Bothall
Castrum de Belfurth
Castrum de Dichant fortalicium
Castrum de Shawden
Castrum de Kippitheton fortalicium

'*Nomina Fortaliciorum infra comitatum Northumbriae*' (Number of small castles and towers in the county of Northumberland).
Turris de Whitle ixuta Tinmowth
Turris de Sighale
Turris de Seton de la uale
Turris de Kirklawe
ffortalicium de Harnhamhall
ffortalicium de Shortflate
Turris de Meldon
Turris de Walington
Turris de Northmidileton
Turris de Whitton Iuxta Aquam
Turris de West herle
Turris de Babington
Turris de Stranton
Turris de Howicke
Turris de Preston
Turris de Hopyn
Turris de Ederston
Turris Thomae Bradforth in Elwicke
Turris Thomae de Elwyke in Eadem
Turris de Lowicke
Turris de Barmor
Turris de Holburn
Turris de Haggarston
Turris de Berrington
Turris de Skremerston
Turris de Cornhill
Turris de Langton in Glendall
Turris de Hethepulle
Turris de Ildirton
Turris de Krawlawe
Turris de Whittingham
Turris de Newton Juxta Edlingham
Turris de Eslington

Survey of the Mars and Tevedale 1509 *(Figure 9)*

The next survey or return of any importance was made in 1509 and gave the names of the 'Owners Inhabytanttes or Officers'. It also mentioned how far each building was from the 'Mars' and 'Tevedale'. The Merse is the name given to the area north of the River Tweed inland from Berwick and is about 20 miles long.

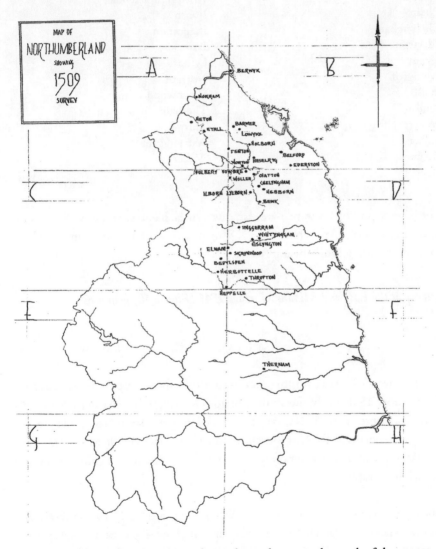

Figure 9: This map shows the survey of 1509, listing houses in the north of the county. The survey also gave their distance from the border.

The buildings are listed here in alphabetical order:

Barmer	Herbottelle
Bedylsden	Heselryg
Belford	Hetton
Berwyk	Holborn
Bewyk	Horton (in Glendale)
Chatton	Ilborn
Chelyngham	Inggerram
Ederston	Lowyke
Elnam	Lylborn
Eslyngton	Norram
Etall	Skrynwood
Fenton	Thernam
Fowbre	Thropton
Fulbery	Wittynggam
Hebborn	Woller
Heppelle	

The 'Garnysons' or horsemen are also given in each entry, along with the 'sum of the number of thys men M^{le}CCLXX men', a total of 1270 men in the whole county, excluding Norham and Berwick.

Survey of the East and Middle Marches 1541 *(Figure 10, seep p.87)*

EAST MARCH

A document of great importance is the one drawn up at Newcastle on 2 December 1541. Only the actual portions relating to the strongholds themselves are printed here. This survey is recorded in two parts, reproduced here, the first giving details of the East March and the second the Middle Marches.

Marginal notes appearing on the original document are appended at the end of each paragraph:

The townes[1] lyinge upon the northe and west syde of the river of Tyll wthin the said East Marches of England foranempst Scotland and howe the same be at this present peopled and plenyshed and what castells towres and fortresses be at this daie wthin the said percyncte and howe the same be maynteyned and reparellyd with certayne other devyces for the repayring and fortefyinge and strngthenynge of those borders muche necessary to be releved in brefe tyme.

1. Towns and c. in the East Marches

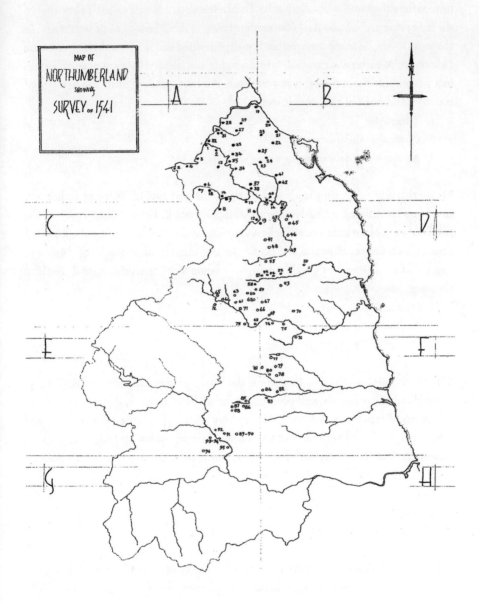

Figure 10: Drawn up on 2 December 1541, this survey is of great importance as it gives details of each house and owner.

Fryste upon the Ryv' of Twede and upon the west side of the ryv' of Tyll nere unto where the same ryv' falleth into Twede standeth a towne called Tylmothe[1] of the'inherytaunce[2] of one [...] Claverubge being at this P'sent a childe wthin age. In the same towne be tenne husbandlands well plenyshed and in yt standeth a pece of an olde tower[3] whiche was casten downe brenghte and defaced by a knyghte of Scottes in a warre tyme more then fortye yeres paste And yet standeth more the half p'te of the vawt and walls of the same tower.

1. Tilmowthe
2. Claverings inheritance
3. An olde tower defaced by the warres

Nexte thtereunto wthin a myle and a half of the said ryv' of Tyll standeth in the towne of Heaton[1] of xij husbandlands well plentyshed. In the which standeth the ruinous walls of an olde castell[2] lykewyse rased and casten downe by the kinge of Scottes in the warre aforesaid and bothe the said castell and towne be of thinhery-taunce[3] of [...] Grayce of Chyllingham now being a childe wthin age and warde to the kings mats.

1. Heaton
2. A ruinows castle defaced by the warrers
3. Gray of chillingham's inheritance

The tower of Cornell[1] standing upon the banke of the said river of twede in yt be twelve husbandlands well plenyshed and a tower newe embatted cov'ed and put in good reparacon[2] by one Gylbert Swynnowe gentlema'[3] the owener and inherytur of the said tower and towne of Cornwe; who entendeth also as his powers may serve to buylde a barmekyn about the said tower and doth prepare stuffe for the same.

1. Cornell
2. A tower in good reparacon
3. Gilbert Swynnowe's inheritance

The towne of Warke[1] standeth also upon the banke of the said Ryv' of Twede in the which town bene xj husbandlands well plenyshed if the kings maties of inh-erytaunce.[2] There ys also a castell of the said kings matie of thre wardes whereof the utter most warde s'veth for a barmekyn the said castell ys in great and extreme decaye[3] as well by reason that yt was never p'fyte;y fynyshed nor the walls of the pryncypall tower or doungeon thereof was nev' cov'ed as by occasion of a battyre made upon the utter walls of the same wth great orden'nce at the last sege lade there-unto by the duke of Albyony.

1. Warke
2. The princes inheritance
3. A castle in great decay

The Townshippe of Carrame[1] conteynes [...] Hereyn ys a lytle tower[2] wythout barmekyn or iron gate metely for the defence of thinhabytants of the said towne in a soddenly occurrante skyrmyshe and in tyme of warre they may resorte for theyr relefe to the said castell of Warke.

1. Carrame
2. A littell tower for a sodayne rescue otherwise hath warke for refuge

The towneshippe of Downeham[1] conteyned in tyme passed viij husbandlands and when yt lay waste by occasion of warre[2] Sr. Cuthbert Ogle clerke purchased yt and hath buylded thereyne an newe tower[3] as yet but of two house heighte and not fully feenyshed by one house heighte and imbattlements nor hath not as yet any barmekyn and the said Sr. Cuthbert occupieth the said towne nowe but wit two plowes of his owne.

1. Downeham
2. Layed waste by warres
3. A towre built by Sr. Cuthbert Ogle

The towneshipe of Pawston[1] conteyneth xij husband lands now plenyshed one Garrarde Selbye gent. Of late purchased this towne and in yt buylded a lytle tower wthout a barmekyn now fully fynyshed.[2]

1. Pawston
2. Garrard Selbyes inheritance a little tower unfinished

The towneshsippe of Hethepol conteyneth vj husband lands newe plenyshed and therein ys a lytle stone house[2] or pyle which ys a greate releyffe to the ten'nts thereof. And the most parte of thys towne ys of th' inherytaunce of Sr. Roher Graye[3] and other ffreholders have p'cell of the same.

1. Hetheppole
2. A little stone house
3. Most Sir Roger Graye's inheritance

At East Newton thres ys a lytle towre and a stone house joined to the same the walls of which stone house ys so lowe that in the laste warres the Scotts wane the said stone house and sett fyer on yt and had thereby almost brunte the tower and all. The experience whereof sheweth that yt were expedyente to rase the walls of the said stone house higher and fortefye the same able for the defence of common skrymyshes.[1]

1. Requireth more fortification for common forrayes

The towneshippe of Aykeld conteyneth xvj husband lands all plenyshed and hath in yt a lyttle fortlett[1] or bastle house wthout a barmekyn. The towneshippe of Wouller[1] conteyneth xx^{ti} husbandlands all plenyshed and had a lytle towre standynge strongely whiche dyd muche releyve as well as the Inhabytants of the same towne as of two or three vyllages nere adjoyninge thereunto yt stode in a mervelous conevemyent place for defence of the countrye thereaboute. And the half od yt ys fallen downe for lacke of reparacons nowe lately this same year.[2]

    1. Wowller

    2. A little towre in dacay

The towneshippe of Yerdle conteyneth x husband lands and hath in yt a bastell house wthout a barmekyn. The towneshipps of Mydleton Hall conteyneth iiij husband lands plenyshed and hath in yt two stone houses or bastells. The towneshipps of Langton conteyneth xij husbandlands plenyshed and in yt standeth a great p'te of the walls of an olde tower whiche was rased casten downe[1] by the kings of Scotts in a warre time.

    1. An old tower cast down by the Scots

The towneshippe of Brankstone conteyneth xvj husbandlands plenyshed and in yt ys a lytle tower wthout a barmekyn which was lykewyse rased by the Scotts and ys newly repared agayne. The towneshipps of foweberye[1] conteyneth viij husband lands well plenyshed and hath in yt tower wthout a barmekyn in reasonable good reparacons.

    1. Fowberye

The towneshipps of Chatton conteyneth xxx^{tj} husband lands plenyshed of the kyngs ma ties inheytaunce late of the Earle of Northumberland's lands. In yt be two lytle towers without barmekyns thone of thunherytaunce of the said Richard Fowebery and thither ys the mansion of vyccaredge.[1]

    1. Fowberyes and the vicarage

Also that a new tower and a barmekyne be made at Kilham and that the towneshippes be so assyngned unto such fortresses and barmekynes as they with their goods may be releved in tyme of necessyte and to be so apporconed and rated that at the lest fourty persons or mo be assigned to every fortresse. At Twdemouthe upon the southsyde of the ryver of Twede foranenst Barwyke there ys two lytle towers in reasonable good reparacons the one belongeth to the hospital of Kepeyere within the byshoppryke of Durrysme and thother ys of thinherytaunce of [...]

At Scrymmerstone upon the sea coste a myle from the said river of Twede ys a great olde towre muche decayed for lacke of contynuall necessary reparacons. At Cheswyke but two myles from the said ryver of Twede there ys a lytle tower of the inherytaunce of one Thomas Mannors and others beinge lykewyse in decaye for a lacke of reparacons. At Braggarstone beinge thre myles from the said ryver of Twde therestandath against the stronge tower of thindherytaunce of on Thomas Haggarson and yt is in miserable good reparacons. At Ancroft two myles from the said ryver Twede there ys a lytle fortresse standinge nere unto the churche of the saide towne of thinherytaunce of Gray of Chillingham scarcely being in good repare.[1]

    1. A little fortresse scarce in reparation

At lawyke foure myles from the said ryver Twede there is a towre on thinherytaunce of Mr. Swynburne of capthteton.[1]

    1. Swinborne of Cap Hetons

At Byermore beynge of lyke distance from the said ryver of Twede there ys a tower of thinherytaunce of Mr. Muschyens in extreme decaye and almost ruinous for lacke of reparacons.

    At Berrynton[1] beynge thre myles from the said ryver of Twede ethere was a towre of thinherytaunce of therle of Rutland wth for lacke of reparacons ys lately fallen to extreme ruyne and decaye.

    At Shoreswolde but a myle from the said ryver of Twede standeth a pece of a tower that was rased and casten downe by the Kinge of Scotts in a tyme of warr'xl[ti] yeres and more passed and belongeth to the college of Duresme.[2]

    1. A pece of a towre defaced in the warres
    2. The colledg of Durhams

The castle of Norrham standinge nere unto the said ryver of Twede belonging to the byshoppe of Duresme ys in very good state both in reparacons and fortefiac'ons on well furnyshed[1] and stuffed with artillery munyc'ons and other necessaries requysyte to the same.

    1. A castle well furnished – the B of Durrams

At Thornebie[1] there is a lytle towre in reasonable good reparac'ons[2] yt standeth within a myle of the said ryver of Twede and ys of thinherytaunce of Sr. Wyll'm Herons[3] heyre.

    1. Thornbye
    2. A little towre in good case
    3. Hrons

At Newebygginge[1] nere to the said ryver of Twede there ys a towre in reasonable good reparacons[2] of thinherytaunce of George Orde esquier[3] and at a place in the felde of the same towne called the great hewghe there ys a stronge stone house or bastell newly made by one John Smythe.

1. Newbrigging
2. A towre in reasonable reparacons
3. Mr. Ordes

At Twysle[1] nere unto the said ryver of Twede there ys standynge the walls of an old fortresse or castell rased and caste downe by the Kinge of Scotts in aware xl[ti] yeres[2] and more since.

1. Twisle
2. An old castle rased by the Scotts 40 years

At Gryndonrygge[1] there ys a lytle tower[2] of thinherytaunce of John Selbye gent.[3] in reasonable good reparac'on and is a myle and a half from the said ryver of Twede.

1. Grindon Rigge
2. A little tower repayred
3. Mr. Selbyes

At Duddo[1] there standeth a pece of a towre that was rased[2] and casten downe by the Kinge of Scotts in the said warre xl[ti] yeres since and more and yt is of the inherytaunce of Claveringe[3] and two myles from the said ryver of Twede.

1. Duddo
2. A twore rased
3. Clavering's inheritaunce

The castell of Etayle[1] beinge of the Erle of Rutlands inherytaunce standeth upon the Est syde of the said ryver of Tyll thre myles from the said ryver of Twede ys for lacke of reparacons in very great decaye[2] and many necessary houses within the same bacome ruinous and fallen to the ground.

1. Etayle
2. Decayed

The castell of Forde standinge lykewyse upon the Est syde of the said ryver of Tyll was bronte by the laste Kinge of Scotts a lytle before he was slayne at Flodden felde some parte thereof hath bene reparelled againe sythence that tyme but the great buyldinges and most necessarye houses resteth evet sythens waste and in decaye[1] the whiche if they were repared were able to receyve and lodge an hundredth and mo horsement to lye there in garrison in tyme of warree and for that purpose yt is a place muche convenient and standeth well for servyce to be done at any place within the said Est marche.[2]

1. A castle decayed
2. Fitt to lodge 100 men and for any service on the Est marches

There ys also in the same towne a lytle tower which was the mansion of the parson-age[1] of the same and a quarter thereof was casten downe by the last King of Scotts at the tyme aforesaid and Sir Cuthbert Ogle parson of the churche there beganne to reedyfie[2] the same againe and rased the wall thereof two houses highte and there so yt resteth and yt were muche requisite to be fynyshed for defence of that towne.[3]

1. A little towre the parson's mansion
2. Unfinished
3. Much for the defence of the towne

At Fenton[1] lykewyse standinge upon the Est syde of the water of Tyll there ys a grett towre wth a barmekyn in great decaye[2] in the rooffe and floores and the walls of the barmekyn wth other necessary houses wthin the same and yt were much requyste that yt were kepte in reparations for yt standeth in a very convenient and apte place for lyinge of an hundredth men in grarryson[3] in tyme of warre against Scotland.

1. Fenton
2. A great tower with a barmekyn in decay
3. Mete for a garrison of 100 men

At Nesebytte[1] there was a towre[2] of thinheritaunce of Sir Roger Gray[3] but yt is longe synce for laske of reparacons decayed and fallen and no fortresse there now remayneth.

1. Nesebitt
2. A towre utterly ruined
3. Sir Roger Grayes

At Wetewood[1] there is a lytle towre[2] of thinheritaunce of one [...] Wetewood gent.[3] in measurable good reparacons.

1. Wetewood
2. A towre in reparacions
3. One wetewoods

At Horton[1] there is a great towre wth a barmekyn[2] of Sir Roger Grayes Inherytaunce and his chefe house in great decaye for lacke of contynuall reparacons and a great petye yt were that yt should be suffered to decayye fro yt standeth ina very conveni-ent place for the defence of the countrye thereabouts.[3]

1. Horton
2. A great tower with a barmekyn in decay
3. A place mete for defence and Grayes

At Holburne ys a towre[1] and a barmekyn of thinherytaunce of Thomas Holburne esquier[2] in measurable good rep'acons.

1. Holburne a tower and barmekyn
2. Holburns inheritance

At Hesellerygge[1] ys a lowe towre wch was never fully fynyshed of thinherytaunce of Thomas Haggarstone esquire kepte in measurable good rep'acons.

1. Heselrigge a low tower not finished one Haggerstones

MIDDLE MARCHES

The descipc'on of the p'sent state of all the Castells Towers Barmekyns and other Fortresses standinge and scytuate nere unto the utter border and frounter of the mydle m'ches of England wth certayne devyses for the repayringe and fortefyinge of the said borders where moste need requyreth aft'our fantasy and opynyon Fyrste in the town of West Llyburne[1] there bene two towers the western toure whereof ys of thinherytaunce of one Cuthbert Proctour gent. And for lacke of contynuall necessary repac'ons ys fallen in great ruyne and decaye[2] for all the roves and floors therefore by wasted and fallen downe and nothing standynge but the walles. The Esterne toure of the same towne ys the Inherytaunce of Sr. Cuthbert Ogle clerke and the rooffe and floores thereof were lately bronghte by sodden fyer Lyonell Graye porter of Barwyke ys the fermer and occupier of bothe the said toures.

1. West Lilburne
2. Two towres decayed

The Castell of Chyllingham[1] of thinheritaunce of younge Raffe Graye of the same beinge in the Kings Mate warde and order during his mynorytie and none ages ys in the measurable good repac'ons[2] for Sr. Robt. Ellerker knighte havynge the custody and gov'nauncce of the said castell hath of late newly reparelled the same.

1. Chillingham a castle
2. Grayes inheritaunce well repayred

At Hebburne[1] ys a lytle toure of thinherytaunce of Thomas Hebbune in reasonable good rep'ac'ons. At Bewyke[2] ys a good tower of the kings mate Inherytaunce as of the augmentac'ons of his graces crowne late belonging to the subpressed monastery of Tynemouthe. A parte thereof ys newly cov'ed wth lead and thither p'te ys not well cov'ed nor in good repac'ons and yt is much requysyte that the said tower were kept in convenient reparll for yt standeth in a fytte place for the defence of the countrye thereabouts and is able in tyme of warre to conteyne fyfte men in garrison.[3]

1. Hebburne a little tower repayred
2. Bewike a good tower the princes inheritaunce
3. A good place for a garrison of 50 men

At Ilderton there ys a great tower wth a stronge barmekyn of stone[1] of thinherytaunce of Rauffe Ilderton gentlemen whiche for lack of contynuall necessary rep'ac'ns[2] ys a fallen in extreme ruyne and decaye and all the roofes and flores thereof wasted and nothinge standinge but the barre walles.

1. Iderton a great tower with a strong barmekyn of stone
2. Out of reparacons

At Roddome[1] there is a lytle toure wthout a barmekyn of thinherytaunce of John Roddom[2] esquier the roofe ys decayed for lack of necessarye repaco'ns.

1. Roddon a little tower unrepaired
2. Roddons inheritaunce

At Crawley[1] there is a lytle toure[2] of thinherytaunce of the daughter and heyre of S. Wll'm Heron in great decaye for lack of contynuall reparaco'ns.

1. Crawley
2. A little towre unrepaired

At Tytlyngton[1] ys a lytle toure[2] of the kingre mate Inherytaunce late belonging to the Supp'ssed monastery of Kyrkeh'm decayed in the rooffes for lacke of repac'ons and the imbattlementes thereof were nev'fynyshed.

1. Titlington
2. A little towre the princes inheritance decayed

At Shawden[1] ys a toure of thinheritance of Cuthb't Proctour in measurable good repac'ons.[2]

1. Shawden
2. A towre in reparacon

At Whyttyngame[1] bene two towers[2] whereof the one ys the mansion of the vycaredge and thother of the inheritaunce of Rb't Collyngewood esquire and both be in measurable good repac'ons.

1. Whittingame
2. Two towres repayred

At Callayle ys a toure[1] of inheritaunce of Claveringe in measurable good repac'ons.
   1. Callyle a tower

At Eslyngton[1] ys a toure wth a barmekyn[2] of the Inherytaunce of one [...]
Heslerygge esquire and in the tenor and occupaco'on of Robt. Collingewoode esqui'
who kepeth the same in good repac'ons.
   1. Eslington
   2. A towre with a barmekyn

At Ingrame[1] ys a lytle toure[2] wch ys the mansion house of the P'sonage there and for
lack of contynuall necessary repac'ns ys fallen in great decaye in the cov'ynge and
Rooffes thereof.
   1. Ingrame
   2. A little towre decayed

Also a lyrle by west the said toure of Ingrame the ryv' or water[1] of Brymyshe
by rage of floodes hath worne sore upon the southe banke thereof that
except there be shortly made a were and defence of the same yt is very lyke
in continuance of a tyme to were awaye both the said towne of Ingram and
tower aforesaid.
   1. The water like to wear the towne of Ingram

At Great Ryle there hath one Thomas Collingewood gent' newly buylded a toure[1]
upon the Inherytaince if Robt Collingewood and is mynded to buylde likewise a
barmekyn about the same as his power may serve thereunto.
   1. Great Ryle a towre

At Prendyke ys lykewyse a lytle toure[1] newlye buylded by one Thomas Aldye gent.
Thinherytaunce of the same.
   1. Prendyke a little towre

At Alname[1] be two lytle toures[2] whereof thone ys the mansion of the vycaredge
and thother of the inherytaunce of the kinges matie p'cell of the late Erle of
Northumb'landes lands beinge scarcely in good reparac'ons.
   1. Aylnane
   2. Two little towres oute of reparacons

At scrynwood[1] is a toure and a barmekyn[2] of the Inherytance of John Horseley
esquire kepte in very good repac'ons.

1. Screynwood
2. A towre and a barmekyn

At Byttylsden[1] ys a toure and a barmekyn[2] of the Inherytaunce of Percyvall Selby esqui' in good repac'ons and nere unto the same ys an other lytle toure at a place called the Cotte walles in measurable good repac'ons of the said p'cyvall Selbyes Inherytaunce.

1. Bittilsden
2. A towre and a barmekyn

At Borrodone[1] ys a great toure[2] of thinherytaunce of George Fenwycke and Percyvall Lysle in the righte of his wife whiche for lacke of necessary repac'ons ys fallen into extreme ruyne and decaye.

1. Borrodne
2. A great towre in ruine

At Clennell[1] ys a lytle toure[2] of thinherytaunce of one p'cyvall Clenell gent newly reparelled and brattyshed by the same p'cyvall and also he ys making of a newe barmekyn about the same as his power will extende thereunto.

1. Clennell
2. A little towre

At Allaynton[1] is a lytle bastell house of stone[2] the mansion of the vycaredge scarsely in good repac'ons.

1. Allaynton
2. A little stone house

At the Lynne brigge[1] there hath bene a stone house of thinherytaunce of one Rog' Horeseley but yt was bronnte and casten down by the Scottes in tyme pste, and the owner hathe gathered the stones thereof unto a place of more strength nere unto the same, and to buylde a new bastell house as his power wyll serve hym Indeendeth.

1. The Linnebrigg

At Tharnam[1] is a toure of thinherytaunce of one Rog' Horseley in measurable good reparc'ons.

1. Tharnam

At nether Trewhytt[1] ys a toure of thinherytaunce of Edward Gallon in measurable good reparc'ons.

1. Nether Trewhitt a toure

At Hephell ys a toure of thinherytaunce of the lord Ogle decayed[1] in the roofes and scarcely in good repac'ons.

1. Hephell a towre decayed

At Throptone ys a lytle toure[1] of thinherytaunce of Sr Cuthb't Ratclyffe Knighte

1. Throptone a little tower

At cartyngton ys a good fortresse[1] of two toures and other stronge stone houses of the Inherytaunce of the said Mr Cuthb't Ratclyffe Knight and kepte in good repac'ons.

1. Cartington a good fortress

Apon the Southe syde of the ryv' of Cockett ys a strongest place and metely for the defence of all that countrye aswell against the Invasion and incourses of Scottes in tyme of warre as for defence of the thefts and spoyles of the Ryddesdayle men standeth the castell Harbottell[1] wythin the said country of Ryddesdayle and ys of the Inherytaunce of the lord Taylboys heyres and is for lacke of necessary repac'ons fallen into extreme ruyne and decaye.

1. Harbottle castle in great decay

At Barrowe a lytle above the Harbottell[1] upon the southe syde of the same ryv' of Cokett standeth the olde walles of a lytle fortresse[2] of the Inherytance of one Garrard Barrowe which in tyme pst was brounte and rased by the Scottes in a warre tyme and so remaineth still waste because the oweners therof have bene but poor men and not able nor of power sythens to reparell the same.

1. Barrow
2. A little fortresse ruined by the warres

At a place called the here clewgh[1] one Rog' hangingeshawes hath lately buylded upon his owne Inherytance a strong pele house of stone[2] in convenyent place for resystence of the Incourse of ytheves of Ryddesdayle and he ys not able in defaulte of substance to p'forme and fynyshe the same.

1. Haare Clewgh
2. A stone pile not finished

At Great Tosson[1] is a tower[2] of the lorde Ogles Inherytance and not in good rep'ac'ons.

1. Great Tosson
2. A Towre

At Whytton[1] nere unto Rothberye is a tour and a lytle barmekin[2] being the manc'on of the P'sonage of Rothberry and is in good reparacon.

1. Whytton
2. A towre and a little barmekyn

At Elyburne[1] p'cell of the lordeshippe of Rothbeyre is a strong pele[2] house of the kings maties Inherytaunce as of thaugmentac'ons of his graces crowne and p'cell of the late Erle of Northumberlands lands.

1. Elliburne
2. A strong pile

At Rhytton[1] is a stone house[2] and a lytle barmekyn of the kinges maties Inherytance p'cell of thaugmentac'ons of his graces crowne lately belonging to the supp'ssed monastery if Newemnestre scarcely in good repac'ons.

1. Rytton
2. A stone house oute of reparacons

At Grenelyghton[1] is a lytle stone house wth a barmekyn[2] of the same Inherytance and not in good repac'ons.

1. Grenelighton
2. A little stone house with a barmekyn

At Rotheley[1] is a lytle towre[2] of the same inheritance in measurable good reparacions.

1. Rotheley
2. A little toure

At Harterton[1] hall ys a stronge bastell house[2] of the Inherytaunce of Sr John Fenwyke in measurable good rep'ac'ons.

1. Harterton
2. A strong house

At the Sawnes[1] is a lytle pele[2]house or bastell of thinherytaunce of the said Sr John Fenwyke in measurable good rep'ac'ons.

1. The Sawnes
2. A little pile

At Wallyngton[1] is a stronge toure[2] and a stone house of thinherytaunce of the said Sr John Fanwyke in good re'ac'ons.

1. Wallington
2. A strong towre.

At Kyrke Whelpyngton[1] is a little toure[2] the mansyon of the vycaredge in good rep'ac'ons.
1. Kirk Welpington
2. A little towre

At Hawyke[1] ys a bastell house[2] of thinherytau'ce of one […] Bellyngiam in good rep'ac'ons.
1. Hawike
2. A bastell howse

At Swetehope[1] is an other bastell house[2] of thinherytance of Sr John Fenwyke knight in good rep'ac'ons.
1. Swetehope
2. A bastell house

At Fylton more[1] is a bstell house[2] called the Whyte house of the kings maties Inheritance p'cell of the Augmentac'on of his graces crowne belonginge to the late supp'ssed monastery of Newminster in measurable good rep'ac'ons.
1. Filton more
2. A bastell howse

At Carre Cottes[1] in the said Fylton more is an other bastel house[2] of the same Inherytance in measurable good repac'ons.
1. Carre Cottes
2. A bastell howse

At lytle Swyneburne[1] is a lytle toure[2] of thinherytaunce of Thomas Mydleton of Belso esqui' decayed in the roofes.
1. Little Swinborne
2. A little towre decayed

At Mykle Swynburne[1] hath nebe a great toure[2] of the Inherytaunce of Sr John Wetherington knighte but all the rooffes and floores thereof bene decayed and nothinge standinge but the walles.
1. Mickle Swinborne
2. A great towre decayed

At Gonnerton[1] is a toure and a stone house[2] of thinherytaunce of Sr John Fenwyke knighte in good repac'ons.
1. Gonnerton
2. A towre and a stone howse

At Chypchase[1] ys a fare toure and a manor of stone warke[2] joyned thereunto of thinherytaunce of John Heron of the same esquire kepte in good repac'ons.

1. Chipchase
2. A fayre towre and manor of stoneworke

At Symondburne[1] ys a stronge toure of foure house height of thinherytaunce of Sr Wyll'm herons heyre and yt standeth of a very stronge ground[2] a myle from Chypchase upon the west side of the ryv' of northe tyne and ys in measurable good repac'ons.

1. Symondburne
2. A strong towre in a very strong ground

And in the same towne of symondburne ys a nother lytle towre[1] the manc'on of the p'sonage there in measurable good repac'ons.

1. A little towre

At the hall barnes[1] in the same towre ys a bastell hosue[2] of the late inheritance of Sr William Heron in good repac'ons.

1. The Hall Barnes
2. A bastle howse

At Hawghton[1] two myles southeste from the said towne of symondburne standeth the walles of an olde castell or fortresse very stronge but the roofes and floores thereof bene decayed and gone[2] and an olde barmekyn p'tely decayed in the walles thereof of thinherytaunce of Sr John Wetherington knighte and in great decaye.

1. Hawghton
2. A fortresse very strong but decayed

At Teckett[1] ys a strong stone house[2] of thinherytaunce of Wyll'm Rydley in good repac'ons.

1. Teckett
2. A strong stone house

At the Carrow[1] is a toure and a stone house[2] ioyninge to the same of the kinhes matues Inherytaunce p'cell of the augmentac'n of his graces crowne late belonging to the supp'ssed monastery of Hexham and my a lete dymytted unto Sr Reynold Carnabye knighte for certayne yeres yt lyeth in decaye[3] and not inhabyted nor in good repac'ons.

1. Carrow
2. A towre and a stone house
3. In decay

At Sewyngeshealles[1] in an old towre[2] of thinherytaunce of John Heron of Chypchase esquire in great decaye in the rooffes and flores and lyeth waste and unplenyshed.

1. Sweyngesheales
2. An old toure wast

At Bradley[1] ys a stone house[2] of the inherytaunce of Nycolas Carrow and Lyeth waste and unplenyshed.

1. Braydley
2. A stone howse

At Satlyngestones[1] ys a toure[2] of thinherytaunce of Will'm Carnabye esquire in measurable good rep'ac'ons.

1. Saltingstones
2. A towree

At Thyrlewall[1] is a toure[2] of thinherytaunce of Rob't Thyrlewall of the same in measurable good rep'ac'ons.

1. Thirlewall
2. A towre

At Blenkinsoppe[1] ys a toure[2] of thinherytance of John Blenkensoppe and is decayed in the roofe and not in good rep'acons.

1. Blenkinsopp
2. A towre decayed

At Bellester[1] is a bastell house[2] in thoccipac'n of one Blenkensoppe and is in measurable good rep'acons.

1. Bellerster
2. A bastell house

At Fetherstonhaugher[1] ys a toure[2] of thinherytaunce of Alexander Featherstonehaugh of the same in good rep'ac'ons.

1. Fetherstonhawgh
2. A towre

At Hawtewysle[1] is a toure[2] of thinherytaunce of Sr Will'm Musgrave knighte in measurable good rep'ac'ons.

1. Hawtewysle
2. A towre

At Willymonnteswyke[1] ys a good toure and a stone house[2] ioyninge thereunto of the inherytaunce of Nycolas Rydley Kepte in good rep'ac'ons.

1. Willimowteswike
2. A good towre and a stone howse

At Langley[1] standeth the walles of an olde castell[2] of thinherytaunce of the kinges maties as p'cell of the augmentac'ons of his graces crown late of thinherytaunce of therle of Northumb'erland. All rooffes and flores thereof be decayed and wasted and gone and nothinge remaining but onely the walles.

1. Langely
2. An old castell defaced

At the Newbrough[1] is a toure[2] of thinherytaunce of the lorde Burrowe in measurable good rep'aco'ns.

1. Newbrough
2. A towre

In all the said countrye of Tundall there ys not any other towne or place of Comon resorte where vyttalles ys to be solde for money but onely at Bellingeame[1] aforesaid nor there ys nowe standinge wthin the said countrye of Tyndall any towers save one lytle tower at Heslesyde of thinherytaunce of one [...] Charleton sone to Edward Charleton deceased.

1. Bellingeam theyr towne and assembling place

There was wthin the said countrye of Tyndall an other tower called Tarsett[1] hall of the lorde Burrowes Inherytaunce the which was brounte by the said Tyndalles xvj yeres sythence and more at a tyme when Sr Rauffe Fenwyke lay wth a certayne garrison in the tower at Tarsett for the reformac'on of certayne mysorders wthin the said countrye of Tyndale.

1. Tarsett hawle defaced

There ys also an olde mansion and apparence of a fortresse that hath bene in tyme passed at a place in Tyndall called Warke[1] wythin twoo myles or lesse of the said Bellingeam of the kinges maties Inherytaunce.

1. Warke the Chefe seignory of Tindale and al the contrye between north tine and south tine

In which naturall strength and fortyficac'ons of such places almost inaccessible the said Tyndalles do much rejoice and Imbolden themselfes and when they be affrayed do rether trust in the strength of such places wthout their houses then to the surety or defence of their houses And yet surely the heddesmen of them have very strong hosues[1] whereof for the most p'te the utter sydes or walles be made of great sware oke trees strongly bounce and joined together wth great tenons of the same so thycke mortressed that yt wylbe very harde wthoute great force and laboure to breake or caste downe any of the said hosues the tymber as well of the said walles as rooffes be so greatt and cov'ed mott p'te wth turves and eathe that they wyll not easily burne or be sett on fyere.

1. Theyr howses strong

Survey of 1541 (Figure 10, see p.87)

This survey is in two parts with the buildings on the East March listed first, followed by the Middle March. This map shows the buildings in numerical order, following their actual entry in the survey. The two marches are picked out using a different symbol for each.

THE EAST MARCH

1. Tylmothe Tower
2. Heaton, an olde castell
3. Cornell Tower
4. Wark Castell
5. Carrame, lytle tower
6. Downeham, a new tower
7. Pawston, a lytle tower
8. Hethepol, a lytle stone house or pyle
9. East Newton, a lytle tower and a stone house joined
10. Akeld, a lytle fortelett or bastle house
11. Wouller, a lytle tower
12. Yerdle, a bstell house
13. Mydleton hall, two stone houses or Bastells
14. Langton, old tower
15. Brankston, lytle tower
16. Foweberye, tower
17. Chatton, two lytle towers
18. Kilham, new tower and barmekyne

19. Twedemouthe, two lytle towers
20. Scrymmerstone, great old towre
21. Cheswyke, a lytle tower
22. Braggarstone, a strong tower
23. Ancroft, a lytle fortresse
24. Lawyke, a towre
25. Byermore, a tower
26. Berrynhton, there was a tower
27. Shoreswolde, pele of a tower
28. Norham castle
29. Thornebie, a lytle towre
30. Newebygginge, towre
31. Gret Henghe, stronge stone house or bastell
32. Twysle, old fortresse or castell
33. Gryndonrigge, a lytle tower
34. Duddo, a pele of a towre or a twore rased
35. Etayle castell
36. Forde Castell and lytle tower mansion of the parsonage
37. Fenton, a grett towre with a barmekyn
38. Nesebytte, a towre utterly ruined
39. Wetewood, lytle towre
40. Horton, a great towre wth a barmekyn
41. Holburne, a towre and a barmekyn
42. Hesellerygge, a lowe towre unfin

The Middle March

43. West Llyburne, two towers
44. Chillingham Castell
45. Hebburne, lytle toure
46. Bewyke, a good tower
47. Ilderton, a great tower and strong barmekyn
48. Roddom, a lytle toure
49. Crawley, a lytle toure
50. Tytlyngton, a lytle toure
51. Shawden, a toure
52. Whyttyngame, two towers
53. Callalye, a toure
54. Eslyngton, a toure wth a barmekyn
55. Ingrame, a lytle toure mansion house of the P'senage
56. Great ryle, a toure (barmekin proposed)

57. Prendyke, a lytle toure
58. Alname, two lytle toures
59. Scrynwood, a toure and a barmekin
60. Byttylsden, a toure and a barmekin
61. Cotte Walles, lytle toure
62. Borrodone, a great toure
63. Clennel, lytle toure and newe barmekyn
64. Allaynton, lytle bastell house of stone (vicars)
65. Lynne Brigge, a stone house Bronnte and casten downe
66. Tharnam, a toure or tower
67. Nether trewhytt a toure
68. Hephell a toure
69. Thropstone a lytle toure
70. Cartitngton, good fortresse of two toures
71. Harbottell castle
72. Barrowe, olde walls of a lytle fortresse
73. Hare clewgh, pele house of stone
74. Great Tosson Tower
75. Whytton, toure and a lytle barmekin
76. Elyburne, a strong pele house
77. Ryttonn, a stone house and a lytle barmekyn
78. Grenelyghton, lytle stone house wth a barmekyn
79. Rotheley, lyrle towre
80. Harterton, a strong bastell house
81. Sawnes, pele or bastell
82. Wallyngton, strong toure and a stone house
83. Lytle harle, a towre
84. Kirk whelpyngton, lytle toure (vicars)
85. Hawke, a bastell house
86. Swetehope, bastell house
87. Fylton More, bastell house
88. Carre Cottes, bastell house
89. Lytle Swyneburne, lytle toure
90. Mykle Swyneburne, great toure decayed
91. Gonnerton, toure and a stone house
92. Chypchase, a fare tower
93. Symondburne, strong toure and a lytle tower (vicars)
94. Hall Barnes, a bastell house
95. Hawghton, olde castell and barmekin
96. Tecket, a strong stone house

The Survey Book of Norham and Islandshire 1560–61

The survey Booke of Norham and Islandshire, taken and made in the third yeare of our Soveraigne Lady Elizabeth, Queene of England, France and Island, Def.of the faith and c. by Anthony Roone, esqr, one of the Queene's mats Auditors; and Thomas Baytes, Gent. Surveyor of her Mata. and in the County of Northumberland. Ex recognicione.
Norham Castle

Newbiging
In the same towne is one tower in good reparacions, and a good barnkin about the same.

Twizell
There hath beene in the said towne one towre, or pile, which is of auncyent tyme decayed and cast downe, and there remayneth one part or quarter thereof, and a barnkin about it; and in the same hath beene a certayne demayne, and ten husband lands, and vi cotags, with appertenne.

Tilmouth
In the same towne is a little tower or pile much in decay, and a little barnekin about ye same.

Cornehylle
There is in the same one tore, or pile, with a barnekin about the same, and is in indifferent good reparacions.

Heaton
In the same towne is the scite of a fayre castle decayed, which was destroyed by the Scotts in tyme of Kinge Henry the Seaventh, and neur syne repaired, so that there remayneth no buildings save ye vauts of ye same, and a dwelling house for ye fermor, and a barnek.

Duddo
In the same is one pile, or tower, which is decayed by reason it was cast downe by the Scotts at Floddenfield and nyver repayred senths, and there standeth bot the halfe yr of, about the which is one barnekin, and there is in it viij husbandlands.

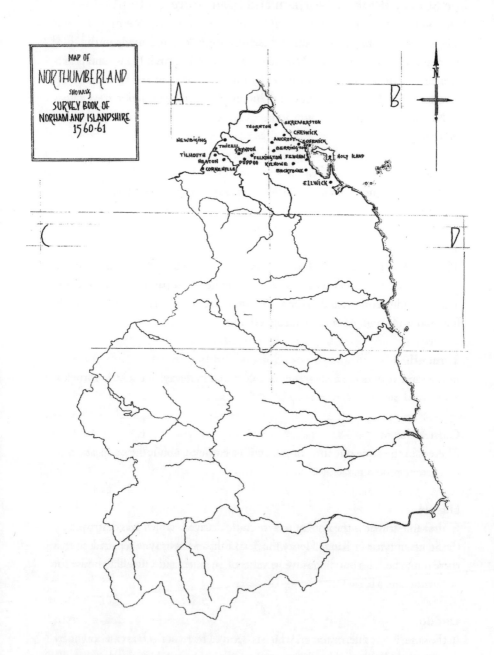

Figure 11: The survey book of Norham and Islandshire was 'taken and made in the third yeare of our Soveraign Lady Elixabeth Queen of England, France and Ireland 1560-1561'.

Gryndon

There is at Grindon Ridge a towre in good reparacions, and in the towne is vj husbandlands and cotags.

Ancrofte, Felkington and Allerden

In the same towne of Ancroft is one pile, builded to the end of the church, and dyvers good howses beside; and in the same is xij husband lands and cottages. In the towne of Flekington is noe tower, or pile, but one bastell house of smale strength.

Ellwick

There is in the same towne twoe towres and ijdemaynes, viij husbandlands and iiij cotages.

Fenham

There is in the same towns one towre in good reparacions, and viij husband lands.

Thornton

There is in the same one towre which was cast down at Flodden field by the Scotts, and is not yet well repayred, bot yt one peece y't is in decay, and barnkin about it, and is in the same vj husband tenements and a demaynes.

Gosewick

There is one good pile there builded uppon the enheritaunce of Thomas Swinhoe, and in good reparacions, and there is in the same x husbandlands, cotages &c.

Skremerston

There is in the same towne on good towre, with a barnekin in good reparacions, and there is a demaynes, xii husband tennaunts and cotages &c.

Cheswick

There is a little towre, ruinous and in decay of the inheritaunce of Thomas Maners; and there is in the same towne xvij husband tents.

Kylhowe

There is in the same towne one towre in good reparacions, and viij husband lands and cotages.

Beale

There is in the same noe tower nor howse of defence, but certen little howses of stone and lyme that some of the tenaunts have builded for theire owne safe gard.

Berrington

. There hath beene in the same towne on towre, which was all utterly decayed, and is now of late some what repayred, and mayd two house hight by John Revelye, farmor of the demaynes there, which if it were finished wold be good strenghth bothe to the towne and the rest of the quarter of the countrye; and there is in the same one demaynes and xx husbandlands.

Bucktonne

Brian Grey holdeth there freely one tenement, wheirevpon an tower is builded, with a close and certaine lands in the fields, et red. Per annun. Ad eosd. Term. Vjs.

Fenwick

In which towne is the scite of an old manor, a parke adioynig to the same, and xv husbandlands, or tenements, and one cottage, an the same is no towre, nor house or strength, save howses as tenants have builded for there owne securitite.

Holy Ilande

And in the same Iland is also one forte builded vpon an hill called Beblawe, which serveth very well for the defence and saveguard of the haven, the which haven is a very good and apt haven both of the harborowe and landinge.

Christopher Dacre's Plat 1584

This Plat, or plan, is unlike present-day maps where north is at the top; here west is at the top and north is to the right.

Shown on the map and noted in the attached report are castles and other fortified houses, their condition, proposed new works and their owners. Perhaps the strangest thing, not shown, is:

the new devised dike or defence ... Which is to pass through the said East and Middle Marches endlong the plenished ring of the borders leving and out certaine places which cannot conveniently be brought within the same, to the joyinge of the dike or defence that already devised and begunne.'

While we can trace the black dyke that runs north-north-east from Hadrian's Wall, roughly parallel with the Pennine Way, through Wark Forest and the much later Roman wall itself, there is to my knowledge no trace of Dacrers Dyke. That is unlike the bold earthworks of the Scots Dike, of 1552, just north of Carlisle, where it runs west to east for 4 miles between the Rivers Sark and Esk. Here the dyke consists of an earthern mound originally 8ft high with deep ditches either side. This was not meant to be a national boundary but was devised by a French diplomat to keep the feuding Armstrongs and Grahams at arm's length from each other.

On 8 September 1584 a committee headed by Sir Henry Hudson, which included C. Dacre; Ro: de la Vale' Jho. Selbye; Frauncil Russell; Thomas Gray; John Forster; Henry Woodrington and William Reed, forwarded a book to the queen, which 'viewed the decayed castles, towers and fortresses meet to be rapaired and such other new fortresses and enclosures as are meet to be newly made and enclosed in the county of Northumberland'.

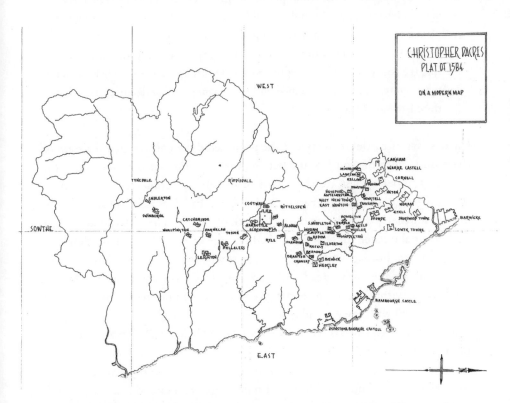

Figure 12: Christopher Dacre actually produced a map or Plat in 1584 and proposed a 'new devised dike or defence'. His survey is shown on a modern map of the county.

The towers and castles mentioned were Dustanboroughe, Bamboroughe, Shorswoode, Towre, Norham, Hton, Cornell Towre, Warke, Howtell Towre, Lancton Towre, Etell, Foord, Wooler Towre, Berwicke Towre, Lowyke Towre and Harbuttle. New fortresses to be built 'if it might so please her majestye' were 'thre newe towres and fortifications between the said river of Twede and her majestyes said castle of Harbuttle ... and another between the said castle of Harbuttle and the west border ...'.

On 11 September, Christopher Dacre forwarded a plan of a proposed dyke directly to secretary Walshingham 'for the better understanding of the plat or carte which is herewith sent, the articles here following will declare':

1. First by the said plat all the castles and fortresses decaied which are thought mete to be repared shall ...
2. Secondly within what compasse the new devised fortresses upon the east and middle marches are thought to be planted howe farre from the border of Scotland ...
3. Thirdly by what townes and places the new devised dike or defence is to goe, which is to passe through the said east and middle marches endlong the plenished ringe of the borders leving our certaine places which cannot conveniently be brought within the same, to the joyninge of the dike or defence that is already devised and begunne to passe through the west borders, and what is intended to be conteined within the same dyke or defence, and what to be left out of the same.

Dacre's Plat of castles, towers and the proposed dyke consists of a diagram of the county, with the south at the left and the sea at the bottom. Starting at the left-hand upper corner are the towns or towers of 'Cholerton, Swinburne, Whelpington, Catchersyde, Farnelaw, Leighton, Fallalees and Tosson'; stretching in a northerly direction and to the south of them is a note that states, 'Here doth want about ten myle west to the ioyninge of the dike or newe defeence upon the west border which serveth from towne to towne as well as the rest.' Below them to the east we read, 'All from these townes east and south and south and by west within this intended defence all to the west border for the most part well plenished with townes and towres but little enclosed.'

At the top of the map is 'Harbuttle Castell' and below it, 'All from Harbuttle to the west border is Riddisdale and Tynedale so moche as is inhabited betwene these townes hereunder and Scotlande beynge about twentye myle directly from Harbuttle to the west border with many great and hoodg waiste grounds and mountains of small profitt not possible to be inclosed.' By 'Harbuttle' is the note 'All waist to Scotland Sixe myle'. North of 'Harbuttle' in a group are the following towers: 'Bittelsden towre, Coutwall towre, Screenwood towre, Alnam, Ryle towre, Prendick, Ingram, Refely, ffawdon, branton, hedgley' and then beginning with 'Rodom towre', a line runs north as follows: 'Rosden, Elderton towre, south middleton, north middleton towre, Yardle (with the note 'Here at Wardle the east and mydell marche is divided') wooler towre, homelton, akeld, yevering, east Newton, West Newton, Kellum, pawston, mindrum, prswen, caram.' Above these is the note 'the Hiles of Cheviot all waiste from these townes of the ringe seven myle to Scotland' and the towers of 'Antechester and Hethpole towr'. Along the Tweed beginning at Carham are: 'Warke castell, Cornell towre, Heton castell, Noram castell, Shorswood towre and Barwicke'. At the bottom, along the coast, are 'lowyke towre held by a Collinwood, bambourgh castle and Dunstonebourghe castell'.

At 'Shorswood' is the note, 'Tweede not to be passed but at certaine places' and 'Here is no castles, towres nor townes set out in this plot betwene the plenished ringe and the sea and the Innermost part of the border but the castles and townes decaied and the townes by which the dyke or intended defence is to goe'. Along the line of the River Till 'not to be passed but at certain places', are 'lancton towre, Howghtell towre, Bewike towre, fforde castell and Etell castell'.

The Time Chart

The time chart is intended to show the periods in time when the various types of fortified house were being built and used.

The symbol used ◁▷ is not an indication of the number of buildings in each group, only showing when they were first built, when they were at their peak usage, and then an estimated time when they fell out of favour.

The periods indicated are only estimated, with peles and bastles and their derivatives in particular being beset with problems.

The Distribution of Castles, Towers, Peles and Bastles

All the maps in this work are divided into sections A, B, C, D, E, F and G, to assist in locating the buildings listed in the gazetteer.

Figure 13 (see p. 114) shows the map with block graphs at the side giving the number of castles, towers and peles/bastles to be found in each section so that, for example, section E (North Tyne and Redesdale) has seventy peles or bastles while section A has only two for Norham and Wark.

Section D has fifty-one towers but only fifteen peles/bastles; a larger graph gives the total number of each building type for the county by adding the numbers in each smaller block graph.

TiME CHART

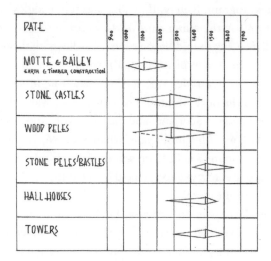

DATE	900	1000	1100	1200	1300	1400	1500	1600	1700
MOTTE & BAILEY EARTH & TIMBER CONSTRUCTION									
STONE CASTLES									
WOOD PELES									
STONE PELES/BASTLES									
HALL HOUSES									
TOWERS									

The chart shows the periods when motte-and-bailey castles, peles and bastles, hall houses and towers were in use and indicates their decline.

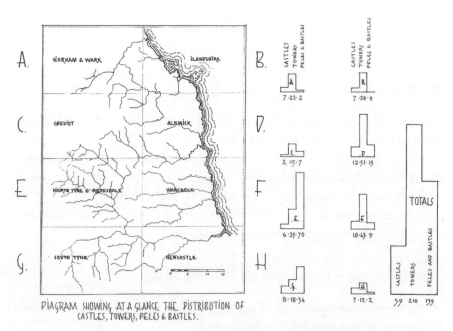

DIAGRAM SHOWING AT A GLANCE THE DISTRIBUTION OF CASTLES, TOWERS, PELES & BASTLES.

Figure 13: This map shows the county cut into eight areas, A to H, with the number of castles, towers, peles and bastles shown in each, also giving the totals for each county. While these figures will vary with time, they are an indication of the distribution of the various types of fortified house. Two houses that appear to be much removed from any kind of fortified house are Fowberry Tower and Capheaton Hall. Fowberry Tower hides within its fabric the remains of two earlier houses, while Capheaton was built using the stone, timber, lead and glass of a castle that stood only metres away.

Chapter IV

Gazetteer

How to Find a Castle

As the alphabetical entries show, Northumberland abounds with castles along with the smaller towers, peles or bastles, and finding one in the gazetteer is simple. Finding them in the field ranges from only too easy to difficult as not all stand out like Bamburgh or are open to the public, only remaining as humps and bumps in a field, parkland or under a coppice of handsome trees.

Many of our 'country houses' are associated with much older, more dour houses built for defence rather than comfort. Some conceal their heritage within the walls of magnificent houses, hiding their ancient roots at the rear of the fashionable, much more comfortable, period house usurping the site. Remains of once proud, thorny facades that cried out defiantly to any marauding enemy are tucked away, surviving as cellars at Wallington or a scant section of an old masonry in the courtyard at Hesleyside.

In the case of Lemington and East Shaftoe Hall, an almost complete tower house was incorporated, swallowed by later houses in such a way that makes them almost invisible at first! Other owners were so proud of their ancient heritage they gave their new house a firm foot in the past by incorporating their old towers in a main elevation so that we can, to this day, tell that this house has witnessed many of the important events of the history of the country.

There is another group, which used the ancient family seat as a quarry to help in the building of a completely new house situated not many metres away, leaving only mounds in their well-manicured parks. Capheaton was one of many that rose up proudly in this way, with the building contract giving Trollope 'all the materials, as stone, timber, iron, lead and glass in the said ole castle' with which to build the new house in the spirit of Isaiah (Bible, Ch. 2. V.4) by beating 'their swords into ploughshares, and their spears into pruninghooks'. The Swinburns were now proud owners of their own Arcadia, a private paradise, set within the stout walls of their park.

A complete list of book references is given on p.293 but to help readers find a given reference, such as AA 3-XXI-40, first find the third series of *Archaeologia Aeliana*, then take Vol. XXI, p.40.

Hodgson's *History of Northumberland* consists of three parts but has seven volumes; part 1 has one volume; part 2 has three volumes; and part 3 also has three volumes: to find Hodgson 2-III-107, find Part 2, Vol. 3, p.107.

Map References

Each site or building in the gazetteer has a map reference such as B.16, C.18 or H.27, or is labelled within a certain section such as A, E or G. To find a site, say that of Melkridge, which has the reference G.41, you must find the section of the relevant map marked G and then site No. 41. The relevant map can be determined by establishing either the type of building (for example, a pele or bastle may be found on the map showing the distribution of peles/bastles, *Figure 3*, p.49) or the historical document the entry was recorded in (for example, the map of the Survey of 1415, *Figure 8*, p.83) and choosing the relevant map. Many of the sites are marked with name and symbol while some have only a number with a symbol.

How to find a castle: Capheaton Castle, standing in its manicured park, hides within its fabric a castle – built as it was using 'all the materials as stone, timber iron, lead and glass in the old castle'. The Swinburnes are now proud owners of their own Arcadia, a private paradise set within the stout walls of their park.

Abberwick Tower. West of Alnwick. D
Northumberland County History VII-134, 200.

The tower was mentioned in a lease of 1572 and in a deed of 1689, but it has now almost vanished. The field west of Abberwick Farm cottages is called Dunkirk field and in a hollow was a stone, which legend says was the step of the old church door. There are many mounds around this spot and this may be the site of the tower.

Acton Bastle. Supposed remains at Acton Hall. D.65
Northumberland County History VII-371.

Four tenants of Acton town appeared at a muster taken on the Moot Law on 26 March 1580 and a survey made about 1585 mentions that the old bastle house was ruinous or ruined: 'There is the seyte of a mannor where the mannor house emongst the tenaunts, and the demayne landers not known in any parte, but all occupied in tenements as followeth …'. A list of tenants follows and ends with: 'Est ibidem in villa una damus constructa prople defensionem contra inimicas vocata le Bastle modo ruinosa. Et reddit per annum … Nil.'

Adderstone Tower. South-west of Bambrough. B.25
Northumberland County History VI-223.

In 1415 Thomas Forster is recorded as owner of this tower and in the time of Henry VIII it was 'in the possession of Sir Thomas Forster, owner of a hold and tropp of 60 horseman', prior to the Battle of Flodden. Little else is known of this tower.

Akeld Bastle or Tower. West of Wooler. C.3
Northumberland County History XI-240. Hodgson 3-II-185. AA 3-IX-35–43. P.F. Ryder.

On Akeld Hill, in the farmyard there is a two-storeyed structure incorporating the vaulted basement of the 'lytle fortelett or bastle house without a barmkin' mentioned in the border survey of 1541.

There is no indication of a staircase to the upper floor, but the basement door remains in the west wall. The basement measures externally 62ft N–S by 24ft 6in E–W, and is 16ft wide in the interior, having a small window at each end as is usual in most towers and peles.

The first lord of the manor was Robert of Akeld and in 1522 Lord Dacre proposed to place ten men in the tower under John Wallis for the defence of the border. This points to a superior house, not a run-of-the-mill bastle or pele.

This fine doorway (*right*), the main
entrance to Capheaton, depicts
at the base of the columns a rich
man giving food to a poor man at
his door.

This plan and section (*below*) shows
Akeld to be one of the largest houses
listed as a bastle. In elevation, the
mass of Akeld is obvious. The walls
to the upper floor and the roof
are modern.

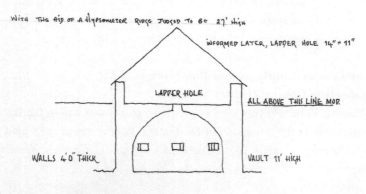

WITH THE AID OF A Hypsometer RIDGE JUDGED TO BE 27' HIGH

INFORMED LATER, LADDER HOLE. 14" × 11"

LADDER HOLE

ALL ABOVE THIS LINE MOD.

WALLS 4'0" THICK

VAULT 11' HIGH

AKELD BASTLE/PELE.

B. Long 1968

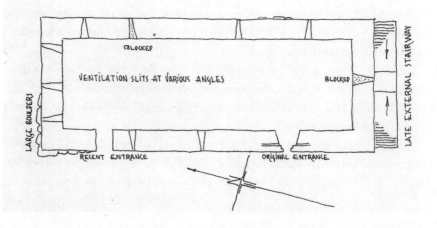

BLOCKED

VENTILATION SLITS AT VARIOUS ANGLES

BLOCKED

LARGE BOULDERS

LATE EXTERNAL STAIRWAY

RECENT ENTRANCE

ORIGINAL ENTRANCE

Alnham: Two Towers. In Upper Coquetdale. C
Pevsner. Bates. Hodgson. Dixon. *Northumberland County History*
XIV-573.

Vicars: This tower, mentioned in 1541 as the mansion of the vicarage, was very small and much like those at Ford, Corbridge and Whitton. It was ruinous in 1663 and still in ruins in 1758 when the vicar lived at Ilderton. The walls were 9ft thick and it had the usual vaulted basement. The windows were unusually ornate, but these were replaced when the parapet and the adjoining modern wings were added about 130 years ago. Hodgson's sketch of 1821 records its former appearance and he noted that it was of good masonry but that the mortar was inferior to that at Tosson Tower. He also described it as being rather low and squat and 'Though it be snugly it is certainly very unsecurely situated'.

Earl of Northumberland Tower: This tower once belonged to the Earl of Northumberland but was surrendered to the Crown and was first mentioned in 1405. In 1415 it was again in the hands of the earl. In 1532, 'Scots to the number of 300 personages and above hath brunte a toune of mine called Alnam ... with all the corne hay and househols stuff in the said toune and also a wome'. In 1586 we read, 'the land hath there a faire strong stone tower of ancient tymem builded and strongly vaulted over and the gates and doors be all of great strong iron bars and a good demayne adjoining thereto. The house is now ruinous and in some decay by reason the farmer useth to carry his sheep up the stares and to lay them in the chambers which roteth the vaults and will in shorte time be the utter decaye of the same if other reformacion be not had.'

The tower disappeared but its foundations may be traced on a hill opposite the church.

Alnwick Castle. D.35
Guidebook. Pevsner. Tate I-372. Davison 22.

'Alnewic' was mentioned in 1138 when it was 'strong' and William the Lion of Scotland was captured while laying siege to the castle in 1147, yet in 1212 it was ordered to be demolished!

The first castle of Alnwick was a motte-and-bailey and enclosed an area of about 7 acres. A shell keep erected on the levelled motte in the early twelfth century stands in the centre of the castle between two baileys, one on the east and one on the west as at Windsor. There are also remains of the moat and its retaining wall round the keep.

In around 1309 Henry Percy built the semicircular towers still to be seen on the north and east of the keep and also the barbican of the outer bailey. He also repaired the curtain and added strong towers such as the constables, the postern

ALNWICK CASTLE IN ITS ANCIENT STATE,
From the North-East.

This engraving, from the north-east, shows Alnwick Castle in its ancient state.

The gatehouse and barbican at Alnwick is said to be the best example in the country. Between the flanking walls is a moat with a drawbridge, which along with the gatehouse has double gates.

in the middle bailey and the abbots in the outer bailey. By the mid-thirteenth century the castle had reached its present plan.

The gatehouse and barbican are said to be the best in the country. The gatehouse has double gates with a portcullis, in front of which a drawbridge used to lift. This drawbridge was to span a ditch between the flanking walls of the barbican, which also has double gates flanked by square towers at its outer end.

The south walls of both baileys have been built up with offices and stables and cannot be seen in their original state from the outside. Between the baileys is a wall with a fourteenth-century gate and once through this, the polygonal flanking towers (fourteenth century) of the Norman entrance to the keep can be seen.

Alnwick shows work of every period on the line of its original motte-and-bailey plan. Henry, the 6th Earl of Northumberland, had more than his share of misfortune all his life. While quite a young man he fell in love with Anne Boleyn but Henry VIII forced him to renounce her. For Anne's trial the earl was appointed a member of the commission to try her – an instance typical of the brutality of Henry VIII. The earl avoided the office on a plea of sickness.

Alnwick Castle: this image shows the shell keep. Modifications over the centuries hide the fact that this had its own barbican.

Alton Side. Haydon Bridge. G.24
Pevsner.
One and a quarter miles south-east of Haydon Bridge is Alton Side, which is a much-improved bastle or pele of the sixteenth century. The upper doorway on the north front is of special note with rather elaborate moulding.

Alwinton. Bastle House of Vicar. C.13
Holystone and Alwinton Parish: Above Rothbury in the Vale of Coquet.
Dixon 225. Bates.
This bastle is in the list of 1541, when it was occupied by the vicar, but by 1635 it was no longer used by the clergy as it was falling into decay and was inhabited by farm workers. The site is no longer known.

Ancroft Tower. North of Belford. B.7
Raine 215–6. Pevsner 76.
This tower was built on to the church (which originally did not have one) for the vicar and for the protection of the villagers during Scottish inroads. Its dimensions are 22ft 6in × 26ft 6in and it is of the late thirteenth or early fourteenth century. It was built on to the west end of the church, blocking the door. There is the usual vaulted ground floor and a spiral stair in the south-east corner behind the south door. There were three storeys above and in one of these is a fireplace. The lintel of a doorway is formed by a coffin lid, upon which there is the rude carving of a sword.

Angerton Strong House or Pele. F.59
Pevsner.
East of Angerton Hall, hidden by a group of nineteenth-century buildings are the remains of a strong house or pele. The remains are scant, consisting of its west gable with a round arch to the byre doorway. This house is well outside the 'Pele Area' and the round arch to the doorway is a feature of peles or bastles south of the River Tyne.

Anick Pele. G.25
Pevsner.
High above the north bank of the River Tyne stands Anick Farmhouse, a good example of the conversion from a dour pele to a much more comfortable house. Evidence of both byre and first-floor doorways are to be found in the south wall.

Antichester (Antechester) Tower. C
Bates.

This tower is marked, along with Hethpool Tower, on the 1584 plan of border defences as being outside the 'Ring of Fortresses'. Like Hethpool, it would have been for use by the local inhabitants in a short and sudden emergency. Its location is not known. See Hethpool.

Aydon Castle. North of Corbridge. H.3
Northumberland County History X-33. Pevsner. Bates. Guidebook.

The licence to crenellate was granted in 1305 but there was a building on the site thirty years earlier. This was a fortified mansion of the late thirteenth century, the plan of which, an irregular pentagon, was governed by the site.

The north side was protected by a fosse while the other three sides were protected by a ravine falling to the Cor or Aydon Burn. The castle consisted of two baileys and a courtyard. The main buildings stood to the south on the edge of the ravine with the outer bailey and gate to the north, where the site is exposed to attack.

There is no keep at Aydon and that gives it its outstanding architectural importance as it is a very early case of a fortified house rather than a castle. The hall, reached by an outer stair as are most peles, is the earliest work on the site. In 1305 the inner bailey was built, with a new range of offices on the west. The house was captured by the Scots in 1315 and again in 1346, and these events resulted in the strengthening of its defences, namely the outer bailey and courtyard.

Some of the walls still have holes at 10ft intervals for supporting the hoarding. Two hundred marks and two palfreys were once paid by a female owner of Aydon to King John for permission to marry whom she pleased.

English Heritage produces an informative booklet on the site.

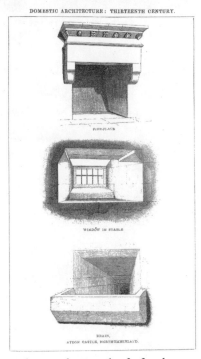

DOMESTIC ARCHITECTURE: THIRTEENTH CENTURY.

Aydon Castle: Details of a fireplace, stable window and a drain. Engravings by W. Twopeny, Parker's *Domestic Architecture*, 1853.

Aydon Castle: Engravings by W. Twopeny, Parker's *Domestic Architecture*, 1853.

DOMESTIC ARCHITECTURE: THIRTEENTH CENTURY.

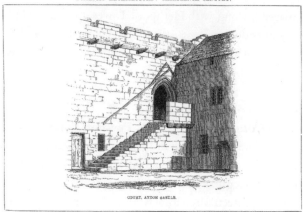

COURT, AYDON CASTLE.

DOMESTIC ARCHITECTURE: THIRTEENTH CENTURY.

AYDON CASTLE, NORTHUMBERLAND.

DOMESTIC ARCHITECTURE: THIRTEENTH CENTURY.

AYDON CASTLE, NORTHUMBERLAND.

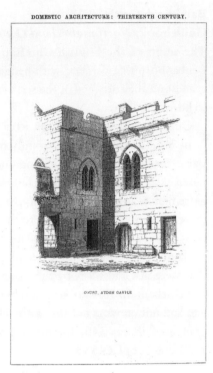

Aydon Castle: Engravings by W. Twopeny, Parker's *Domestic Architecture*, 1853.

An engraving by T. Allom of Aydon Castle.

Bamburgh Castle. B.18

Guidebook. *Northumberland County History* **I-17. Bates. Pevsner.**

The reign of the English Chieftain Ida began in 547 when he 'timbered Bebbanburn that was erst with hedge betyned and thereafter with wall'. Ida's grandson Ethelfrith (end of the sixth century) gave the stronghold of Dinguaray to his wife Bebba:

Queen Bebba – Bebbanburgh – Bamburgh.

In 744, 'Bebba is a most strongly fortified city, not very large, being of the size of two or three fields, having one entrance hollowed out of the rock and raised in steps after a marvellous fashion. On the top of the hill it has a church of extremely beautiful workmanship … to the west on the highest point of the city there is a spring of water sweet to the taste and most pure to the sight, that has been excavated with astonishing labour.'

Bamburgh is one of the three places between the Humber and the Tweed that were not laid waste by the Conqueror in 1070, the other two being York and Durham. In 1164 the keep was built at a cost of £4 and four years later, £30 was laid out on works of the castle. Henry III directed the building of a 'good grange' of 150ft × 34ft after his visit of 21 March 1221. This was completed in 1222 at a cost of £46 18s.

10 April 1774.   (D L sculp.

Bamburgh Castle is an eye-catcher from any direction and perhaps the best known of all the magnificent coastal castles in Northumberland.

The tower of Elmunds Well and the barbican before St Oswald's Gate was repaired in 1250 and the great tower of the three gates within the castle and the great drawbridge outside the great gate on the south side were repaired three years later.

The keep is 35ft high and measures 69ft 1in N–S and 61ft 7in E–W. The angles are covered by pairs of pilasters 12ft wide that continue above the parapet as the outer walls of four square turrets. The doorway is in a like projection near the north of the east wall and on the ground floor; a remarkable and rare feature, showing how secure the builders must have felt on their dolerite rock. There is the usual vaulted basement and a straight in the thickness of the walls, also a spiral stair in the north-west corner. The original arrangement of rooms is uncertain, as too much was changed by Sharp, Archdeacon of Northumberland, who was responsible for alterations in the mid-eighteenth century. Bamburgh and Carlisle Castle keeps are similar and of early date, and it is interesting to compare them with the later keeps of Newcastle and Dover. The site is long and narrow in an E–W direction and comprises 8 acres, a twelfth-century keep, three baileys and a gatehouse at the east end with traces of an earlier one at the west end.

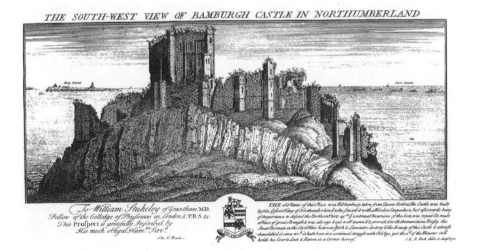

An engraving of Bamburgh Castle from the village by S. and N. Buck in 1728.

This view of Bamburgh Castle from the village cricket pitch, at the bottom of the main street, shows a stout but calm protected area to play cricket.

Another view of Bamburgh Castle shows why it has been used by so many film makers as it bristles with defensive works.

Massive and moody, you can choose the vantage point that is best for your storyline.

Bamburgh Siege Castle. B.18
Lawrie, Ancient Scottish Charters XV.
In 1095 William II built a motte-and-bailey siege castle recorded by Lawrie as 'Nove Castellum Apod Bebbanburg'. Just where it was sited is not known.

Tower of the Master of the Augustinian Cell. Bamburgh. B.18
Hodgson 3-I-30. *Northumberland County History* **VI-113. Bates. Pevsner.**
In the list of 1415 a tower belonging to the Master of Bamburgh is recorded as the Touris de Bamburgh. The base, being 33ft in length, may still be seen in the wall separating the churchyard from the house called 'Bamburgh Hall'. The masonry is of very solid character and projects at a short distance beyond the rest of the wall.

Bardon Mill, Grandys Knowe. G.26
Pevsner. Ryder. Grundy.
South of the B6318, Military Road, south-west of Housteads Roman Fort, are the remains of Grandys Knowe pele with the usual stout walls now partly obscured by the ruins of a later farmhouse once used as a bothy by the climbing club. The original basement doorway was in the west gable and there are later vents in the north and south walls. These walls are 3ft 4in thick and overall the building was 30ft × 20ft.

Barmoor Tower. B.11
Northumberland County History **XIV-106. Hodgson 3-II-190. Pevsner.**
Edward I stayed here in 1206 and Edward II in 1319. During a raid of the Scots in 1367 Thos. Muschamp lost eight oxen, two horses, gold and silver and other goods. In 1341 a licence to crenellate was granted and later it could house thirty horsemen, while in 1541 it was 'in extreme decaye and almost ruinous for lack of reparacions'. The walls of the old tower are incorporated in the present building and are 4ft to 6ft thick. The survey of 1415 describes the building as a fortalice.

Barrasford Pele or Bastle. (The Head House.) E.57
Northumberland County History **IV-315.**
The drawing on p.131, based on an old print, shows a pele much like a gatehouse with its external stair ending short of the threshold to the first-floor entrance and the elegant window to the right.

In 1289 the site of the manor house was worth nothing because it had been burnt by the Scots. The Head House was a pele much the same as that at Gatehouse; it had a stone house added to it at a later date. This simple dwelling is not of manorial status.

Barren Know
See Stokoe Crags. E.64.
This site is known for the many names used for it over the years:

Stokoe Crags, Crag Cottages, Craig
Barren Know
Skittering Lin
Broon Hills
Smalesmouth

Head House, Barrasford: While there is an obvious pele behind the haystack, the other building looks as if it was also a pele.

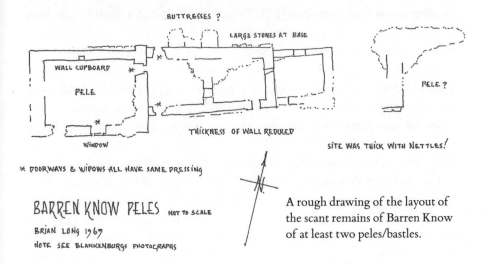

BUTTRESSES ?

LARGE STONES AT BASE

WALL CUPBOARD

PELE

PELE ?

THICKNESS OF WALL REDUCED

WINDOW

SITE WAS THICK WITH NETTLES!

* DOORWAYS & WINDOWS ALL HAVE SAME DRESSING

BARREN KNOW PELES NOT TO SCALE

BRIAN LONG 1969

NOTE SEE BLANKENBURGS PHOTOGRAPHS

N.

A rough drawing of the layout of the scant remains of Barren Know of at least two peles/bastles.

Barrow Tower. C
Northumberland County History XV-488.

There is now only the farm on this site, marked on the map as a pele, but no trace remains of the old pele or tower. In 1522 a garrison of twenty was kept here, but in 1541, in spite of the garrison, it is reported as being burnt down in times past.

Barty's Pele (Bog Head). E.25

Northumberland County History XV–271; Headlam's Three Northern Counties 334. Ryder. Blankenburgs Collection.

This pele derives its name from one of the 'Tindale thieves', Bartholomew Milburn, although some people allocate it to Hodge Corbit and call it Corbit Castle, alleging that Barty lived either on the other side of the Tarset Burn where a farmhouse named Combe stands, or less probably, at Shilla Hill. According to one legend, Shilla Hill was the home of Hodge Corbit, or Corby Jack, who was a friend of Berty Milburn.

The pele stands on a narrow strip of land between the Highfield Burn and the foot of Shilla Hill. Visible remains consist of walls to a height of 15ft in quite good condition on three sides, apart from a shortage of pointing. The north wall has been split and partly thrust out by the collapse of the basement vault, which has now been cleared to show the basement floor. The walls on the first floor will be seen to be 4ft thick and all the courses have large quoins, while the basement door on the west end is of 'almost cyclopean' masonry. As in many other peles, the doorway is small, being only 2ft 2½in wide. Traces of a small loophole in the east end can be seen but nothing is now left of the external stair to the first-floor living area. If this stair ever existed it would have stood on the side to the left when facing the basement door, but it is possible that access was gained by a retractable wooden ladder. As peles originally had only the wooden ladder, the stone stair would be built when more peaceful times came to the border.

On the same plot stand the remains of a later two-roomed cottage and a larger but not so strongly built seventeenth-century cottage of three rooms. Also at hand are enclosures, which would have been 'night folds' or enclosures for sheep, etc.

The thieves of Tindale, Bartholomew Wilburn among them, achieved a notoriety of which they were excessively proud. Border warfare came to an end in the early seventeenth century, but individuals were still indulging in raiding towards the close of the century. One morning it was discovered that Scottish thieves had driven off all Barty's sheep. He set off in pursuit with his friend Corby Jack over Carter Bar to Letham but lost all trace of his animals. Not to be outdone, they selected a quantity of the best sheep of the inhabitants of Letham and made off home with them, only to be pursued in turn by two brave fellows of Letham. On the site of Catcleugh Reservoir the argument began and was a grim affair. Barty was wounded in the thigh and then saw that Corby Jack was dead, and this so enraged him that with one mighty backhand stroke he struck the head of his slayer clean from his shoulders, so that 'it sprang along the heather like an onion'. The other Scot fled at the sight, so Barty lifted his dead friend on to his back, collected the sheep and drove them the remaining 15 miles over the heather to the pele you now see.

Bavington Tower. E

The Turris De Babington was listed in the survey of 1415 but its actual location is not known. At first glance there is nothing older than the house of the Shafto family, much altered and extended by Admiral Delaval and now known as Bavington Hall. Is the tower, or its remains, incorporated within the house?

Baxter's Tower. Corbridge (Low Hall). H
Northumberland County History V-155. Pevsner.

Of this tower, probably built in the late fifteenth century, the vaulted basement still remains and the entrance is on the west side. The staircase, in the wall, is very cramped and before reaching the first-floor level it breaks away in circular form. Most of the windows are of a later date. A hall was built on the west side in the later seventeenth century and it was then that the windows were altered in the tower to match the rest of the building.

Beadnell Tower. South of Bamburgh. D
Northumberland County History VI-327. Pevsner.

The building known as the Craster Arms still preserves much of the old masonry and has an eighteenth-century front of two bays with a coat of arms. Pevsner says, 'Beadnell Tower is small and well preserved, with the usual tunnel-vaulted basement and spiral stair and one original fireplace.' This was a late construction and was first mentioned in 1587 but has the date 1751 on a door sill.

Beal. B.30
Hodgson 2-III.

The survey book of Norham and Islandshire dated 1560–61 records that at 'Beale there is in the same Noe tower nor house of defence but certen little houses of stone and lyme that some of the tenaunts have builded for theire owne safe gard'.

The designation 'stone house' in contemporary surveys is used to emphasis that a building is not of perishable wood but has some durability and strength. Evidence of this is to be found in the various ways it was used from 'strong stone house, little stone house or pile, bastell house of stone, strong pele house of stone to stone house attached to a tower'. These stone houses at Beal were at the bottom of the security scale, if they were even on it.

Beaufront Tower. North-east of Hexham. G
Northumberland County History IV-198. Bates. Pevsner.

Occurs in the lists of 1415 and 1541 and in 1547 is styled a manor. The remains are incorporated in a house of 1837, which also incorporates a Georgian house.

Bebside Hall (Tower). F
Northumberland County History IX-296.
This old hall was 100ft E–W × 40ft N–S, and had incorporated an earlier tower in its south-west angle, where the remaining masonry is thickest. The tower had an external measurement of 20ft E–W × 30ft N–S. Most of this old hall and its kitchen wings, etc. were demolished in 1853, but the farm buildings on the site are built of the old stone.

Bedlington Tower. F
Pevsner.
A tower house of the sixteenth century was demolished in 1959 to make way for the new council offices. The windows were hood moulded and had mullions. There was no sign of battlements, but there was a hall range. Having started life as a motte-and-bailey castle, a much later hall house with a small solar tower followed. In 1827 John Dobson of Newcastle built a mansion on to the old house.

Belford Tower or Fortalice. B.20
Northumberland County History VI-364. Pevsner. Hodgson 3-I-2–7.
At Belford West Hall farm, the site of a tower or fortalice, some human bones and spurs of Henry VI's time were found in the moat when it was made into a duck pond in the late nineteenth century. In 1900, not only the moat could be seen, but also some other works under green mounds.

Bellingham Tower or Castle. E.38
Mackenzie II. *Northumberland County History* XV-234. Ryder. Grundy.
There is now no trace, but it may have been on a green mound near the Hareshaw Burn and this may be the remains of the motte-and-bailey castle. Mackenzie says that it was in ruins in 1825. It was mentioned as belonging to the King of Scotland's Forester, one Bellingham of Bellingham, in an early document.

Bellingham, Bowes Hill Pele or Bastle
Incorporated into field walls, north of the cottage, are the scant remains of the north and east walls of a pele. The only detail left is a slit bent in the centre of the east wall.

Bellingham, The Riding
This house was formed by extending a pele, the remains of which sit in the south-west corner of the existing property. The original basement and first-floor doorway were in the long south wall. The basement entrance is poorly hidden behind a twentieth-century stone porch, while the upper doorway has been much knocked about.

Bellister Bastle or Fortalice. G.23
Hodgson 2-III-344. Pevsner.

Attached to a house are the ruins of a square tower called a bastle in 1541 – the date of the house being 1669. Hodgson says, 'Bellister is a grey and goodley pile of ruined towers, with modern inhabited additions, in the castellated style, and good taste. A moat or ditch now green and dry, sweeps around it and the fair mount on which it stands is partly natural and partly artificial.'

Belsay Tower (Fortalice). F
Bates. Hodgson 2-I-359. Pevsner. AA 2-XIV-416. Guidebook, Sir A. Middleton's Account.

A very impressive rectangular tower with short wings at the south-west and north-west ends. The entrance is in the re-entrant angle of the south-west wing, as is the staircase. The main tower has three rooms, one above the other; the lower one with a pointed tunnel vault was the kitchen. On the first floor was the great hall and above that the upper hall, both having fireplaces. The small wings have more floors in them than the main block, that to the north-west having four and that to the south-west having six. In the south-west wing the lower two rooms are vaulted and also the two topmost ones. The top room of this wing is well above roof level and has to be reached by an external stair. The battlements are machicolated and there are corbelled-out bartizans on all four corners. The tower is approximately 56ft × 47ft, being one of the largest in the county. Prior to the tower, there was a manor house fit for a king (Edward I), which was englarged and made secure by the tower in 1370. A more comfortable Tudor house was added to the west side in 1614, followed by another wing in the eighteenth century. Subsequently a new hall was built, beginning in 1807, which left the original tower and castle abandoned.

Beltingham Pele (Ridley). G.28
Pevsner.

Some forty years ago, the owners of this house were having problems with the wrestler ridge and the ingress of rainwater into their attic and requested permission to replace it. I contacted the local authority, saying how rare this kind of roof was and that it should be preserved at all costs. Further to this, I suggested they should at least advise the owners how to overcome the water problem and even pay to renovate the ridge and preserve it, it being such a rare and important architectural feature. I was never informed of the outcome but the ridge survives to this day. Under this roof, the house, White Heather Cottage, is a converted pele with massive boulders in its walls, but no other detail.

Remains of Ancient Wall-Painting   (Lower part completed from fragments).

Ornament round Window.

C Section of Rib
to show treatment
of Window Heads.

Shield on North Wall.   Lower South Wall.

Mural Decorations on Wall of Great Hall.

Not many murals survive in the castles and towers in the county but Belsay Castle, now an English Heritage site, has some that hint at just how magnificent they could have been. The tower at Cocklaw has remains of a more classic nature.

Benwell Tower. Newcastle upon Tyne. H
Northumberland County History XIII–211.

Benwell Tower was pulled down in 1829, and the present building was erected in 1831. The medieval tower belonged to Tynemouth Priory but passed to the Crown at the dissolution. In 1608 it is described as 'the stone tower being the manor house and other edifices … with a garden and a garth'.

Berrington Tower. B
Raine 207/8.

In the list of 1541 the tower is mentioned as being in ruins and now not a trace of it is left.

Berwick Castle. B.1
AA 2-I-92. Scott. Hodgson 3-I-26.

This castle stood at the south-west corner of the town walls but its ruins were almost completely swept away to make way for the railway station. Very little now remains, the most interesting section being the white walls with the water tower, which juts out into the river. Underground chambers were discovered in 1951 and some of the curtain walls still remain in places. (The castle was first mentioned in 1167 when Henry II rebuilt, with stone, what must have been a typical Norman motte-and-bailey castle of wood and earth. In 1396, the castle had been in a ruinous state for some time and in 1560 most of its buildings were pulled down to make the new town walls, which were being built at that time. The remains were also used for a church and other buildings in the area. The following account was made in the reign of Henry VIII:

'The Castell'

First the entre from the Percy Tower into the said castell, unto the draw brige is the distance of 1ᵗⁱ yerdes, and the same draw bridge is iij yerdes over. And betwixt the same draw bridge and the dongean, beinge the entre into the Court of the castell, is xxj yerdes, which entre conteignith in bred … yerdes, and is mayd of lyme and stone, and a parte thereof shronk in and revyn. Item: Betwixt the saide Dongeon and the counstable Tower, stondinge southward from the same, is the distaunce of xxvj yerdes and the same Counstabill Tower conteignit in Wydenes within xvj foote for the gunners to occupye their ordenance, and the thickenes of the wawll in the lawer parte iiij foote and above the vaults ij foot.

Item: Between the same tower and the Posteron Tower on the south syd of the castell is the distaunce of xxᵗⁱ yerdes which tower is dampned within, and a great part of the same tower toward the castell, inward, is fallen down, and the rest of the same will fawll verray shortely outward. And nyegh the same tower, on the west syd, is a Posteron of ieron, with a woode gait without, good and stronge.

Item: Bitwen that tower and the Chappell Tower is the distaunce of twentie and thr yerdes. The same tower conteignith in wydenes within … foote, and so soore decayed as at every great wynd is doith shak so dangerously as no man dar aventur to lye in the lodging of the same of the over part, and by all likelihed will fawll to the ground right shortely.

Berwick Castle in an engraving after Turner, produced in postcard form.

Berwick Castle from Tweedmouth on the south bank of the Tweed.

Item: Bitwen the same Chappell Tower and a Buttres mayd, with a Tower casten owt apon the tope, myd against the Hawll, is xxix^{ti} yerdes, of the same south syd, an is in right soore decay booth at the ground and the most part of the same upward and a great parte therof in a danger of fallinge. The compase of the same botterase is iiij yerdes.

Item: Bitwen the same Butteres and the wawll called the Whit Wawll, going streig from the outwart corner of the castell to the watter of Twed, is the distaunce of xl yerdes, a great part wherof beinge the wall of the Hawll and the Lodginges for the Captaigne, is in exstreme decay, and many steannes fawllen furth of the same, without spedye repayringe wherof it will put a great part of the same wawl in danger of fawllinge.

Item: The said Whit Wawll, goinge southwart frome the utter corner of the castell down, to the watter of Twed, conteigneth of length iiij^{xx}xiiij yerdes, in the myddest wherof is oone yeron Posteron to issue into the feldes; and at the end of the same wawlll is a tower mayd for occupyynge of ordenance, and the stondith in the wattir, the foundacion wherof is under myned by the watter, and the corners of the same driven away, whereby the same tower by all likelyhed will right shortely fawl into the watter. The same tower conteigneth in wideness within ix foote, the wawll in thikenes iiij foote. The entringe into the same frome above the wawlle was covered with tymbre, and the tower self wiwth falgges of stone. The tymber is rotten and decayed so as ther dar no gunners neither lye within the same as hath ben accustomat, ne yet occupy any ordenance, for doubt of fawllinge therof.

Item: Frome th'end of the said wawll called the Whit Wawll, adjoined to the castell, to a Botteres of the west syd of the same castell northwart frome the same Whyt Wawll is the distaunce of xix yerdes, which wawll in diverse places reven and shronkin. And the same botteres in compase x yerdes.

Item: between the same Botteres and the wawll goinge down frome the castell to the stanke, northward, is the distaunce of lx yerdes, diverse places wherof is crashed and reven, and needful to be maendyt. And of the same west syd, and that part of the wawll, is one yeron Posteron, to issue furth of the castell in to the feld.

Item: without the saide posteron is a Barmekin, of stone, for the defence of the posteron and of that parte of the castell, the most part whereof is decayed and fallen to the ground, and so lyyth oppyn.

Item: The same waulle goinge down, northwart, frome the castell to the stanke, conteigneth in length … yerdes.

Item: Bitwen the hed of the same wawll and the Bakhowse Tower is the distaunce of x yerdes, and the same tower is dampned and fylled with erth frome, the grounde to the yddest. The entre into the same tower, through the myddest of the Countermoore is xij foote in length, and in brede v foote. Which tower is overheled with two and countermoored above, and the same tymber is rotten and fallen down, and a part of the countermoor into the said tower, and haith stopped the same so as neither ther can any ordenance be occupied within it, ne discharged upon the tope of the same, for doubt of fawllinge of the rest (of the rest) of the said countermoor. The same tower conteigneth in wydenes x foote, the mayne wall in tikenes vj foot.

Item: Bitwen the same tower and the Boukil Tower is the distaunce of xx yerdes. The entre into the tower is v yerdes in length, under the Countermoor, and in bred ... yerdes. The same tower conteignith in widenes within xvjth footte, and the mayne wawll in thikenes ix foote. The vawlt of the same tower is so craysed, as for doubt of fallinge therof, there is a prope of wod set upe to the same, and the gunner dar unneth occupe any ordenance within it. The same tower frome the vawlt upwarte is fylled with erth and dampned.

Item: Bitwen the same tower and the Gunners Tower is the distance of xxiij yerdes. The entre into the same is in length ... foote, and in bred ... foote. The same tower conteigneth in wydnes within xx foote, and the mayne wawll in thikenes iiij feete.

Item: Bitwen the same Gunners Tower and the Dangean is the distaunce of xxxv yerdes of slender wawll; and the same dungeon of the utter parte contetnith xxxxvj yerdes, the wideness of the yaite of the same, beinge the passage into the castell, is x foote; and the same dungeon is in wydenes within xv yerdes, and in diverse places craysed and decayed. And forsomuch as ther is not within the said castell neither brewhowse, myln, garners for keping of store of corne, ne howse to keep an ordenance, so as yf any haisty danger should come unto the same castell, or that the town should be woon, as Gode forbed, or yf th'inhabitanttes should reball against the Captaign, all the kinges ordenance, saving such as sar stondinge upon the wawlles of the castell, should so be in ennemyes hands, the mylnes and the brewhows barred from the castell, and the capetane his store of corne beinge in garners within the town, the great danger of the same and the strength of the ennemyes. For the avoding of all which dangers it wer verray necessary and expedient that a myln, with a brew howse, a garner, and a howse for the kepinge of the Ordenance wer mayd and set upe within the said castell.

Item: It is to be noted that the same Bakehowse Tower and Boukill Tower is now covered above, by reason whereof the rayne wattir discendith throwgh the countermore and moostith the towers, so as the ordenance nor power can be keped dry within the same.

Item: It is also to be noted that the castell stondith in such forme and so lowe under the town, as yf the town by any meanes be against the castell, either woon by enemyes or by rebelling of th'inhabitauntes against the captene, the said castell can no waies hurte or danger the town and the town greatly hurte and danger the castell.

Item: There is a wawll at the entringe into the haven called Holdeman Wawll, which was maide for savegard of the same haven. And the same wawll is now decayed, by reason whereof the mowth and the entringe into the same havyn gatherith and is filled so with sand, that oneles spedy remedy be provydyt for the same, the said haven shall within breve tyme to come be clerly stopped and sanded.

Item: Over and above thes special noticions of decayes, declayred in the articles above writtyn, ther ar divers playces of the said wawlles of the town and castell, which had much neid to be pynned, pynted, and brittished with stone and lym, the doing wherof in tyme shall save the kinges hieghnes the oone half of the charges which within breve tyme he shalbe inforced els to maike for the repayringe of the same.

Today, no trace of the early Norman castle handed over to Henry II in 1174 survives.

Bewclay (Bukeley) Pele. E.60
AA 3-XIII-13.

John Warburton made a list of the ruined towers and chapels in Northumberland *c.* 1715, and in it is an almost indistinguishable entry: 'Bukeley and Portgate … two ancient piles.' Could the 'Nightfolds' a mile to the west be on the site? See Portgate.

Bewick Tower. D
Tate I-222.

A tower standing at Bewick was mentioned by the historian Tate, who produced his two-volume *History of Alnwick* in 1866–1869. See Old Bewick.

Bickerton Bastle. D.60
Dixon 314. Mackenzie II.

Bickerton Bastle lay east of Hepple between Hepple and Tossen. Dixon says there were many bastles, remains of which are under green mounds in a field adjoining the farm, which also incorporates some old work in its north wall. Mackenzie says that Bickerton was formerly the property of four persons, all of them Snowdons, whose bastle houses are still standing.

Biddlestone Tower. C
Pevsner. *Northumberland County History* **XIV–418. Raine. Ryder.**
The remains, standing next to the hall, were converted into a chapel in the early nineteenth century. The original vaulted basement of this tower has gone, as has all trace of its barmkin, but traces of a built-up doorway in the east wall remain. The walls were 6ft thick and the tower was 42ft E–W × 32ft N–S. A passage was discovered to the thickness of the wall in 1879. The first mention of this building was in the survey of 1509 and it was also in that of 1541. A plan of the remains is on p.46 of Ryder's *Bastles and Towers*.

The Birks, Tarset. E
There are the remains of a stone house on a good defensive site known as 'Birks Barrow' just over the stream from the present mansion house.

Birtley Tower. E.52
Northumberland County History **VI–361. Pevsner.**
The present remains were built as late as 1611, but the mention of the chief message in 1307 is the earliest notice of Birtley Hall, whose ruined walls remain in the vicarage garden. It is not on the lists of 1415 or 1541 but the date of 1611 with the letters 'JH' remain on a stone built into the walls. The walls stand 8ft–10ft high. No decorative features survive, and the stair was in the north-west corner. At Tone Hall, 2 miles north-east, are the remains of a bastle converted into a tidy five-bay house having walls 4ft thick. The original byre doorway, though blocked, still exists in the east gable. This house was much larger than the average pele or bastle.

Bitchfield (West) Tower and Barmkin. F
Northumberland County History **XII–341. Pevsner. AA 3–XVIII–103.**
This is a fifteenth-century tower, measuring 31ft × 23ft, with a seventeenth-century mansion on its east side, where the date 1622 can be seen on the inside. There were traces of a barmkin wall and a moat on three sides, the moat being fed by a spring on the east side. The basement is vaulted and there were corbelled-out bartizans at the corners. The building has been restored and is occupied. The photograph on p.144 shows the house prior to its restoration in 1935.

Black Cleugh (Unthank) Pele. G.29
Pevsner.
High up on the open fells south-east of Unthank Hall is a ruined pele with its basement doorway in one of the long side walls. Unusual for such a house,

there is a gunloop in the remaining gable end. The grass-covered remains of other buildings are a little distance away.

Black Middings Pele/Bastle. North of Bellingham. E.22
Pevsner. *Northumberland County History* XV-271. Bates. Ryder.

Measuring 25ft × 14½ft, this basement has a door in the east wall that is only 2ft 3in wide. There is an outside stair to a door in the middle of the south wall, the head of which was made from an older lintel with holes for three iron stanchions. To the east are remains of an eighteenth-century cottage built on the heavier foundations of a much older house, which no doubt preceded the pele in more peaceful times. There are two eighteenth-century doors on the ground floor in the south wall, one each side of the stair. Also to be seen are the remains of the original roof timbers, which were partly cut away when the present roof was put on. Just up the hill are the foundations of another pele or bastle 22¼ft × 30ft with walls from 4ft 3in to 4ft 6in thick. Shown on p.35 are my drawings depicting the plan, elevation and section of Black Middings pele/bastle, made in 1971. On p.144 is my field sketch showing the relationship of the buildings. Good photographs are to be found in the Blankenburgs Collection held in the County Records Office. Just over the stream are remnants of what may have been an early pele, a low mound within a shallow dry moat.

Blanchland Abbey. Two Towers. G
Northumberland County History IV-312.

1. Tower at north of west range (Lord Crewe Hotel). The Old Tower of the Forsters converted into an inn was originally part of the conventional buildings until it passed into the hands of the Radcliffes and Forsters at the Dissolution. The walls on the ground floor are medieval and may have been the guest house of the abbey. The north chamber has a semicircular vault and the door is on the east or cloister side of the tower, the opening at the north-east corner being modern. The outer walls surmounted by the battlemented parapet are all of post-Reformation character and the upper floors are destitute of medieval work.

2. Tower and gate. The gatehouse has suffered from much rebuilding but it has a fireplace of *c.* 1400. All the windows were on the south or inner side of the yard, and foundations of a wall connecting it with the north-west angle of the Lord Crewe Hotel have been found. The roof is enclosed by a battlemented parapet. The foundations of the Lord Crewe Hotel are of *c.* 1225 and those of the gate are late fourteenth century.

Bitchfield Tower, just south of Belsay, is depicted as it was prior to its restoration by
W.D. Caroe and Lord Gort in 1935.

BLACK MIDDINGS PELE

Black Middings Pele/Bastle with its roof intact. Beyond are the remains of the later
cottage, all built on the foundations of an older house.

Blenkinsop Fortalice. G
Pevsner. Bates. Hodgson 2–III–128.
The castle or fortalice is mentioned in the surveys of 1415.

Bog Hall Bastle. Rothbury. F.2
Dixon 473.
This was a fortified house demolished some years ago (early twentieth or late nineteenth century) and it was the 'last one left in the Forest of Rothbury'.

Bog Head. E.25
See entry for Barty's Pele.

Bolam Castle. F.40
AA 4–XXII–146.
The enclosure on top of Bolam Hill was once a motte-and-bailey castle and the site was used for the later tower, which has now disappeared. See Bolam Castle Tower.

Bolam Castle Tower. F
Hodgson 2–I–337. Pevsner.
The main tower of the 'castle' was 40ft × 30ft outside and some of it and the walls of other buildings remained until Bolam House was built, when it was used as a quarry. It stood in an ancient earthwork and with walls and ditches contained about 7 roods. The site is a high hill by the name of Bolam Hill, and when the trees were planted there, a lot of hewn stones were found.

Bolt House: Bastle/Pele and Tower. Kirkwhelpington. F.27
Hodgson 2–I–189. Bates.
This pele or bastle had the usual accommodation, with the cattle below and the living quarters above. These had a boarded floor and a garret, both approached by a stair on the outside. They were in this case covered by a very dangerous thatch roof. The door to the cow house or basement was under the landing of the stairs and was fastened by a strong bolt on the inside, for which purpose there was a trapdoor in a corner of the upper floor. Hodgson also mentions 'the little tower, the mansion of the vicarage', which stood next to the church, but the only strong house existing in his time was the above pele.

While the historian John Hodgson mentions a tower as well as the pele, in his time only the pele with its dangerous thatched roof existed.

Bolton 'Pila'. D.66
Bates (Footnote, p.11). Pevsner.

Bates mentioned that in 1317 the peles of Bolton and Whittingham were taken from partisans of Gilbert De Middleton. Father Nicholson told me of two towers, the 'one at Bolton and one at the hospital at Whittingham, which had a licence to crenellate'. A 'pila' in 1317 would not have looked like one of the many peles and bastles to be found today, but could have been moated earthworks with timber superstructures or the towers mentioned by Father Nicholson. The Bolton house incorporates a three-storey, tower-like structure, perhaps a tower or strong house.

Bothal Castle. F.19
AA Pevsner. Hodgson 2-II-151. Bates.

Bothal, a square gate keep with flanking towers, was granted licence to crenallate in 1343. Above the gate between the flanking octagonal towers is a very fine display of shields, arranged in the order shown below, and on the battlements above were stone figures.

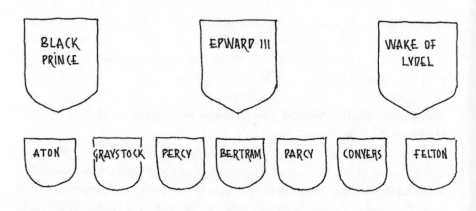

The Black Prince. Edward III. Wake of Lydel.

The passage under the gatehouse was 33ft long × 12ft and had a portcullis and gates and a set of meurtrières (arrow holes) in the roof. The courtyard ran 60yd south of the keep toward the River Wansbeck and had all the usual offices built against its walls, of which little is left. The plan is that of a motte-and-bailey but in this case the gate is also the keep, as at Morpeth and Bywell. The mason's marks on the gate are similar to those on the barbican at Prudhoe.

Of great importance is the site of this castle, which like Newcastle and Berwick, guards a bridgehead and therefore stands on the north bank of a river. Only three castles in the whole county stand on the north side of a river, all others using the river for defence against raids from over the border. The term 'bothel' is thought to be derived from the old English for a dwelling house, here being of such a high status that it did not require any prefix or suffix to identify it. Other houses in the county incorporating this old root in their names are Harbottle, being translated as 'the dwelling of the hirelings', while Shillbottle was 'the dwelling of the Shipley people'. Shipley is only a short distance away and is thought to be 'where the sheep lay' or 'pasture for sheep'. Wallbottle is simply 'the homestead on the Roman wall'.

Bothal Castle.

Boughthill Pele/Bastle. E.33
Northumberland County History XV–249. Ryder.

All that remains is a heap of stones high up on a hillside above the left bank of the Tarset Burn. There is a sketch plan of the site suggesting a later building or extension on the east end and the position of an external stair on the long south wall in Ryder's *Bastles and Towers in the Northumberland National Park*.

Bower Pele/Bastle. West of Bellingham. E.33
Tomlinson 220. AA 3–XIII–14.

A list of *c.* 1715 states, 'The Bowre: an ancient pile on ye north side of ye river Cherdon'. This is now incorporated in the present farm. William Charlton, or 'Bowrie' as he is known, was at Preston with the Earl of Derwentwater and would have joined the 1745 Jacobite Rebellion if his friends had not had him put in prison. In 1709 he was responsible for the death of Henry Widdrington and Widdrington's followers carried the body to Bellingham Church and had it buried at the entrance to Bowrie's pew. They did this thinking that Bowrie would have to step over his victim every time he went to his devotions, but this was not to be. Bowrie, being a Papist, found it no hardship not attending a Protestant church, so stop he did.

Bower Shield. Elsdon. E.66
Pevsner. Ryder. Grundy.

Now part of some stock pens, the east gable of a pele-like structure is all that remains.

Boweshill. Bellingham. E.38
Ryder. Grundy.

A little distance from the nineteenth-century cottage are the scant remains of what looks like a pele/bastle with only the slit vent in the east wall as evidence of refinement.

Bradley Hall Peles/Bastles. Henshaw. G.4
Hodgson 2–III–17. Ryder. Pevsner.

The farmhouse here is in a wild, windswept part of the county and harbours a secret in that its heart may be not one but two peles or bastles built end to end. Edward I stayed here on 6–7 Sept 1306, so it must have been of some standing, perhaps a hall house later to decline in status. About a mile west of Bradley stood a pele on Peel Crags but no trace is left.

Branshaw Pele. E.9
Grundy.
Only the vaulted basement of this pele remains and it is in poor condition, being open at both ends. From the outside it looks like a mound of stones as it is buried in the debris of its own upper walls. Near at hand are remains of later buildings, but its own dimensions were 30ft × 15½ft.

Branton Pele/Bastle. D.31
Northumberland County History **XIV–403.**
A mansion is mentioned in 1695 and it may have included a pele, but if so it was one of the latest built in Elizabeth I's reign as it is not mentioned in any pre-Reformation records. In 1730 it had been 'destroyed by a fire 50 years before', and in 1864 its foundations were still visible opposite the Presbyterian chapel.

Branxton Tower. A
Northumberland County History **XI–106. Hodgson 3–II–168.**
The tower is of a date before 1522 and is famous because of its connections with the Battle of Flodden Field, or the 'Field of Branxton'. It was a 'lyttle tower' destroyed by the Scots but was repaired again before 1541, when it was mentioned in the survey of that time. On 9 September 1513, 40,000 Englishmen fought the most famous battle ever on Northumbrian soil, against 60,000 Scottish soldiers under King James IV. This ended in the death of James and victory for England. Correctly called 'The Field of Branxton', it is now known as Flodden Field and the brave of both nations are remembered every year by a service on the spot.

The Brig Pele. Corsenside. E.89
Pevsner.
Within the farmstead is a pele, now used as a barn, yet still in a reasonably good and complete state when I visited in 1975 after surveying the old house at Corsenside.

Brinkheugh. Brinkburn. F.60
Pevsner.
On the other side of the River Coquet to Brinkburn Priory and a little further upstream is Brinkheugh, which is an unusual pele, having both basement and first floor doorways in its east gable.

Brockley Hall Bastle. F.2
Dixon 474. Pevsner.
The remains of this building are incorporated in the farm of Brockley Hall, and
an overmantle frame in the kitchen with the words 'Thomas Warton 1666' was
built into the gable of one of the farm buildings.

Buckton Tower. Islandshire. B
Raine.
This tower was in the survey of 1415, but little else is known of it, other than that
it fell to the rank of a farm in 1581–82.

Burnbank. North Tynedale. E
***Northumberland County History* XV-249. Ryder.**
Foundations on a plateau between the Tarset and Tarret Burns may be of two or
more towers in the one range. There are steep slopes on three sides of the plateau,
with a marsh on the fourth, protecting it from slightly higher ground. It is on
this fourth side that the remains of a ditch and a range of buildings can be traced.
This range consisted of two towers or a kitchen range and tower. A farmhouse
was built in the seventeenth century on the site of the present West Burnbank,
but it is not known if the tower was inhabited until then. There must have been
a barmkin or some form of stockading.

Burnlaw. Allendale. G.53
Ramm et al. 80.
This house has pele-like elements about it but has been much enlarged and remodelled. Where it falls down is in the thickness of its long walls, they being only 2ft 6in
thick, while its end walls are just over 3ft thick. Is this a pele, bastle or a 'bastle derivative'? Measuring 43ft 6in × 23ft externally, it has on the inner face of the south-east
end wall a recess that may mark the position of the original basement doorway.

Burradon Tower. Coquetdale. C
***Northumberland County History* XV-424. Raine.**
The ruins of this tower were visible in 1850 but the only record of it is in the
survey of 1541, when it was 'a great tower in decay'.

Burradon Tower. North of Newcastle upon Tyne. F
***Northumberland County History* IX-47. AA 3-XIII-15. Bates.**
Burradon was a small tower with exterior dimensions of 23ft 3in × 22ft 6in and
stood three storeys high. It has rubble walls with long quoins at the angles. There

was a parapet on one corbel and a *bretesche* on three corbels over the door, which was at ground level and in the east wall. The basement is vaulted and has a slight point, and the stair is in the wall on the left side of the door.

Butter Knowes Bastle or Tower. F.2
Dixon 474. *Northumberland County History* XV–357, 359.

There is no trace of this bastle, or tower, left and the site is uncertain. All but one or two of the towers, bastles or peles that were in Rothbury Forest are now lost without trace.

Bywell Castle. H.6
Bates. *Northumberland County History* VI–75. **Pevsner.**

In 1464 Henry VI found shelter in the castle of Bywell. It did not guard a bridge-head or take advantage of high land, but seems merely to have enclosed a large, irregular-shaped barmkin with high walls. Bywell, like Dunstanborough, Bothal and Wilimoteswyke, is a stronghold in which the gatehouse was the dominant feature of fortification, but Bywell is the only one with a gatehouse and very

The small tower at Burradon, north of Newcastle, has a vaulted basement of 25ft 3in by 22ft 6in. Externally are the remains of corbelled-out machicolations positioned so as to protect the basement entrance.

little else. The gatehouse, a rectangle of 59ft × 38ft facing the Tyne, had a portcullis and gates, with machicolations over the entrance, the passage being 10ft 8in wide with a doorway in each side at the inner end.

The battlements and turrets are of great interest. The turrets are gained by straight outer stairs resting on the east and west walls, with the battlements carried to a great height to screen them. The sides of the turrets facing the field have meurtrières in their floors and there are machicolations over both outer and inner gates. A little curtain wall with two slits remains between the tower and the modern house, which has a fifteenth-century vaulted basement. A large number of Roman stones were used in building this castle. Guy de Balliol, one of the men who came over with William the Conqueror, was made Lord of Bywell in the reign of William Rufus. This was a great family and one member founded Balliol College, Oxford, and one was King of Scotland.

Bywell Motte-and-Bailey Castle. H.17
Pevsner.

A little north-west of Styford Hall, high above the Rive, is a motte 21ft high with a ditch on three sides. No ditch was required on the fourth and final side, it being a steep drop to the river.

Bywell Castle (H.6): The remains indicate that this was a rather fine house with a rectangular gatehouse keep 59ft by 38ft that faces the river. The drawing shows the house in 1786.

Callaly Castle and Towers. North of Rothbury. D.42
Northumberland County History XIV-529-62. Pevsner. Hodgson 3-II-210. Bates.

Traces of a motte-and-bailey castle can be seen 650yd north of the house on the opposite bank of the burn. In the twelfth century the occupants moved to the south bank and started to build a tower on top of the 'castle hill'. A ditch 40ft wide was quarried but the fortress seems never to have been completed. The foundations of the two rectangular buildings survive.

The survey of 1415 says there was a castle at Old Callaly, which suggests that the tower around which the modern house is built was either completed or under construction and the old one was still in use as a place of defence.

The new tower was approximately 40ft × 40ft and had diagonally opposite turrets or small towers attached (on the east and west). There was a vaulted basement of two spans and a twin gabled roof was removed in 1440. The south-west angle of the modern house incorporates three walls of the new tower and in one corner are the remains of a spiral stair.

Cambo Pele or Bastle. F.23
Pevsner. Bates. Hodgson 2-I-281.

Cambo 'Tower' is now the village shop and post office. The building we see today is a stout pele or bastle with traces of the first-floor entrance above the shop front.

Camp Cottage. Tarset. E.35
Pevsner, Grundy.

On the north bank of the River North Tyne are the scant remains of one gable end of a pele. The outlines of the other walls are under grass mounds.

Capheaton Fortalice. F.43
Hodgson 2-I-213, 3-I-28.

The first mention was in the survey of 1415 but a new house was built in 1668. The new house was a short distance from the old site and in 1779 it was noted that the fortalice had had a moat and a drawbridge. The old site is west of the hall (see p.116).

Caraw Tower. E
Hodgson 2-III-397.

There was a tower of the grange of Hexham at Caraw, to which was added a stone house in 1406. The surveyors of 1541 noted that both house and tower were in decay at that time. A herdsman's cottage is all that now remains on the site.

Carham Tower. A.12
Bates. Pevsner.
Carham Tower is mentioned in the survey of 1541, but it has now completely disappeared. Bishop Aldon is said to have died of sorrow at the deaths of so many of the children of St Cuthbert when in 1018 the men of Northumbria were defeated at the hands of Malcom, King of Alban and Eggenius, the King of the Strathclyde Brythons. This battle was witnessed by the inhabitants of Carham. See Pressen.

Carrshield Peles. G.31
Pevsner.
At the north end of the village is a ruined pele attached to the farmhouse of Whiteley Shield. North of the village by about one mile at Hartley Cleugh is a much better-preserved example.

Carrycoats Bastle. E.45
Northumberland County History IV-405. Hodgson 3-II-215. Pevsner.
Mentioned in the list of 1541. As part of the suppressed monastery of Newminster it may have stood on or near the site of the present hall. Much sixteenth-century masonry survives at the rear of the present-day Carrycoats Hall.

Cartington Castle or Fortalice. Rothbury. D.52.
Bates 307. *Northumberland County History* XV. Dixon 350. Pevsner.
Hodgson 3-I-29, 3-II-212. AA 2-XIV-397, 3-VIII-12.
This castle consisted of a square courtyard with a palace range on the north, the east end of which was a large fourteenth-century tower. This tower had a well opening on to the first floor from a vaulted basement and bartizans on its two east corners. On the south side of the courtyard are two towers, the south-east being the first built and older than the north range; it houses a garderobe. The south-west tower may have housed or guarded the gateway. The large north-east tower followed this but was extended to make the palace or hall before completion. The entrance to this tower was on the west and there are the remains of a stair in the south-west corner. The hall to the west was divided into smaller rooms in the late fifteenth century. The present remains were excavated and partly rebuilt in the late nineteenth century, and due to these excavations, the foundations of the intended north-east turret can be traced south of the large fourteenth-century tower at the east of the hall range. The castle has belonged to the Cartingtons and the Herrons, great Northumbrian names.

Catcherside. Kirkwhelpington. F.27
Pevsner.
Just north of Knowesgate is a cottage that started life as a pele, with a blocked
basement doorway in a gable end. Having a round-arched lintel, it is more typical
of examples in the south-west of the county.

Catcleugh Pele. C.21
Hodgson 11-I-153.
'All those summerings called Catcleugh ... the highlands called Spithope ... and
the peel of the highland summer lands' were mentioned in a deed of sale. The site
is not known but it sounds as if it was only used in the summer, when the animals
were taken out to the hills.

Causey Park Tower. F
Hodgson. Pevsner. AA 2-XIV-22.
A fortified mansion built in the early fifteenth century, the remains are incorpo-
rated in the old house, where two spiral staircases remain.

Charlton Pele. West of Bellingham. E.36
Northumberland County History **XV. AA 4-XVI.**
The pele of Charlton is shown on the Map of Medieval Northumberland and
Durham in *Archaeologia Aeliana*, and the remains could still be seen in the late
eighteenth century.

Charlton (South) Tower and Pele. North of Alnwick. D.18
Bates 21. *Northumberland County History* **II-309. Pevsner.**
A tower was built in the mid-fifteenth century by the Earl of Northumberland for the
safety of the village in the time of war. This has now vanished but was on the end of
the chapel, like that at Ingram, Long Haughton and Ancroft. It is strange to find
the remains of a pele in the hamlet, it being so far east in the county, but the old
school, though much remodelled, exhibits the usual stout wall and a byre door in
its east gable and the door to the first floor is in the wall to its left (south) as in other
parts of the county.

The location of Chesterwood pele in the village.

Mr and Mrs Keen standing outside Chesterwood pele, their home.

Chatton Towers. D
Northumberland County History XIV-207.
The vicar's tower mentioned in 1415 and 1541 has now gone. In 1566 it was described as 'the site of the vicar's house with an orchard and two other gardens without a wall'. Later in the same survey it is stated that it is in great decay. New vicarages were built in the early eighteenth century and again in 1844, but the tower is incorporated in the present house.

Chatton. Fowberyes Tower. D
This tower was built on the village common for the protection of the inhabitants, and was known as Fowberyes Tower in 1566. It was also mentioned in the surveys of 1415 and 1541. The last mention was in 1616 when it was held by John Collingwood, but now even its site is unknown.

Chesterwood. Haydonbridge. G.32
Pevsner. Tomlinson.
As shown by this old postcard of *c.* 1920, Chesterwood was a small hamlet set round a green. Tomlinson, in his *Comprehensive Guide to Northumberland*, said that it was 'chiefly composed of old fashioned buildings known as peles' but only a few remain today. Golf House is the best preserved and still has an external stair on the south wall and the basement doorway on the north – not the usual arrangement if original! On the north side of the green is another pele, which has its upper doorway now blocked up. To the west are what could be the remains of two more, but much reduced in height. On the south side of the green is more stout masonry, which may be the remains of yet another. Is this an example of the grouping together of peles for greater defence?

Cheswick Tower. Islandshire. B
Bates. Raine 234. Pevsner.
The tower was built around 1400 and in 1541 was a little tower, but in 1560 it was in ruin. The site was north of the village, but no trace is left. Ladythorne House at Cheswick has the date 1721 inside, but the stepped gable looks older.

Chibburn: Moated Preceptory. Widdrington. F.5
AA 2-V-113, 2-XVII-263. Pevsner. Parker.
First mentioned in 1313, this group of buildings is one of the few houses the Knights Hospitallers had in this part of the country. It consists of a moated courtyard with a chapel on the south, and west of that, the hall and living quarters. The principal entrance was by an arched gateway in the north range.

The east wall had no buildings on it but had a small door or postern. The moat, which was around the whole, enclosed an area of approximately 100yd in diameter, but everything is now overgrown. The Knights Hospitallers of St John of Jerusalem were founded in 1092 with the building of a hospital at Jerusalem, their object being to provide assistance to pilgrims visiting the Holy Land and to protect them on their way. A military order, they built their first house in England in 1100 and more than fifty-three lesser houses were to follow. Their modern counterpart, indeed descendant, is the St John Ambulance Association.

Many of the county's most prominent historians have written papers on Chibburn Preceptory, including W.W. Tomlinson, John Hodgson, F.R. Wilson and Raine, with excellent steel engravings in John Henry Parker's *Domestic Architecture of England* (1853).

Tomlinson produced an article in 1899 telling of the raid by French naval hero Jean Bart, who put the house to the torch in 1691. During the Second World War

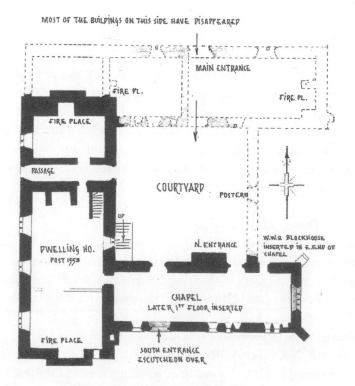

CHIBBURN PRECEPTORY

Attached to the tower at Chibburn is a manor house of 1621.

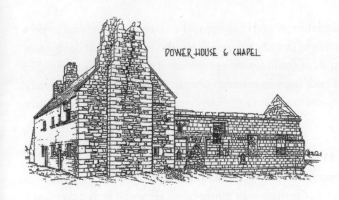

DOWER HOUSE & CHAPEL

The massive tower at
Chibburn is boldly
corbelled and
machicolated.

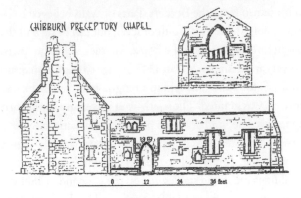

CHIBBURN PRECEPTORY CHAPEL

0 12 24 36 feet

The Second World
War left its mark
on Chibburn with
this gun-firing
loop built into the
chapel wall.

B. LONG.

a pillbox was inserted into the east end of the chapel and was only removed in 1994 as part of the consolidation of the site. One of its loopholes was rebuilt during this work to ensure the history of the house was perpetuated. Other wartime defences in the area consisted of tank traps and aircraft obstructions that have since mostly been destroyed by open-cast coal mining, when even the moat and fish pond were quarried for coal.

Chillingham Castle. D.9
Northumberland County History **XIV-330. Hodgson. Bates. Pevsner.**

This castle was a mansion in the thirteenth century, and Henry III stayed there on 4 and 5 September 1255, on his return from the Borders. Parts of walls believed to be of this mansion are not now visible above ground-floor level, but can be seen in the basement and may be of or before 1296, when the house was sacked by the Scots. The castle is square with towers at the angles, and in 1344 licence to fortify 'mansun of Chevelynham' with a wall of stone and lime and to strengthen it, crenellate, and convert it into a castle or fortress was granted. The south-west tower and lower parts of the other towers belong to this date, probably also part of the curtain wall.

Sir Thomas Herrons' fortress consisted of a courtyard with a tower at each corner, an entrance on the south or west side, a great hall on the east and windowless curtain on the north. A block of buildings including stables was on the west and in 1514 the castle could billet 100 horsemen, the same as Etal (also fortified in the 1340s) and more than Ford could accommodate. Mentioned in the survey of 1541, it was in good condition as it had been restored recently. The castle remained in its medieval state until the mid-seventeenth century, when it was made more fitting as a gentleman's house, and in 1753 the grounds were landscaped.

Chipchase Tower ('Castle'). E
Northumberland County History **IV-333. Hodgson 3-II-216.**

This is unusually well built for the mid-fourteenth century and must have belonged to a family of importance and wealth. Its dimensions are 51ft 6in N–S by 34ft × 50ft to parapet walk and 10ft more to the top of the angle turrets. Very boldly corbelled and machicolated battlements crown the walls, and the turrets were treated in a like manner. The ground floor is vaulted and the upper floors (three of them) were of timber, supported on corbels. The main area of each floor formed a single apartment, and in addition, there were a number of well-lit and conveniently arranged rooms in the thickness of the walls.

The original door was on the ground floor in the east side, the site of the later mansion. There was a stout door and a wooden portcullis, operated from a room directly above. There is a trapdoor in the roof of the vault at the north end.

CHIP CHASE CASTLE, NORTHUMBERLAND.

FISHER, SON & Cº LONDON & PARIS.

Chipchase Castle.

A manor house of 1621 is built on to the east side of the tower, which was first mentioned in 1415, and traces of medieval work in the courtyard may be the remains of an earlier manor house.

Sir George Heron of Chipchase was slain at Reedswire in 1575 and the Scots were so pleased that they gave all the prisoners they had taken that day a falcon, saying a live hawk was a noble exchange for a dead 'heron'.

Chirdon Pele. E.33
AA 3–XIII-14. *Northumberland County History* XV-273–74. Bates.
In 1237 Hugh Bolbeck complained to Henry III that Sir David Lindsey was building a strong house in the form of a tower on the King of Scotland's land in Tynedale and that such a tower would prove a danger to the English. No place is named and the tower may have been at either Chirdon or Dally Castle.

Chollerton Tower. E.91
Bates. Pevsner.
Christopher Dacre recorded, in 1584, towers to be incorporated in a line of strong, fortified houses of towers, being a defensive line against incursions from north of the border. This line was also to include a 'new devised dyke or defence'

but neither the dyke nor Chollerton Tower are to be found today. At the entrance to the churchyard is a rare survival in the form of a stable and hearse house in which can be seen reused medieval stonework; can this be from the tower mentioned in 1584?

Choppington (Chopington)Tower. North of Bedlington. F
Hodgson 2-II-364. Raine 371.

The tower of Choppington has now disappeared and the site is unknown, although it may have stood on the site of the Glebe Farm. The first mention of this tower was in the survey of 1541 and it was built by Gawen Ogle, Esq., around 1500.

Clennell Tower and Barmkin. C.12
Northumberland County History XV-434. Pevsner. Bates.

The first mention was in 1541 and it was small, with the usual vaulted basement and a barmkin. The door is in the south wall, with a stair in the wall at the west of the door. It also had an upper floor and perhaps an attic. In 1568 a wing was built running west with half of its face projecting from the south face of the tower. At the same time, another storey had been added to the tower. An addition, now removed, was also built to the east side and a door cut at first-floor level of the tower to reach it. The old tower door was made into a window.

Cocklaw Tower. North of Hexham. E.59
Northumberland County History IV-180. Bates 370. Pevsner.

The entrance is from the south through a passage about 10ft long × 4ft 6in high, the outer door of which is secured by a fall bar only. On the right of the passage is a door to the wheel stair, which occupies the south-east corner of the tower. The other side of the passage has been broken through into the dungeon, 5ft × 8ft with an opening in its vault. At the end of the passage is another door to the basement vault. A door in the east wall of the first floor led to the chapel and another building, the foundations of which can be traced. The stair may have ended in a turret above the rest of the tower, so affording access to the battlements. There were turrets on all four corners at roof level with machicolations placed over the entrance, supported by four three-projection corbels. Cocklaw has traces of refinements, which are wall decorations in the hall, etc., and these included a frieze in which a crude acanthis ornament is predominant.

Cockle Park Tower. North of Morpeth. F.16
Hodgson 2-II-39. Pevsner. Bates.

This is a rectangular tower of the mid-fifteenth century with bartizans corbelled out on the two north corners. There are machicolated battlements between the

Cocklaw Tower.

bartizans and traces of gables above. Including the later south wing, the dimensions are 54ft N–S × 30ft E–W. The ground floor is vaulted and there is a spiral stair in the south-east corner but it is of a later date. The arms of one of the Ogles (*c.* 1461) can be seen on the east front and help to date the building.

Coldmartin Tower. D
Northumberland County History XIV-215. Bates.
To the north of the shepherd's house of Tower Martin is a steep hillside in which is a disused quarry. The tower stood on what is now the west verge of this quarry. In the wall along the top of the hill were a few yards of solid masonry, which breaks off at that quarry edge showing a core of cement and rubble. That is all that is left of the tower. Bates says a fragment of wall 9ft high × 6ft thick was standing at the south-west in 1891 and that the tower was approximately 27ft square outside. It was mentioned only once (in 1584) as 'one towre of stane and lime of Roger Fowberry gent. Utterly decayed notwithstanding it hath land belonginge to it able to keep two men and horse fit for service.'

Coldtown Pele. Corsenside. E.88
Pevsner.
It was while surveying the old house at Corsenside in 1975 that I first visited the two farmhouses of Brig and Coldtown and discovered two peles, one at each. Now very much part of a working farm, they are (were) almost complete but I never got back to survey them.

Cockle Park: Now part of Newcastle University, this large tower has a good example of machicolated battlements set between the bartizans.

The main entrance front has a restrained Gothic Revival treatment of much older windows.

Combe Pele. North-East of Bellingham. E.22
Northumberland County History XV-271.

The combe, a farm that incorporates a pele, stands on the north bank of the Tarset Burn, while on the south side stands the remains of two peles, Shilla Hill and Barty's Pele. For many years it was said that Barty's Pele was the pele of Hodge Corbet or Corby, and was therefore known as Corbet Castle, but this is in fact the Combe.

Coquet Island, Tower of Monastic Cell. D
Northumberland County History V-319. Pevsner.

On the island are the remains of a large range of buildings, including the vaulted basement of a tower. Trinity House converted this into a lighthouse in 1841, adding an extra floor to raise the height. Too small to have been a tower house, it was perhaps a detached solar reached in times of emergency by a bridge not unlike the much stronger Cocklaw Tower.

A tower of a Benedictine monastic cell mentioned in 1415, it is now encased in Trinity House work of 1841. Like Cocklaw Tower, did this have a bridge allowing access to the first floor from the range behind it?

Corbridge Low Hall. H

A most interesting house of the late thirteenth or early fourteenth century, having a ground-floor hall with the solar at the east end. In the fifteenth century this solar was raised to form a small tower. There is the usual vaulted basement and a stair that starts off in the thickness of the wall but in the fifteenth-century extension continues as a conventional newel stair. See Baxter's Tower.

Corbridge Vicar's Pele Tower. H
Northumberland County History X-209. Bates. Pevsner.

Built of Roman stones about 1300, the tower appears in the list of 1415 and in Clarke's survey of 1663. Well made and of one date, many of its stones show original Roman cramp holes. The tower is a good example of a smaller tower with vaulted basement and two other floors, which exhibit in a very complete manner the details of interior arrangements. Its external dimensions are 27ft 4in E–W × 21ft × 30ft to parapet walk and 5ft further to the top of the parapet. Square bartizans corbelled out at the corners had machicolations. The entrance on the ground floor was in the east side, and the old door still remains. It stands across the line of the present churchyard wall, which abuts on its east and west sides.

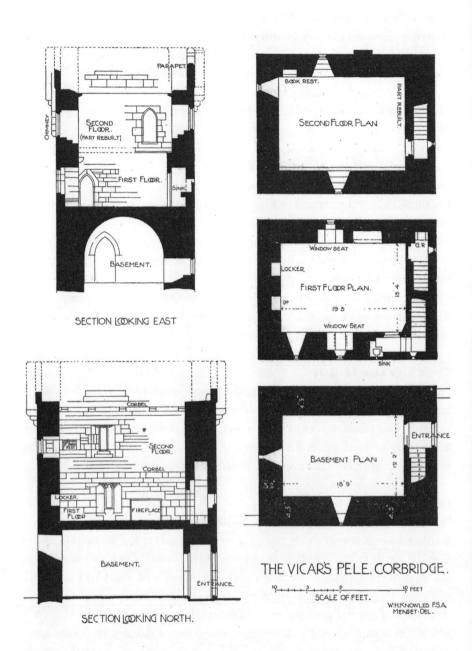

The Vicar's Pele, Corbridge.

Cornhill Tower and Barmkin. A.15
Raine 321. Bates.

A tower stood at Cornhill in 1385 when the Earl of Fife destroyed it, but it was rebuilt and described as new in 1541. The owner at that time was also busy building a barmkin around the same. The tower was still standing *c*. 1560 but only traces of earthworks survive in the wood by the river to mark the spot today.

Corsenside House, North of West Woodburn

Standing next to the small Norman church of St Cuthbert is a brave and early example of a non-defensible house. Pevsner puts a date of 1686 on it but I read the date above the door as 1680, while my field notes suggest an earlier date. Three storeys high, it has a four-centred arch to the centrally placed doorway. The windows have been messed about a bit, starting with two lights in those to the left of the door and three lights in those to the right. Mullions have been removed and sashes inserted on the ground floor. Iron bars still remain in small windows to the gables and back of the house.

This is not a bastle derivative but a forward-looking development by a builder embracing the domesticity enjoyed in more settled parts of the country. The occupants of peles/bastles within walking distance would have viewed such a house with envy.

Originally the vicar's house, it passed into the hands of the Reeds, with William and Frances making considerable alterations as recorded above the door. A new parsonage was built in 1736 on the road to East Woodburn.

Cote Walls (Coat Walls) Tower. Alwinton. C.22
Bates 43.

Coat Walls Tower is first mentioned in the list of 1541 and is included in the ring of fortresses shown on Dacre's Plat of 1584. The site of this tower and barmkin is now unknown. The entry for Byttylsden in the 1541 survey says that 'nere unto the same ys another lytle towre at a place called the Cotte Walles in measurable good repac'ons'.

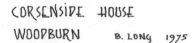

CORSENSIDE HOUSE
WOODBURN   B. LONG   1975

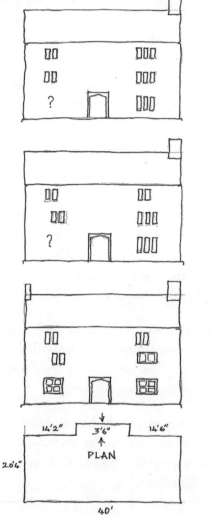

HOUSE AS BUILT AFTER THE FASHION
OF A MEDIEVAL PRIEST HOUSE

1680- TOP WINDOWS MOVED BUT SAME
STONE USED TO REBUILD

1800- SASH WINDOWS INSERTED IN
GROUND FLOOR

14'2"   3'6"   14'6"

PLAN

20'4"

HOUSE 40' × 24'4"

40'

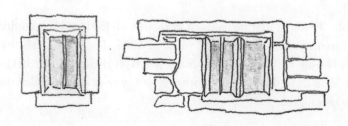

Coupland Tower. A
***Northumberland County History* XI-227. Bates.**

In 1514 there was 'nether fortresses nor barmekyne'. The character would imply that it was not built until the late sixteenth century or early seventeenth century; in any case, it followed the commission of 1584, which recommended the chain of forts to protect the frontier. It is L -shaped with the staircase in the minor arm of the L, and immediately within the entrance is a door giving access to the basement. The staircase reaches only to the first-floor level. The access to the second floor is by a smaller stair above the entrance and in the angle of the L, its foot being corbelled out and carried up as a circular turret. Above the second-floor apartment is a gabled roof erected on the inner edge of the main wall and around it was a walk, protected by a parapet and supported by projecting corbels. The staircase tower had a similar parapet and both have projecting gargoyles to carry off the water.

The most famous Lord of Coupland was John, who came to fame in 1346 when he captured David, King of Scotland, at Neville's Cross. He was made a knight banneret and whether as a result of this action or not, he was henceforth constantly in the king's service. There are some fine stone carvings set in the oak panels in the hall: two coats of arms and 'a picture'.

Coupland Castle is a complete tower house incorporated in a later mansion.

Crag Pele. North of Elsdon. E.19
Dixon 287. Ryder.

Crag formed part of a chain of peles and its remains show it is typical of many others in the county. They are situated in a farmyard above Elsdon in a line with three others. The ruins are attached to the north-east corner of a nineteenth-century farmhouse, where the west gable has the usual entrance to the ground floor but on its right is a stair in the thickness of the wall. The east gable has a wall cupboard and a slit vent. The basement is vaulted, which along with the external stair, helpS it rise above the ordinary. As a rule, the existence of an internal stair meant that an external stair was not required, yet what may have been a first-floor doorway (now blocked) can be seen in the east gable.

Craster Tower. Embleton. D
Northumberland County History **II-166. Bates. Pevsner.**

The original remains are now only a small part of a modern house, but it was built before 1415. Edmund Craster owned it at that date, according to the survey of 1415. It is of excellent masonry, and has a vaulted basement and a wheel stair in the south-east corner, where the wall is 6ft 5in thick (this stair may still remain, but it was blocked off when the modern house was built). The basement is 27ft 7in × 15ft 5in and the vault is somewhat flat and 10ft high. Modern battlements have been added and windows inserted.

Crawley Tower. D
Northumberland County History **XIV-408. Pevsner. Bates.**

Of early fourteenth-century construction, it is now an L-shaped house, much repaired and puzzling. The remains stand in the corner of a rectangular earth-work. Licence to crenellate was granted in 1343. The ground-floor loop holes have been made into windows and the door has gone. The tower is on the list of 1415, but was in great decay in 1541. The south front is 50ft and the west front is 36ft 6in. In the eighteenth century it became an ornament, an eye-catcher, on the estate and even provided an estate worker with a house built within its stout walls. The tower had been part of a much larger complex and may have had a substantial barmkin. Could this be the tower shown in Dacre's Plat of 1584 because the triangulation of map markers of the period was not great?

Cresswell Tower. F
Hodgson 2-II-204. AA XIV-22. (2). Pevsner.

The tower of Cresswell is 21ft 6in × 16ft 6in within and is vaulted in the basement, the two floors above being approached by a spiral stair. Of the old mansion house, which was attached, nothing now remains. An old picture shows the tower with turrets corbelled out at the corners and the mansion house attached. The house was demolished in the early nineteenth century, and the tower was subject to a detailed survey in 2003 which exposed features of considerable interest.

Dally Castle, Tower or Fortalice. E
Northumberland County History XV-273-7-9. Bates 55-56. Mackenzie II-250.
Built in 1237, the castle stood on a ridge with a ditch at either end of it; it was in two portions:

1. A building 30ft × 15ft east of the main one, date and use unknown.
2. A rectangular block 56½ft × 26ft 8in internally with attached turrets on the two north corners and a large turret or wing on the south, which has almost vanished. There are traces of masonry outside the east ditch.

The work is early thirteenth century with loop holes now blocked and buttresses added in the late thirteenth century as well as other additions of the fourteenth century and unknown date. The tower was presumably entered by the first floor. The stone was used to build Dally Milly and now only the foundations remain.

Darden Lough Pele. East of Elsdon.
See entry for High Rigg Pele.

Darques 'Peel'. Otterburn. E.67
Ryder.
While the remains of this house are in the garden of Dunns Cottage and are so fragmentary as to make it difficult to work out any detail, it is evident that masonry was massive with walls 6ft 8in thick; could this have been a tower?

Detchant Fortalice or Tower. North of Bamburgh. B
Northumberland County History I-402. Hodgson 3-I-27.
There was a tower or fortalice here, of which no trace now remains, but it is mentioned in the list of towers compiled in 1415 and was then in the possession of Richard Lilburn.

Dilston Tower. South-West of Corbridge. G
Northumberland County History X-286.
There is now no trace of the thirteenth-century manor house, which was probably unfortified as there is no mention of it in the list of 1415. The existing tower, which formed the nucleus of the later mansion, is mentioned in a deed of 1464.

The tower of 38ft 9in × 23ft 3in resembles the larger Cocklaw Tower and shortly after completion, an additional 13ft 2in × 18ft 4in was projected at the south end. This has three upper floors in the same height as the two of the tower.

The entrance, which is in part of the second addition of the mid-sixteenth century, gives on to a spacious stair around a square newel post. The original stair and entrance were also in this corner, the north-east. The remains were incorporated in a later mansion that has now almost disappeared and the tower is in ruin.

The Pretender James Stewart had a brave follower in the Earl of Derwentwater, who at his execution examined the block, and finding it rough, directed the headsman to smooth it off 'lest it might offend my neck'. In 1805 the commissioners of Greenwich Hospital had the vault at Dilston opened and found the earl's body and head, which had been embalmed, and the marks of the axe could still be seen.

Doddington Bastle. B.23
Northumberland County History XIV-156. Pevsner.

Doddington Bastle is now much overgrown, with a tree inside it. The ruins are in the centre of the village and it exhibits a departure from peles and towers in the greater comfort of its plan and in its external aspect. It was built in time of peace (1584) but contained defensive features common to houses on the border and incorporated on the exterior the then prevailing style of domestic architecture. Built in 1584, it was one of the latest border towers and was rectangular with the staircases, etc., projecting from the centre of the south side. It was three storeys high with a ridged roof and embattled parapet to the side walls, which also served as a gutter. It was not as big as Hebburn Bastle but more like Low Hirst Tower. The walls were not very strong (3ft) and had to be strengthened inside and out by the adding of buttresses. The east end has now been removed to leave an L-shaped plan. Originally it measured 57ft × 25ft externally; all the floors were supported by wooden joists and there was no basement vault. The attic had dormers with a door opening on to the parapet walk, and the stairs ascended to roof level and communicated with the various floors.

Donkley Wood. Tarset. E.68
Ryder. Pevsner. Grundy.

A small hamlet on the 'back road' (north of the River North Tyne) from Falstone to Tarset has the remains of a pele that juts out into the road. Only the eastern end is recognisable but later building obscures much of it. On the same back road is Camp Cottage with only the most fragmentary remains of a pele.

Downham Tower. A
Northumberland County History XI-85. Hodgson 3-II-183.

Very little is known of this tower, but it was built by Sir Cuthbert Ogle. Completed up to the second floor and in 1541, it was to have another storey with embattlements and a barmkin round it. At 9 p.m. on 20 October 1596, a band of Scots hewed up the gate of the barmkin 'which helde them tyll cock-crowe in the morninge'. And the defence offered was such that they went off empty-handed to try their luck at Carham.

Duddo Tower and Barmkin. A.11
Raine 316. Hodgson 3-II-191. AA 2-XIV-53 and 409.

A tower at Duddo was destroyed in 1513 or 1496, there being conflicting reports as to the date, and the remains of the later one, believed to have been built in the early seventeenth century, can now be seen. Raine, in his history, says that a large, old-fashioned barn building was standing in 1821 and had, in 1852, just lately been removed.

Dunstan, Two Towers. D
Northumberland County History II-188. Pevsner.

The two towers of Dunstan stood on the site of Proctor Steads and little now remains but foundations that were built over many times up to 1959. The west tower was very small at 17ft 10in E–W × 15ft N–S and had whinstone foundations with fourteenth-century ashlar on the upper walls. The whinstone in some places may be a modern replacement for ashlar that has been removed. Other stonework may be fourteenth century and may have been connected to the east tower, but the connecting wall looks as if it is of a later date.

Dunstanburgh Castle. D.21
AA *Northumberland County History* II-196. Pevsner. Hodgson 3-I-30. Bates. HMSO Handbook.

The modern approach is over the mouth of an old harbour, from which a ditch 80ft wide × 13ft deep ran north under the west walls of the castle to Embleton Bay, thus making the castle in effect an island. The old road came from inland over the ditch by way of a drawbridge and up the bank to an outwork or barras, which had to be disposed of before attackers could, by turning at right angles, direct their undivided attention on the gatehouse.

Some 80ft high, the keep was originally the gatehouse and to it was added a barbican, of which the foundations are still to be seen. A little distance from this to the south stood the barras mentioned above. This arrangement of gatehouse/keep was not suitable, so a gate tower was built in the west curtain and a small bailey was built in the internal angle formed by the keep and curtain. This new gate had a barbican added, which was approximately 21ft × 38ft, and to this was added the mantle wall with a gate that had a drawbridge in the form of a ramp, as the gate was above the level of the road. The outer bailey has four posterns, two on the east or sea wall and one on the Egginglough tower at the east end of the south wall, the other next to the Lilburn tower in the west wall.

A moat was started in front of the south wall but was never completed. The castle is the largest in the county and covers an area of 11 acres; it has walls on three sides but the north is protected by cliffs falling 100ft to the sea. As Berwick was often in Scots hands, a fortress and harbour was required further south to supply the English forces, so Dunstanburgh was built and licence to crenellate was granted in 1316.

Earle (Yeardle) Tower or Bastle. C.6
Northumberland County History XIV-171. Hodgson 3-II-185. Bates.
In 1541 the commissioners on the defence of the Border reported, 'the town-shippe of Yerdle conteyneth X husbandlands and hath in it a bastell house without a barmekyn and ys of thinherytaunce of Thomas Hebburne esqre and Gylbert Scotte'. The map of 1584 shows the tower with a note: 'Here at Yerdle the east and mydell marche is divided.' Nothing can now be traced to mark the site of this tower.

Dunstanburgh Castle viewed from the north is shown in this engraving, with extensive fieldworks to the south and west.

East Ditchburn Tower. D
AA 3-XIII-7.

In the 'Notices of Ruined Towers' in Northumberland *c.* 1715, East Ditchburn is mentioned as follows: 'East Didgburn: A small village on arising ground, belonging to Carrs of Lesbury and Collingwood of Biker: an old tower.'

East Shaftoe Hall Tower. F.67
Pevsner. Hodgson.

The mural painters Peter Harthewer, Robert Crosby and their 'man' George Phillips set up at Capheaton in April 1674 to 'workmanlike draw lime or paint diverse pictures lanskips chimony peeces boards or panels of Wainscott' for Sir John Swinburne. While researching their work, I visited a number of houses in the area of Capheaton where they are thought to have worked and it was then that I first discovered East Shaftoe Hall. I did not find any evidence of their work but discovered a jigsaw puzzle of a house with at its heart a fourteenth-century tower, with a vaulted basement and a projecting stair turret. This, with the remains of a later hall range, are all wrapped in the masonry of a small mansion house with the external appearance of a Georgian house built by an enthusiastic amateur, yet of considerable charm and great interest to an antiquarian.

East Woodburn Pele or Tower. South of Otterburn. E.40
OS Map. Pevsner.

East Woodburn was the house of the De Lisle family and the site of their house is known as Hall-Yards or Town Foot, which still shows traces of a fish pond and other works. Two other peles stand over the river at Highleam and one at the vicarage. In the vicinity is Harewalls, a mile east; a house being a relatively complete pele and still in use as a residence. Cherry Tree Cottage is also a pele, still occupied and standing between East and West Woodburn.

Edlingham Castle or Fortalice. D.43
Northumberland County History VII-122. Pevsner.

There are abundant indications of a 'barmekyne' of fine architectural detail and the remains include a rectangular yard with the keep to the east and the gatehouse to the west. There are also indications of buildings at the north and south-east angles of the courtyard. The keep is three storeys high and the basement was vaulted but is now filled with fallen masonry. Each floor is comprised of a single room and the main first-floor room is very ornate, with a groined roof and the remains of a good fireplace. The main building was screened by a forebuilding on the west and next to it on the north was a newel stair. This forebuilding was two storeys high. The main building has buttresses on the corner diagonal-wise that terminate in circular bartizans. First mentioned in 1396, the castle is now a delightful ruin. The fireplace in the tower/solar has now fallen but it was a fine example of a 'trilobe joggled' lintel.

Edlingham Hall Bastle. D.27
Northumberland County History XIV-396. Pevsner.
This site was no doubt occupied by the usual succession of different types of dwelling during the Middle Ages, but the oldest part of the present building is no older than sixteenth century and has been so much modernised that it is now impossible to say whether it is the remains of the bastle house or not. It was once the home of the Ogle family, and there is an apartment that is pointed out as having been occupied by Cromwell.

Edlingham Tower. D
Northumberland County History VII-149. Pevsner.
The church at Edlingham has a strong tower that was used for refuge in times of strife.

Elliburn Tower or Pele (The Lee). South of Rothbury. F.66
Hodgson 3-II-214. Dixon 474. Bates 45–46.
This tower has now gone but it is believed to have stood on the site of the Lee (on the east bank of the burn). It is shown in this position on many maps, although

Edlingham Castle:
Engraving from
Parker's *Domestic
Architecture*, 1853.

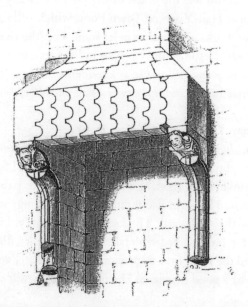

FIRE-PLACE, EDLINGHAM CASTLE, NORTHUMBERLAND

all trace and even the name has now vanished. In the survey of 1541 this tower is called a strong pile and a strong pele house.

Ellishaw. Otterburn. E

The remains of the solar/tower of a hospital here were removed in 1808. The site is just north of Otterburn at the junction of the A68 and the A696 roads. Hodgson mentions this house in Part 2, Vol. I of his *History of Northumberland*.

Elsdon Castle. E.18
Hodgson. Pevsner. AA 4–XXII–116.

The best motte-and-bailey in Northumberland is north-east of the village of Elsdon and was probably built about 1080. The circular mound of the motte stands to the south and is separated from the bailey by a ditch. The bailey is defended by ditch and rampart, east and north, with the ground to the west falling so steeply as to render artificial defences unnecessary. The castle was only made of wood and earth and never of stone.

The photograph (below) was taken from the side of the road from Winter's Gibbet down to the village of Elsdon. The massive earthworks are the finest in the country. Built by Robert De Umfraville, it would have been of earth and timber but some stones found in 1715 may suggest some rebuilding in stone, although these could simply be base stones for some stout timbers. The farm buildings and village are insignificant when compared with the size of the castle mounds.

The motte-and-bailey castle at Elsdon is the finest example in the county.

Elsdon Tower. Elsdon. E
Hodgson 2–I–96. Pevsner. Ryder. G. Taylor.

Elsdon village was once the heart of the largest parish in the county and must have been, as one poet said, 'like world's unfinished neuk'. The Rev. C. Dodgson once wrote of the tower where he lived:

> I have lost the use of everything but my reason, through my head is entrenched in 3 night caps, and my throat is fortified with a pair of stockings twisted in the form of a cravat, the vestibule of the castle [tower] is a low stable, and above it is the kitchen, in which are 2 little beds joining to each other. The curate and his wife sleep in one, and Margery, the maid in the other. I lay in the parlour between two beds to keep me from being frozen to death.

The tower existed before 1436, as is shown by the arms of Robert Lord of Rede in the battlements, and it has a vaulted basement. Externally, it retains much of its original form, having a corbelled-out garderobe and the entrance on the north side. The spiral stair is also on the north side. The Rev. Dodgson would enjoy a three-year stay in the tower now with all the comforts that Mr Taylor, the present owner, has installed. There is some debate as to the date of foundation of this tower, best presented by Ryder in his *Bastles and Towers*.

The diagrams on p.33 show plans, sections and elevation of Elsdon Tower and give some idea of its supposed original layout. Externally the most important features are the corbelled-out part of the battlements (machicolations) over the basement entrance and the change in thickness in the wall 20ft above the base. This 20ft-high string moulding would normally point to a floor just inside, but it would have not been so here as it would only have been 5ft to 6ft above the roof of the basement. The section shows the basement as it is today, and the mural chambers of the first floor, but the other floors are shown in what would be their most probable positions forming from top to bottom:

Vaulted basement used as byre and store room.

Lower hall with chambers in the thickness of the wall.

Upper hall or main room in the house which may have been divided to form kitchen and hall.

Garret or upper room with parapet walk and battlements.

View of the main front of Elsdon Tower, built looking out over the village green. It is now a private house.

All floors and the battlements would be reached by the spiral stair in the corner. The situation of the original fireplaces is not known and chimneys can be seen at both gable ends today, but the diagram only shows one. The two small windows in the stair are used to light the landings of the upper hall and garret.

Elswick Tower. H
Northumberland County History **XII-242.**
This castle or tower belonged to Tynemouth Priory and is mentioned as 'lately belonging' to Tynemouth Monastery in a lease dated 1576.

Elwick. Two Towers. North-west of Bamburgh. B
Northumberland County History **VI-412: Hodgson 3-I-28. Raine.**
There were two towers mentioned in the list of 1415 as belonging to Thomas de Bradford and Thomas de Elwick, and in 1561 'there is in the same towne twoe towres and ij demaynes, viij husbandlands and iiij cottages …'.

Elsdon Tower: Two views of the tower.

Embleton Tower. D
Northumberland County History II–80. Hodgson 3-I-30. Pevsner.

The tower was built in 1395 at a cost of £40. There are two vaults in the basement resting on a partition in the centre. The north of the chamber measuring 16ft 7in N–S by 12ft 4in, has a fireplace, also the remains of the straight mural staircase, which has now been blocked up. The south chamber is 13ft 8in N–S by 10ft 6in. The tower is attached to a modern house and the entrance may have been on the first floor as in the north wall there is a blocked opening. The battlements are there and only 3ft 8in above the water tabling, so would not be much use in defence. The tower would seem to have been the solar of a much more comfortable residence and the only ancient part of the house to survive.

Errington Pele. E.57
Northumberland County History IV-184. Pevsner.

On Armstrong's map of 1769 it is called a castle, but the remains are incorporated in a later house and therefore indistinguishable, other than a much older, single-storey range with thick walls protruding from the rear. This looks as if it was superior to any pele.

Errington Tower. Two Miles East of Chollerton. E.57
Bates. Hodgson. History of Northumberland. Pevsner.

At Errington there is a farmhouse of 1704 that has elements of at least two earlier builds, with to the back of the house an outshot consisting of some very stout walls that may be part of a much older house or tower.

Eshot Castle. F.4
Northumberland County History VII-342. Hodgson 3-I-26. Pevsner.

The site is shown on the OS map as north of the hall, and is marked by a ditch and mound. On 22 July 1310, the king, being at Westminster, granted a licence to Sir Roger Mauduit to crenellate his dwelling house at Eshot. ('Mansum sum de Esshet'), but in 1358 the king gave the castle to Roger Mauduit junior, as his father had fortified it as a rebel to the Crown. The building is also mentioned in the list of 1415. Half a mile north of the hall can be seen remains of a moat and, within, curtain walls with angle towers.

Eslington Tower and Barmkin. D.38
Northumberland County History XIV-515. Hodgson. Bates.

In 1334–35 Robert of Eslington was granted licence to crenellate his house and in 1415 a tower of Eslington was held by Thomas of Hazelrigg. It was found suitable for a garrison of twenty men in 1514 and in 1541 it was a tower with a barmkyn in good reparation. Stormed and taken by the Scots in 1587, nothing now remains of it, but it is thought to have stood a little north of the present mansion where some wrought stonework has been dug up.

Embleton Tower, now a fine house of 1828 by John Dobson. It still retains at its east end the solar of the vicar's pele, the only ancient part remaining

Etal Castle. North of Ford. A.12
Pevsner. Guidebook. *Northumberland County History* XV–460. Hodgson 3–II–191.

The castle of the Manners never reached the fame of that of the Herrons, but it was no mean fortress, as its ruins show. It stands on level ground 30yd from the River Till, which bends around its north and west sides. It was probably built as a challenge to Ford, since licence to crenellate Etal was granted in 1341, just three years after that of the Herrons of Ford. At the time it was a mansion of some importance and even in 1291 the Archbishop of York had lodged there in preference to Ford.

The crenellated house developed into a castle or fortalice in 1355 and a castle in 1368. Save for a skirmish with the Herrons in 1427, we hear little of its history in the Middle Ages but in 1438 the castle was 'ruined and therefore valueless'. This may indicate that it was dismantled at the time. Like Ford, it was a link in the second line of defence and figured most prominently in the sixteenth century. It was frequently garrisoned by the king's forces independently of the owners, as were many other border holds. It was estimated to hold 100 men, although this could be exceeded in time of need, and it was much prized as a position of importance. James IV captured it before Flodden but it was not destroyed. At any rate, it was used to house the captured Scottish ordnance after the battle and it was garrisoned in case of a fresh attack.

In 1541 it was 'for lacke of reparacions in very great decaye and many necessary houses within the same became ruinous and fallen to the ground'. The last survey of 1584 found it 'decaied for want of reparacion of long contynuance' and the estimated cost of repairs was £200.

The remains are scant, yet of great interest. The area enclosed is a rough rectangle approximately 182ft from N–S and 168ft E–W. At the south-east angle is the gatehouse tower and at the north-west stands the keep. There are signs of a tower at the north-east angle of the courtyard. The south-west angle has a small vaulted chamber in it.

The gatehouse is approximately 36ft square, and the entrance was recessed and flanked by towers, which were carried above the battlements. There is a shield above the gate with the arms of the Manners. The entrance was protected by a gate and portcullis, a drawbridge and a barbican, of which very little remains. The omission of the base course, which is carried around the building but not returned at the entrance, and the provision of holes by the upper-floor window suggest the drawbridge.

The ground rooms at each side of the entrance were entered from the tunnel but the courtyard had to be taken before access to the upper floors was won. There is a cavity for the portcullis in the east wall above the gate. The towers flanking the gate housed a spiral stair leading to the second floor and battlements and a door on to the barbican. The other (the south) tower held the camera. The keep was four-storied and resembles the tower at Cocklaw. The forebuilding measuring 17ft 6in wide × 7ft 10in held a spiral stair to the upper floors and battlements, where the stair ended in a square tower above the same. There was a portcullis 4ft from the door as at Chipchase, but this is not common in towers of the size of Etal. The curtain wall is only 4ft 6in thick where it is left standing and only the basement of the south-west tower remains, which is incorporated in a cottage.

Evistones Pele and Strong Houses E.5
Brown I-117. Pevsner. Ryder.
Set high on a hillside sloping down to the River Rede is a group of houses clustered together for protection, as much from the elements as from bands of reivers coming over Carter Bar. At the heart of the group is a communal space, with areas of ride and furrow beyond/ There are at least four peles/bastles and what looks like long houses. Both Frank Graham in his book, *The Castles of Northumberland*, and Brown show the layout much like a Roman fortlet, whilst it is actually a jumble of houses.

Fairnley Pele. F.26
Hodgson 2-I-287. Tate I-222.
Hodgson mentions a tower or pele with a vaulted basement and rooms above for the farmer in a farmyard at High Farneylaw. Tate, the Alnwick historian, refers to it as Highfarlaw; it was mentioned in the 1548 survey by Christopher Dacre. Recently, RSPB wardens lodged in the tower found steps down to a fresh-water spring within its confines while clearing debris from the vaulted basement.

Fairnley Tower. F
Hodgson 2-I-287. Tate I-222.
A tower or pele with vaulted basement and rooms above for the farmer stood in a farmyard at High Farneylaw. Tate, the Alnwick historian, calls it Highfawlaw; it was mentioned in the 1584 survey by Christopher Dacre.

Fallowlees (Dod Heugh) Bastle. F
***Northumberland County History*XV-386.**
The bastle was built after 1541 and the foundations can still be traced by the uneven nature of the site.

Falstone Peles. E.29 and E.31
Pevsner. Ryder.
The remains of a pele are incorporated in Falstone Farm, which shows traces of an inscription (the letters of the alphabet) above the door and the date 1604. I surveyed the house twice, once with Barbara Harbottle, the then county archaeologist, and

again for the owners, the Forestry Commission, prior to the sale. While renovations were in hand, a wooden comb was found in the lime mortar of the north wall of the vaulted basement. There are good photographs in the Blankenburgs Collection held in the Northumberland County Records Office. The ruins of a pele stood a little to the north of Stannersburn but this was removed around 1800 and now there is nothing to indicate the spot where it stood. A pele is also known to have stood on Hawkhope Hill not far from Hawkhope Farm.

Falstone Tower. E
Mackenzie II-242.

The tower of Falstone has now disappeared, but in 1541 there was a chapel at 'the Fawe Stone used for private masses'. This chapel was some miles above Bellingham and the persons for whom private mass was conducted would be either the owners or occupants of the tower, which must have stood close at hand.

Farne Island Tower. B
Raine. Pevsner.

Prior Castel's Tower. This is a tower with no outward projections, but with the usual vaulted basement. It stood at the back of a courtyard with an armed gate flanked by two chapels. A small turret stood on top of the wall above the gate, as can be seen in Speed's map. Built from 1494 to 1519, after the dissolution it was used as a fort in connection with Holy Island Castle and later as a lighthouse, with a coal fire on the roof. One of the chapels was used as lodgings by the lighthouse man. The remains are in good condition, but are not open to inspection. There is a pointed tunnel vault to the basement and a steep mural stair.

Farnham Tower (Thurnham). C
Northumberland County History XV-440. Bates.

The tower was in the lists of 1415 and 1541, and in 1546 fifty men of Teviotdale burnt it. The remains were built into later houses and now all that remains are the well and two curious hoodmould stops, placed the wrong way round at a doorhead.

Fawns (Sawnes) Pele. Kirkwhelpington. F.27
Hodgson 2-I-195. Bates. Pevsner.

In the list of 1541 is the 'Pele of Sawns', which may have stood on the site of the farm. There are some rectangular enclosures or earthworks in the area, but they may be of Romano-British dating and have no connection with the pele. Pevsner says the earthworks are medieval and also mentions masonry of the same date.

Featherstone Castle. West of Haltwhistle. G.15
Hodgson 2–III–357. Pevsner.

There are remains of this castle in part of a house built around a courtyard, the oldest part being in the west range. There is a thirteenth-century door into the yard on the east and three buttresses to the west and the remains of a hall house or hall range. To this range was added a strong tower in 1330. At the south-west angle it is L-shaped, with four three-corbelled bartizans on its battlements and with a vaulted basement. The rest is all make believe, but may be over genuine work. In the reign of Henry VIII, Richard Featherstone, brother of Alexander, was chaplain to Queen Catherine of Aragon. He was too zealous for his own good and was put to death by Henry in 1540.

Felkington Bastle. South of Norham. A.5
Raine 19. Bates.

The Norhamshire survey of 1560 mentions a 'bastall house' of small strength, but no other 'tower, or pile'. This was the first mention of this house and so it must be of a late date, as is Grindon Rigg Tower.

Fenham Castle. B.2
AA 4–XXII–163.

The date of the foundation of this castle is not known and nothing is known of its history, but the remains of a small motte-and-bailey castle stand by the sea on the road from Fenham to the mill.

Fenham Tower. B
Bates 53. Raine 180.

This tower was part of the monks' manor house, which was moated and many-roomed. Built or added to in 1339, it was called a tower for the first time in 1561, when it was leased by the Crown. It was pulled down and made into a farmhouse in about 1780.

Fenton Tower or Castle. A.18
Northumberland County History **XI-339. Bates.**

The tower was only mentioned once before the sixteenth century, in the list of 1415. In 1541 it was '… a grette towre with a barmkyn' but it was 'in great decaye in the rooffe and floores and walls of the barmkyn with other necessary houses within the same'. The repairs must have been executed as in 1542 it was classed with Etal and Ford as 'houses of strenghte'.

In 1549, 100 footmen were stationed at Fenton, but with the close of the sixteenth century they were there no more. The foundations could be traced in the garden of the farm built on the site. The walls of the tower were thick and some remains stand 20ft high. A wing behind the tower has a doorway with a four-centred arch, and various pieces of medieval stonework on the site point to something more than a simple tower.

Fenwick Tower. F
Northumberland County History XII–349. Pevsner.
Licence to crenellate the tower of Fenwick was granted on 26 November 1378, but all that is left of it now is part of the vaulted basement in a farmyard. A labourer engaged in the demolition of the tower in 1775 found a chest of gold coins, which it is said Sir John Fenwick hid. All 226 coins were fresh from a mint and not the accumulation of years of saving. The story that lies behind their acquisition has not been solved to this day.

Filton Bastle. E.44
Northumberland County History IV–405. Bates.
Filton Whitehouse, a bastle 'late belonging to the suppressed Monastery of Newminster', is mentioned in the survey of 1541 and all that now remains is some uneven ground behind the farm.

Flotterton Fortalice. D.54
Bates 18.
This fortalice was built prior to 1415 and is mentioned in the survey of that date. Nothing now remains, but it may have stood on the same site as the present Flotterton House, built in 1826.

Ford Castle or Fortalice. A.13
Northumberland County History XI–410. Bates. Pevsner.
In the second line of defence was a manor house for which licence to crenellate was secured in 1338 by William Herron. Enclosed by high embattled walls, it was raised to the status of a castle in 1340 for the defence of Glendale from Scottish inroads. By 1367 it was recognised as a unit in the border defences. The castle could accommodate forty men and King James of Scotland used it as his headquarters before taking up his position on Flodden Field. He burnt it before he left as it could not be defended due to lack of sufficient preparation, and although it was repaired often, it was never restored to its former strength. In 1541, 'the great buildings and most necessarye houses' had lain 'waste and in decaye' ever since

1513, 'the whiche if they were repared wer able to recyve and lodge an hundredth and no horsemen to lye there in garrison in tyme of warre and for that purpose yt is a place much convenient and standeth well for servyce to be done at any place within the said Est marche'.

In 1549 French and Scots forces assailed the castles with four guns. A brilliant defence ended in the repulse of the enemy but only one tower was left to shelter the gallant garrison. Again in 1580 it was in need of repair and in 1584 'decaid by want of reparacion of long contynuance'. The days of border warfare were nearing their end, and no more was heard of Ford Castle as a fortress. It was a mansion rather than a castle during the Civil War and in 1648 Royalist soldiers plundered it.

Francis Blake bought it and in 1694 started alterations. Plans and other documents of 1716 are still in existence and are very interesting. In 1793 Sir John Hussay Delavel said it was in ruins and uninhabitable, but he at once repaired it at a cost of £10,500, 'so that it became a useful and noble country seat'. Successive owners have destroyed the work of predecessors, with the the Delavels and Waterfords responsible for considerable destruction of ancient work.

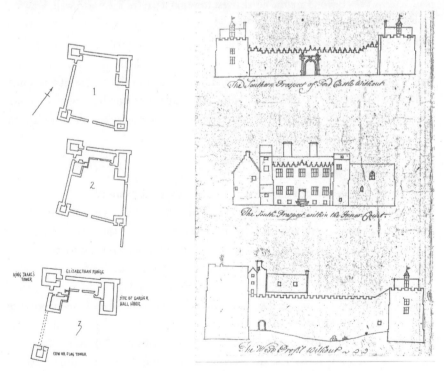

Ford Castle: Three elevations of the castle show the work of the Delavals in its restoration. the plans depict how the house started as a simple rectangle (1), followed later by more comfortable apartments on the north wall (2). A complete change of mind is shown in plan 3, with the buildings on the south-east side removed.

Ford Castle: The west side of the castle, with the south-west tower now isolated, as in plan 3 (see p.187). Beyond are the north-west tower and part of the north wall, now with a mansion of considerable comfort.

The castle consisted of a square courtyard with a tower of rectangular plan at each corner. The two largest towers were to the north and other buildings were built against the wall in between them. The gate was in the centre of the south wall. Only three of the towers remain, the south-east one having gone completely. The south-west tower is isolated from those to the north, which were connected to make a mansion.

Ford, Tower of Parson. A
Northumberland County History XI-362. Bates. Pevsner.

There were allusions to this in early days, but the first description dates from 1541, when it was 'a lytle tower', which was the mansion of the parsonage. Partly cast down by the Scots before Flodden, Sir Cuthbert Ogle rebuilt it to 'two house highte'. Little was left of it in 1663, when there was 'no house for the parson', and what little remained, was almost totally demolished. In 1725 it was 'strong and convenient', and yet a century later it was 'old with small and low rooms but the view is delightful'. The tower is now only one storey in height and is overgrown. Its plan is square, being 33ft 6in on the exterior and 19ft 6in within, the walls thus being 7ft thick. The door is on the east, and there is a staircase 2ft 8in wide in thickness of the wall. The usual semicircular basement vault was lit by a small window in the south wall. The tower is similar in plan to those at Halton, Corbridge and 'King James's Tower', which is at Ford Castle.

Fowberry Castle. D.4
Northumberland County History XIV–218.
About ¼ mile south-east of the hall is a mound known as Castle Hill and thought to be the remains of a motte-and-bailey castle.

Fowberry Tower. D
Northumberland County History XIV–218. Hodgson 3-II-187. Pevsner.
This was a rectangular tower of the fifteenth century. Rebuilt as a more comfortable house in 1666, little of this can now be seen as it was again rebuilt in 1776 or a little later. It was first mentioned on a list drawn up between 1513 and 1517, and in 1532 the Scots had burnt Fowberry. The tower or stone house is again mentioned in 1541 and 1590, but it had no barmkyn.

Gatehouse. Two Peles. E.21
Brown III-115. *Northumberland County History* XV–250. Ryder.
The two peles, one each side of the road at right angles to each other, were both of two storeys with a door at one end of the basement, but no other light. There was a trapdoor to the living quarters, above which was a door in one of the long sides, reached by a stone stair on the outside. There were two small windows on the same wall, south or east according to orientation.

A fireplace warmed one end of the upper floor and there may have been a loft above. The north house is in the best condition as the other was used as a stable and then a garage, and is much altered and damaged. Within a short distance of Gatehouse are a number of fine peles and it is not hard to imagine that at one time it was an area that was not nice to know:

> And if any true men of England get knowledge of the theft or thieves that steal his goods in Tyndaill he had much rather take part of his goods again in composition than to pursue the extremity of the law against the theif. For if the thief be of any great surname or kindred, and he be lawfully executed by order of the justice, the rest of his kin or surname bear such malice, which they call deadly feud, against such as follow the law against their cousin the thief, as though he had unlawfully killed him with a sword.
>
> *Northumberland County History*, XV–250

I know this house well, having been involved in raising funds for its preservation and knowing the two ladies who owned it and lived in the cottage just to the east of it. Monuments such as this repay repeated visits, as in the day when I was a regular visitor, the vent in the south-east wall was not known, it being blocked with masonry looking as ancient as the rest of the structure. Now it is only too obvious, having been unblocked inside and out, and is of considerable interest.

The photographs show the development of the first-floor entrance from a door with no permanent method of access. It is assumed you gained the first floor by a retractable wooden ladder. Later a platform or landing was built leaning against the house but not bonded to it. This platform did not reach the threshold of the door but ended some 2ft below; perhaps this was to prevent an unfriendly visitor building a fire at the foot of the door hoping to burn it down? The next stage was to extend the platform across the slit vent and only when clear of it descending by ten steps to the ground, making the retractable ladder redundant. For some reason the vent was later blocked, only to be reopened in recent years. While most of the upper floor is of stout timber, the area in front of the inserted eighteenth-century fireplace consists of large stone flags. Gatehouse is a small hamlet and I would refer you to Peter F. Ryder's *Bastles and Towers* for an interpretation of its numerous remains.

Girsonfield, Otterburn. E.70
Ryder.

There is not much left of this house, which can be found 600yd north of Girsonfield farmhouse. The north, long wall stands in parts up to 4ft high and traces of its ground-floor entrance still exist in the east gable. There are signs that other buildings stood within a short distance of these ruins.

Gatehouse Pele/Bastle: Detail of an example of a door (*left*) and one of the first-floor windows showing a touch of refinement (*right*).

These views of the
Gatehouse North Pele
show to advantage two
features evident on
many such houses. The
first feature is the larger
window over the foot
of the stair so as to allow
it to be defended. The
second is the distance left
between the platform
(formed by the landing
of the stairhead) and
the foot of the door.
This was to prevent the
build-up of a fire of any
intensity, so protecting
the door.

Goswick Tower. B.4
Bates 53. Raine 187.

Goswick Tower, with its yard or barmkins, stood on the seashore near the mouth of the brook. The yard, being on the north, was entered by a low arch. The addition of new windows and roof at a later date did not prevent it from being pulled down in 1825 to make a new and more comfortable house. There was no tower at Goswick in 1415, 1541 or 1550, but in 1560 there was a 'pile', a fact that proves its foundation within a year or two.

Grandy's Knowe Pele. Bardon Mill. G.33
Pevsner. Ryder. Grundy.

Almost square, the ruins are on the south side of the military road, west of Housesteads. The original door was in the west side/end. There are later vents in the north and south walls, the walls are 3ft 4in thick and overall the building was 30ft × 20ft.

Grasslees. Hepple. E.71
Ryder. Grundy.

On the south side of the road from Elsdon to Rothbury, incorporated in the nineteenth-century farmhouse are the scant remains of a pele. Old stonework in the north-east gable reaches a height of 6ft 8in.

Great Ryle Tower and Barmkin. West of Whittingham. D.39
Northumberland County History **XIV-544. Hodgson 3-II-211. Bates.**

There was a tower at Great Ryle in 1541, newly built by Thomas Collingwood on the land of Robert Collingwood. Thomas 'is minded to buylde likewise a barmekyn about the same as his power may serve thereunto'. The site is unknown and very little is known of its history. There were, in 1549, mercenary soldiers stationed there and in 1587 the Armstrong of Liddesdale made day raids on Prendwick, Ryle, Ingram and Reaveley, and carried off a large booty and thirty-five prisoners.

The map drawn by Christopher Dacre to be forwarded to Secretary Walsingham for Queen Elizabeth I to approve shows a strong line of towers but the modern OS map shows these were far from the tight defensive line he was putting forward for approval. The tower and bastle at Great Ryle and Little Rylee are not to be confused with the hamlet of Ryal, west of Matfen, map ref. F.47.

Great Swinburn Tower or Castle. E.49
Northumberland County History IV-128. Hodgson 3-II-216. Pevsner.
Tradition had it that the castle stood on the lawn of the present house. The ruins of the castle were demolished in the seventeenth century to make the new house, but to the east of this are two old vaults, one behind the other.

Great Tosson Tower. Rothbury. D
Pevsner. AA 2-XIV-392, 3-XIII-13. Bates 392. Dixon 329.
Northumberland County History XV-395.
Great Tosson is in ruins, with all its four walls standing, although the top parts are missing and the ashlar face has been removed from the base to show the rubble core. It had a vaulted basement and a stair in the north-east corner; also the usual slit for air, etc. at the west end. The basement door is in the south-east corner and above the stair a square-headed door can be seen from the outside. The tower is not in the list of 1415 but is in that of 1541, so must have been built between these dates. A very good spring is close at hand and may have been in the barmkin. This was no doubt the reason for building on this site.

Green Leighton Bastle and Barmkin. F.24
Hodgson 3-II-214. Bates.
The stone house or bastle at Green Leighton is mentioned in the survey of 1541, when it and its barmkin were in decay.

Grindon Rigg Tower. A
Raine. Hodgson.
This tower was first mentioned in the survey of 1560 and was of so late a date as to be of the sash window type, with wainscoted rooms and outbuildings for horses and hounds.

Groat Haugh Bastle. A.6
Bates.
This bastle is in the survey of 1541 and is mentioned as being in the field next to Newbiggin. See Newbiggin Tower.

Gunnerton Castle. E.50.
Northumberland County History IV-326. Pevsner.
On Gunnerton Moneye Hill are the remains of the earthworks of a Norman motte-and-bailey castle. On the village street is an old cottage by the name of Close House of *c.* 1600. The main part is two storeys high with a ladder addition

of only one storey to the loft. The walls are 4ft thick and there are three door-ways with Tudor lintels. Built at the right time to be a pele or bastle but a little more refined, what was it? Could it be part of the tower and stone house of 1541?

Gunnerton Tower. E
Northumberland County History **IV-326. Hodgson 3-II-215. Bates. Pevsner.**

In the list of 1541, a tower and stone house is said to be standing here, but the site is unknown. Is 'Close House' on the village street, with its thick walls, part of the tower and strong house?

Haggerston Castle. B.6
Pevsner. Raine.

In 1311 Edward II received homage from the Earl of Lancaster here, and the lists of 1415 and 1541 mention it. Destroyed by fire in 1618, it was repaired and again was in good repair in 1759. Work was done on the later mansion in 1777 and 1805 by pulling down part of the castle and now only one tower remains.

Halton Tower: South elevation of the small tower at Halton with later small mansion house on its east side.

Hall Barns. E.55
See entry for Simonburn.

Halton Lea Farmhouse. Halton Lea Gate. G.34
Pevsner.
Close to the Cumbrian border stands a substantial farmhouse, looking as if it may have originated as a large bastle. Situated next to the A689, it is quite easy to find.

Halton Tower. North of Corbridge. H
Northumberland County History **X-409. Pevsner. Bates.**
Of the fourteenth century, its dimensions are 31ft 3in × 24ft 4in on the exterior (about the same size as Dilston). It has four storeys, including a vaulted basement. There are circular bartizans on the corners like those of Chipchase and the door is in the north wall of the basement. It is in the thickness of the wall and becomes circular at the first-floor level. This stair is very cramped and terminates at the north-east bartizan. The other three bartizans house small chambers with flat roofs. In the fifteenth century a mansion was added to the north side and another on the east in the seventeenth century. There are the remains of very old masonry, which may have been the barmkin on the west.

Haltwhistle Bastles and Towers. G
Hodgson 2-III-119. Bates. Pevsner.
A tower at Haltwhistle was mentioned in the surveys of 1415 and 1541, and indeed the Red Lion Inn is a restored tower. Another inn and houses in the town were also fortified and one of these stands north of the road above the burn to the east. This bastle is of *c.* 1600 and has a triple-corbelled oriel window below

The north face of
Halton tower.

the gable. Hodgson mentions a part-fortified house fast falling into decay with a loop-holed projection on corbels over its door, and these initials and date in its front – wrn 1607. In 1598 the Armstrongs of Liddesdale plundered Haltwhistle town to such extent that the King of Scotland was required to compensate the town. But he sent word to England, saying that the Armstrongs lived on debatable land and were not subjects of his and that it was in the hands of Sir Robert Carey, the English Warden, to do what he could. Off they marched to Cathill in Liddlesdale and as an old ballad says…

Let flee
A cothyard shaft ahint the wa'
It struck Wat Armstrong in the ee,
Went through his steel cap, heid an' a'.

Archdeacon Singleton, writing in the early nineteenth century, said, 'Haltwhistle is full of uncouth but Curtis old houses which betoken the state of constant insecurity and of dubious defence in which the inhabitants of the borders were so long accustomed to live.' Much of the town still presents a stern aspect with many in the way of fortified houses yet to be identified.

Haltwhistle Castle. G.13
AA 4-XXII-164.
Castle Hill at the east of the town was once used as a motte-and-bailey castle and traces of scarping and an earthern mound or wall can be seen.

Harbottle Castle. C.15
Northumberland County History XV-480.
There was a motte-and-bailey castle here and the powerful Umfravilles, Lords of Redesdale, who built it, moved their capital from Elsdon to here in the twelfth century and shortly after 1157 built the castle we see now, very much like Mitford in plan. The bailey was divided in two by a cross wall with the motte crowned by the keep at one end of it, and next to it the gate, then an angle tower at the other end. To the west is the fortified bailey and outside the gate is the unfortified barmkin or outer bailey. The keep was of shell type with a boldly projecting forebuilding on its west side, and flanking towers on the north-east and south-east corners. It was captured by Robert Bruce in 1518, but in 1515 it was habitable and by 1527 not fit to live in. In 1563 the new ward was in reasonable condition, the outer almost down, and the remains became a quarry. It was also used as a fort, the shell keep being filled with debris and guns placed on it.

Hareclough Pele. Holystone. C.20
Pevsner. Bates.

Mentioned in the survey of 1541 as being of stone rather than wood is Hareclough or 'Hare Cleugh' when 'one Rog' Hangingeshawes had lately built a strong pele house of stone' as protection against the 'thieves of Ryddesdale' but did not finish it. What remains are the ruins of a Tudor house incorporating one wall of the pele. These ruins stand about 2 miles south-east of Woodhouses.

Hartington Tower. F.25
Hodgson 2-I-287, 3-II-214. Bates.

In 1541 the tower was called a bastle and in 1552 Hartington Hall. Its remains could be incorporated in the present hall.

Haughton Castle. E.58
Northumberland County History XV-12. **Pevsner. Bates. AA**

Haughton Castle, first mentioned in 1373, is in the list of 1415 and was first a hall of one or two floors, with or without arched buttresses, as these may have been an addition. In 1373 it was called a castle because the arches had been built up with solid masonry and the whole heightened so that the hall could be on the

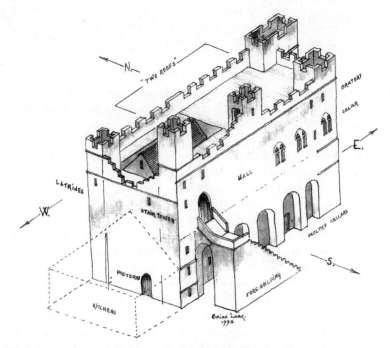

Haughton Castle: Dacre's Plan of 1595 gives dimensions and other details such as the house's two roofs, one at each of the east and west ends.

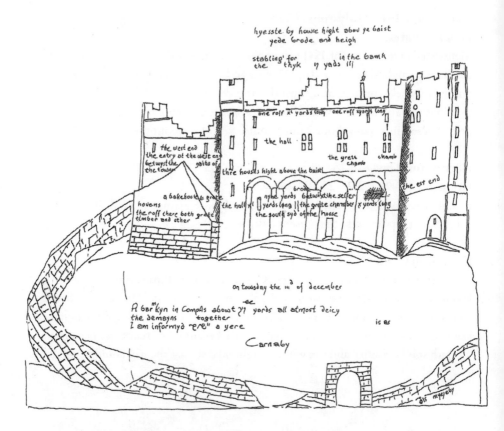

Drawing of Haughton Castle based on that of 1595 (Brian Long, 1992).

Of the later thirteenth century, the original building was a hall house with simple corner turrets. There is evidence to suggest that the entrance to this hall must have been reached by an external stair of some type, perhaps as shown here or like that at Aydon Castle (see p.124).

Each of the 107ft-long side walls had a row of five arched buttresses built on them, perhaps at a later date when the basement vaults were inserted. The arches were in turn blocked, making the house much more secure.

As shown in the drawing of 1595, to the west, were the kitchens, where in 1876 Anthony Salvin built the more comfortable modern residence.

Notes on the 1595 drawing and the lower parapet to the west end gable tell us that the roof was of two different parts. A doorway in one of the arches on the south front appears to be within the wall at the back of the arch not through the later masonry blocking up. All of this makes Haughton a pleasure to interpret.

The position of the hall is indicated by three windows, while the oratory is behind a similar window in the east wall. The entrance is at the west end of the south wall, which was reached by an external stair of some kind. The kitchen was built outside the main structure as a precaution against fire. The 1538 drawing shows it at the west end of the house. It was not unusual for kitchens of the period to be detached.

second floor. The turrets were all carried above the roof and a new turret was added on the south side. The walls were also provided with parapet walks at this time. This castle evolved over many years, having started life as a manor house in the thirteenth century. It was later encased in a series of arches, which carried the walls much higher than they had previously been.

An embattled parapet followed with taller turrets at the corners, with another being corbelled out above the centre of the south side. The wall below the arches was protected by murder holes in the underside of each arch prior to them being infilled to help support the walls above and give greater security. The houses consisted of a rectangle 49ft north to south and 107ft east to west with turrets on the corners. That at the north-west contained the garderobes, while the south-west one contained a newel stair. The drawing of 1538 shows the north-east turret as having another newel stair from the solar to the oratory above. The position of the hall is shown by three fourteenth-century windows.

Hawick Bastle. E.42
Hodgson 3–II–214. Bates.

Hawick Bastle is in the list of 1541, but nothing of it or the village remains. A farm is now on the site.

Hawkhope Bastle/Pele is a late example of its type and shows signs of the basement entrance having been in the long front wall. Internally, there is a modern break in the gable connecting it to the smaller cottage, but no evidence of any older work was found.

Hawkhope. Falstone. E.72
Pevsner.

North-west of the village stands the impressive farmhouse of Hawkhope. To its left is a range of stores and attached to its right gable is a small Victorian cottage. There is no vault but it is two and a half floors high, with the basement entrance in the long front wall and that of the first floor above it. An unusual feature, one I have previously come across on the west coast of Ireland, is that the roof timbers all lean into the prevailing wind. A more recent passage between the house and the attached cottage may have removed evidence of an earlier basement entrance. A Forestry Commission drawing for this work mentions nothing about a pre-existing doorway. My survey and plans of Hawkhope are with the Forestry Commission, Bellingham, and good photographs by Blankenburgs are in the County Records Office.

Hazelrigg Tower. B
Northumberland County History XIV–226. Hodgson 3–II–193.

The tower was mentioned in 1514, when it could hold a garrison of twenty men. However, in 1515 the Scots invaded Hazelrigg with 300 men, burnt the tower and carried off thirty prisoners, four cattle, thirty horses and the insight (goods and furniture). In 1541 there was a 'lowe tower, never fully fynyshed but kept in measurable good reparacions'. By 1546 Hazelrigg was wasted by the Scots but in 1715 there was a good house in Hazelrigg built out of the ruins of the old tower.

Healey Hall 'Bastle'. Riding Mill. H.18
Pevsner.

The hall is shown in an old print as tall and with a lookout turret on a gable end somewhere between Melkridge and Low Hurst in style. See the drawing on p.232. The stable block behind the house has fragments of the old house built into it.

Heaton (Old Heaton) Castle, Norham. A.9
Raine 326. AA 2–XIV–329. Pevsner.

In 1560 only the vaults, a dwelling and a barmkin remained of a 'fayre castle', which had been in ruin since the time of Henry VII. Today the ruins of a 'small' tower thought to have been built in 1580 stand three storeys high. There is a semicircular projection housing a stair that starts at first-floor level. The parapet and cap house to the stair have vanished but part of the vaulted basement survives. Is this part of the 'fayre castle'?

Heaton Tower (Camera). Newcastle. H
Northumberland County History **XIII-279. Pevsner.**
The remains are near Heaton Road and are of the thirteenth century. They consist of rectangular rooms with remains of a doorway and some windows. The original entrance is on the first floor and that seen at the ground level is modern. Behind this simple exterior are remains of much older work, which may be the tower mentioned in the surveys of 1509, 1514 and 1541.

Hebburn Bastle and Tower. Chillingham. D.10
Northumberland County History **XIV-374. Bates. Pevsner.**
A tower was referred to at Hebburn in 1515 and 1541. In 1564 it is referred to as a mansion house, which no doubt was of much greater size than the present remains, as marks of the roof of a wing that has now disappeared can be seen on the south wall. The tower referred to is in fact the bastle. The other tower is said to have stood by the wall of Chillingham Park, not many yards away, and was demolished to build the bastle. Only a few stones now mark the site. The bastle is three storeys high with two vaults in the basement, and also has an attic under two gables. There is also a spiral stair and a pit 8ft deep with a trapdoor over it.

Hedgeley Tower. D
Pevsner.
Hedgeley Hall, 1 mile north-east of Powburn, contains work of many periods but there is little evidence of anything before the seventeenth century. Christopher Dacre marks it on his map of 1584 and in the area are its remains, lost in the confusing jumble of building periods that go to make up the present hall.

Hefferlaw Tower. North of Alnwick. D
Tate II-43–44. Hodgson 11-II-140.
This tower was not built before 1461 as it is not shown on any lists or surveys prior to the date and a coat of arms on it could not be before that date. A strong square tower, it stands high above the north road just west of Alnwick. Tate also mentions Hobberlaw, a small tower in Vol. I, p.223. One mile south-west of Alnwick is the hamlet of Hobberlaw.

Hepple Tower and Bastle. C.19
Hodgson. AA 3-XII-12, 2-XIV-392. Dixon. Mackenzie. *Northumberland County History* XV-380.

The vaulted remains of Hepple Tower are all that is left standing of a more extensive mansion. The west wall has now been removed and it is possible to see into the vaulted basement. The vault is 17ft high and has provision for inserting a wooden floor to form a loft in it. The entrance is in the south side and it has a murder hole over it. At least two upper storeys appear to have been built above the vault. A number of bastles once stood north of the road behind the present row of houses and Mackenzie says that in the middle of the last century (*c.* 1750) the town consisted of cottages, farms and several strong ancient houses and a tower.

Hepscott Tower (or Hall House). F
Hodgson 11-II-439. Pevsner.

It is known that a hall had been built at Hepscott before 1603, and that it had been, with the usual offices, built around an old tower. Hepscott Hall now stands north of the Hepscott burn, which is called Sleekburn, 2 miles further downstream and shows work of many periods.

Hesleyside Tower. E
***Northumberland County History*- XV. Bates. Pevsner.**

Mentioned in the list of 1541, the only remaining old stonework is in the west end of the present mansion. The tower was of the fourteenth century, but a house seems to have been added in 1631 as that date is over an old doorway.

The Hesleyside Spure

Hesleyside, for centuries the home of the Charltons, one of the leading reiving families, houses a relic of the raiding days in the form of the Hesleyside Spure, which the lady of the house would serve up on a salver at the table to remind the men of the house it was time to ride and raid as the cupboard was bare and the next meal was up to them and was still grazing in someone else's field.

One of the murals in Wallington Hall, painted by Sir William Bell Scott, depicts the then matriarch with a hungry family being served, with the famous Spure prompting them.

Hethpool Tower or Pele. C.23
Northumberland County History XI-250. Bates. Pevsner. Ryder.

Hethpool was mentioned in the lists of 1415 and 1541, when it was 'a lytle stone house or pyle which ys a greate releyffe to the tenants thereof'. On the plan of border defences of 1564 it is shown outside the 'ring of fortresses'. Built for strength rather than roominess, indeed it was so small as to have been useless 'save for a sudden and short emergency'. It was evidently for the use of the locality and not part of the defence system of the border. The ground-floor ruins stand in a well-tended garden, with some walling being 20ft high. Ryder gives a sketch plan on p.49 of his *Bastles and Towers* (1990).

Hetton (Heton) Tower or Hall House. Chatton. B.22
Northumberland County History XIV-320. Raine. Pevsner.

The large farm of Hetton is on rising ground on the west bank of Hetton Burn and the remains of the tower are beside it. This may be the latest tower built on the border, probably in Queen Elizabeth's reign as it is not mentioned in any earlier surveys. In reports of 1627, it is described as a tower of stone, three storeys high. The remains of the tower are now part of the Hetton Hall complex and was much like that at Old Heaton (Norham), being of three storeys with a semicircular projection to carry the stair. The top was corbelled out to carry a square cap house, now all missing. To the rear are remains of more old masonry, suggesting that more than an isolated tower stood on the site.

Hexham Castle? G.10
Northumberland County History III-225. Pevsner.

The two towers, the gate tower or moot hall and the prison or manor offices may have formed a castle, if in medieval times they were connected by a curtain wall. The manor office is of early fourteenth-century work and the moot hall is of the late fourteenth century or early fifteenth century. Only one tower is mentioned in the list of 1415 and must be the manor office as the moot hall was believed to be ruinous. There is nothing in the entry to indicate if this was so, or that the two towers may have been classed as if joined by a curtain wall. The prison is a sheer parallelogram with corbels meant to carry machicolations. It has two vaulted chambers in the basement and one room on each of the two upper floors. The original spiral stair has been removed.

The moot hall is T-shaped in plan, with the head of the T being higher than the rest and to the south. On the ground floor in the shaft of the T is a vaulted chamber 30ft × 20ft, which used to house a well in its floor. A vaulted passageway with three sets of gates ran E–W through the top of the T and the upper floors extended above the passageway with small rooms in the south-east and south-west towers. A newel stair in the east led to the former chapel, and a guardroom is also preserved. The moot hall is made of stone from the bed of the River Tyne, while the prison is made of Roman stone from Corbridge. The prison formed an isolated keep and the other tower, with its three sets of gates, the main entrance. The curtain walls would have had towers and the kitchens and other offices would have been within the bailey.

High Bowershield. Elsdon. E.73
Pevsner. Ryder. Grundy.

Bowershield is north-north-east of Elsdon village, while Higher Bowershield is a little to the north of where the ruins of a pele or bastle now form part of a complex of sheepfolds, with one gable wall still existing.

Reconstruction of Hexham Castle. The famous prison is a sheer paralellogram with corbels to carry the missing machicolations.

High Callerton (Rebellion House). Ponteland. F.62
Pevsner. Ryder.

Rebellion House has some interesting features. The first-floor entrance was in the east gable but is now partly blocked, having a window inserted in it. To the right of this is a simple gunloop, a feature not found in many peles or bastles.

High Cromer (or Croner?). Redesdale

This house was recorded in the field notes of W.H. Knowles when he was shown a sketch dated 1791. To help place this house, he also sketched the Raw on the same day. It is shown to be a substantial house of two-and-a-half floors, having a rather fine external stairway.

Highfield Peles. Tarset. E.74

The farm of Highfield, now reduced to smallholding, within Tarset Forest, is on the side of the Forest Road from Black Middings to Falstone. The roadside wall has scant remains of a pele in the form of part of a basement entrance incorporated in it. The track over a field to the house has the remains of a second pele, again in the form of remnants of a basement doorway depicting the usual stout bolt holes. Also in the vicinity are traces of a small mound with evidence of a rectangular structure upon it, all enclosed by a dry moat. Perhaps an example of an early pele? Situated in a forest plantation to the north of the house, this is not easy to locate.

High Leam. West Woodburn. E.75
Pevsner. Ryder.

On the banks of the Cleugh Burn, below the farmhouse of High Leam, are the scant remains of at least two peles.

High Rigg Pele. E.15
Ordance Survey.

High Rigg stood on a hill east-north-east of Darden Lough and all that can now be seen is some rough ground in the fence running over the hill.

Highshaw Pele. E.13
Pevsner. Ryder. Grundy.

This pele stands north-west of the Raw and over a field from Highshaw Farm. Only the basement, which is vaulted and in very good condition, remains, its dimensions being 30ft E–W and 14ft N–S. My field notes give further dimensions and Ryder gives a longitudinal section of the vault on p.27 of his *Bastles and Towers*. The east end of the vault has a series of put holes to carry the timbers of a large shelf or loft. While found in some towers, this is the only example I know of in a pele.

Hill House Moated Site. E.77

In Wark Forest there is a site of medieval date that has a small moated mound, which could be the remains of an early wooden pele. Attached to this is a barmkin or night fold. It was unusual for a pele to have a barmkin but not unusual to find night folds in the vicinity.

Hirst (Low Hirst). Ashington. Two Houses. F.18
Hodgson 2-II-192. AA 3-XIII-16. *The Authentic Tudor and Stuart Dolls House*, Long.

Hodgson mentions 'the castle' at Hirst and informs us that it was incorporated in a farmhouse, as shown in drawings by W.H. Knowles of 1896 that were once in my possession. 'Castle', I assume, was the name given by the locals as it had battlements on one gable end, but nothing remains other than the drawings and details on old OS maps.

The second house and the earthworks associated are also lost, to be rediscovered. The location of these two houses, be they bastles or strong houses, was well outside the normal area where peles, bastles or strong houses were found. Indeed, going off the evidence presented in the drawings, these houses were much more sophisticated than the peles and bastles inhabited by the upland farmers of the period and would be better classified as strong houses.

Hobberlaw Tower. D
Tate I-222.

Tate mentions a small tower; could this be Hefferlaw (see p.201)? Or is this the site of the hamlet of Hobberlaw, a little south of Alnwick?

Holburn Tower. B.14
***Northumberland County History* XIV-137. Hodgson 3-II-193.**

In 1350 the town lay waste due to wars, and by 1415 a tower had been built, which in 1514 was capable of accommodating twenty men. In 1553 it was reported to the queen that the Scots had taken in a foray, 'from a towne called Howburne LX hedde of nolte and VI naggs and taken also at the same tyme diverse persons', despite the fact that ten years earlier the tower and barmkin had been reported 'in measurable good reparacions', a state most border strongholds did not attain. The site of the tower is now forgotten.

Hole Pele. North-east of Bellingham. E.39
Pevsner. Ramm et al. Ryder. Grundy.

This late pele/bastle has a vaulted basement and outer stone stair up to the upper floor. This upper-floor area has a partition in the form of wattle and daub. An impressive house, the later stone stair is of twenty-three steps to the first-floor entrance. The ladder hole from the byre is just inside the first-floor entrance. The basement byre has a fine stone vault still used as a byre from time to time and Mrs Robson, the farmer's wife, informed me that even with the extra ventilation given by more recent apertures it is too hot to keep stock in for any length of time.

'The Hole' stands in the yard of the farm of that name on the road from Woodburn to Bellingham. Much smaller than most peles, it is only 34ft × 22ft 7in externally and 26ft × 14ft 6in inside, but is of very stout construction. This house started as a small but stout pele about 1550, having a vaulted basement and one large upper room with possible storage space in the rafters.

At some later date, the loft was carried up above the original gables on the front and had windows inserted in it. During the same reconstruction the first-floor windows were replaced by larger ones and the large room divided into two, a window being inserted in the back wall to light the smaller of the two.

Just inside the first-floor door and to the right is the remains of a simple stair to the new floor above. The larger of the two rooms on the first floor has a fireplace, not bonded to the gable wall and of the *c.* 1603 reconstruction. The insertion of the fireplace, first-floor stair, larger first-floor windows, second floor with windows, and rear window transformed the pele into a much more comfortable house, a bastle house.

It is buildings such as Woodhouses and the Hole, which started life as simple pele houses and by later alterations become more comfortable bastle houses, that show the differences between the two types.

The Plan of the Hole

This house is quite small, being only 34ft × 22ft 7in, and is important in that it shows the development from a simple pele to a much more comfortable bastle.

The conversion was carried out by first enlarging the windows on the first floor, inserting a fireplace and dividing the floor space by a simple partition. The room formed by the partition had no windows, so one had to be broken through the back wall, getting away from the rule about peles only having windows in the staircase side. The wall on this side was carried up above the gables to make room for windows required to light a room built into the loft area, making a much more commodious house, a bastle house.

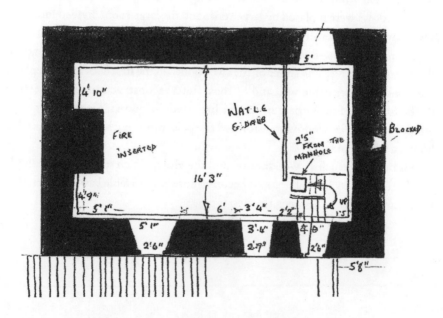

HOLE PELE/BASTLE BELLINGHAM
DETAIL OF STAIR & WATLE & DAUB WALL.

This is a stout but simple house, made more comfortable by giving it a loft area and a stair up to it. This was achieved by raising the roof above the gables.

Holy Island. Two Forts (One Belbowe, One the Heugh). B.28

The two forts on the island were in no way private houses and do not come into the scope of this book, as castles, towers, peles and bastles were private residences first, and fortresses last.

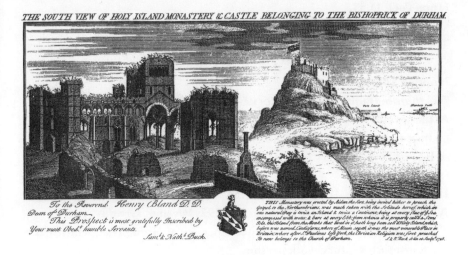

Holy Island: An engraving by the brothers Buck of 1728, showing monastery and castle.

Holy Island: An engraving by J. Gray after L. Clennell.

The Priory, Holy Island.

The Priory church was strongly fortified as early as the thirteenth century. There was a gatehouse and barbican to the cloisters, and also a tower and barbican to the outer yard.

Hope Peel. D.51.
OS Map.

The remains of this pele stand about 2 miles east of Cragside House, Rothbury.

Hoppen Tower. B
Northumberland County History I-244.

At the beginning of the fifteenth century there was a tower at Hoppen, of which no trace now remains, and it is mentioned in the list of 1415 as being in the hands of Robert Hoppen. Very little is known of it.

Horneystead Pele. (Hornestead). E.54
Northumberland County History XV-292. Pevsner. Grundy.

There was a small tower with a vaulted basement at Hornestead, which was of late fourteenth-century workmanship.

Horton Castle or Fortalice. Blyth. F.35
Northumberland County History IX-257. Hodgson 11-II-265.

The castle stood, until 1809, on the site of Low Horton Farm and though some portion of it remained twenty years later, that too has now vanished. In the early thirteenth century a manor house stood on the site and on 28 December 1292, licence to crenellate was granted. The work on the fortifications took about six years and included a double moat enclosing an area of about 190ft × 200ft. The inner moat, which was used as a duck pond until quite recently, has now been filled in. It was 33ft wide on the north, east and west sides and 54ft wide on the south. The Delavals were the last people to live in the castle and they left it in the seventeenth century.

Horton Castle. Chatton. B.24
Northumberland AA 2-XIV-15-29.

The castle has now disappeared except for a few fragments of masonry in the farm buildings at West Horton. In 1415 it was on the survey of the borders and on another of the early sixteenth century, when it could hold a garrison of sixty men. It is again mentioned as a castle in 1568 but was demolished after 1808 to make way for an improved farmhouse.

Housesteads. G.36
Guidebook. Pevsner. Ryder.

The south gate of the roman fort was converted in the late medieval period into a pele of unusual plan. The original west door of the eastern guard chamber was built up, but a new doorway was cut through the south wall to give access to a new larger room. Later, the Roman part of the structure was converted into a corn-drying kiln, pointing to a more respectable way of life than that of the previous occupants, the notorious horse-thieving Nixons and Armstrongs.

Howick Tower. D
Northumberland County History II-338. Hodgson. Pevsner. AA 2-XIV-16–59.

Emeric Hering was in possession of a tower at Howick in 1415, which was described as a 'a little pile, a mile from the shore' in 1538. The present hall was built in 1782, with alterations made in 1809, and stands on the site of a small medieval tower that was pulled down in 1780.

Howtel Tower. A
Northumberland County History XI-207. Pevsner.

First mentioned in 1541 when a 'greatt parte of the walls' were standing, though it had been 'rased and casten downe' in an invasion of 1497. The estimated cost of

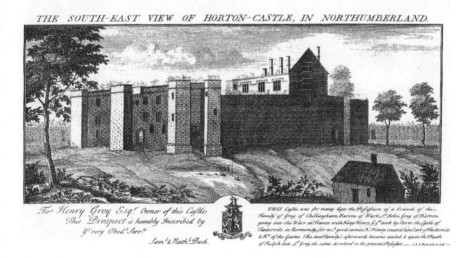

THE SOUTH-EAST VIEW OF HORTON-CASTLE, IN NORTHUMBERLAND.

Recorded by the brothers Buck, Horton Castle was demolished in 1808.

repairs was £40, but it was again in ruins in 1506 and in need of repair. The years 1580 and 1584 found it 'decaied by warres' and the repairs would only cost £50, 'beynge a vereye small thinge'. Howtel was about the same size as Hethpool, its neighbour, with a 33ft × 31ft exterior. There is no remaining evidence of a stair but there is a door at ground level.

The tower had a vaulted basement and the holes for stout timber joists are to be seen for the upper floors. The basement walls are in a very mutilated condition and the south wall is standing to the height of three storeys. Springing stones for a vault can be seen in the north wall.

Hulne Abbey Tower. D
Pevsner. Tate.

In the grounds of the abbey stands a fifteenth-century tower, which is in good condition and has the usual vaulted basement and some rooms and windows, above, which were Gothicised by the 1st Duke of Northumberland. The tower and the wall about the site were given by the duke in 1488 for the defence of the church.

HULNE ABBEY From the NORTH EAST.

This old engraving shows the Hulne Abbey Tower prior to the duke's Gothic makeover.

Humbleton Tower. C
Northumberland County History **XIV–615.**
This was one of the very late peles and in 1541 it was stated that 'the towneshippe of Homyldon conteyneth XII husbandlands, all ploughed and hath yn yt nether fortresse nor barmekyn'. The tower is marked on Dacre's 'Plat of the Borders' in 1584. It therefore cannot have played any part in the Battle of Humbleton Hill. The scene of the hottest fighting was said to have been at Red Riggs, where human skulls and horses' bones have been ploughed up. The foundations of the tower could be traced in 1878.

Humshaugh. A.37
Pevsner.
On the south side of the pretty village street, Linden House started as two peles, while on the north, Dale House and the two cottages next to it contain traces of peles. Is this an example of grouping for security? Even Humshaugh House has some stonework over 4ft thick.

Hurst Bastle. Rothbury. F.2
Dixon 474.
The tower or bastle of Hurst stood in Rothbury Forest, but little is now known of it, other than a few words in *Upper Coquetdale* by D.D. Dixon.

Ilderton Tower, Barmkin and Castle. D.15
Northumberland County History **XIV–266.**
This tower is on the list of 1415 and in 1541 it is very much decayed, but a garrison is sometimes mentioned in Henry VIII's reign. It is marked on Dacre's Plat of castles and fortresses on the border in 1584, but in 1715 Ilderton is described as follows: 'a small village and in it ye seat of George Ilderton a mean edifice at present, ye tower, which was ye ancient mansion house, being in ruins'. The site is not known for certain, but its remains may have been built into the present hall. Not far from the hall, the remains of a motte-and-bailey can be seen.

Ingram Tower. D
Northumberland County History **XIV–471. Bates.**
In 1541 'at Ingram ys a lytle tower which ys the mansion house of the P'sonage there and for lacke of continual necessary repac'ns ys fallen in greatt decaye in the Cov'ynge and roofes thereof'. The same survey gives the probable reason why today there is no tower at Ingram in as much as 'the ryv'or or water of Brymshe by rage of floodes if very lyke in continuance of tyme to were awaye both the said towne of Ingram and tower'.

Iron House Pele. Elsdon. E.12
Pevsner. Ryder. Grundy.
On the south bank of Watty's Sike, a few hundred yards from Highshaw Pele stand the remains of Iron House. The foundations of this house are of massive rough stones and continue to the east beyond the pele for quite a distance. The pele is quite large, being divided in two by a cross wall. The door is in the east end and still retains its hinges and bolt holes. Many mounds of stone to the south may be the remains of night folds or a barmkin. The dimensions of the house are 34ft E–W and 13ft N–S.

Kershope Castle or Tower. E.1
Northumberland County History XV-265.
A few mounds on the south slope of Deadwater Moor is all that is left of this tower, which seems to have been reckoned as being in Scotland, as the documents relating to it are there. This part of the border was very much disputed and known as 'debatable' up to the nineteenth century. What little remains of this tower has been cut through by a forest road and deep roadside drains. The drain to the north-east did have some stonework in it and below the road on the edge of what was a moat were other stones. Field walls or at least traces of them are on the south running down to the River North Tyne. The remaining evidence would point to a rather poor house, much removed from the 'castle' in its name.

This was never a castle and at best would have been a pele or bastle but the name rings out loud in border history. Kershope, Cater Bar and Reddenburn were ancient trysting places where on truce days, under the supervision of conservators, borderers might meet their opposite numbers to sort out grievances. While 'Kershope Castle' was on the English side of the border by half a mile, on the lower sides of Deadwater Fell, Scotch Kershope is about 6 miles south-west, with Kershopefoot being a further 1½ miles downstream. This was an area that witnessed the worst of border reiving, being part of the debatable lands.

Kilham Tower. A.24
Northumberland County History XI-168.
'The township of Kylham conteyneth XXVI husbandlands nowe well plenyshed an hathe in yt nether tower barmekyn nor other fortresse whiche ys great petye' or so it was in 1541. The commissioners recommended that 'A new tower and barmekyne be made at Kilham'. There may have been a tower here before 1584 as at least one is marked on a plan of that year.

When I took a WEA class at Wooler, members of the group proudly told me of their bold ancestors who were at the receiving end of a reivers raid in

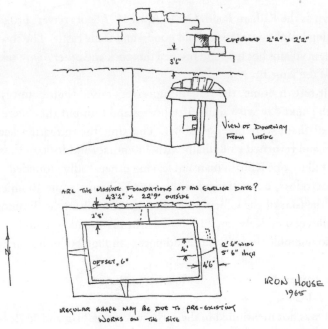

Iron House: A plan and detail of the basement entrance, the detail showing it to have had two bolts to the door. The notes record 'night folds' in the area.

The remains of Iron House, standing on on the wild Otterburn Ranges.

1597 known as the Kilham Raid. On 14 April 1597 Scots reivers broke into the tower, taking insight gear (household goods) and some cattle. The townspeople pursued these villains hot trod and rescued the stock and other items, taking three prisoners at the same time.

On their return home, the remaining reivers raised their countrymen and returned the next day with some fifty horses and foot but they were repulsed and more of them were taken prisoner. This time the retreating Scots raised Teviotdale and returned to Kilham with 160 horses and foot and rescued the prisoners, killing one Kilham man and leaving others badly wounded. Someone did not like to lose, no matter what the cost! Kilham is some 10 miles west of Wooler at the foot of the Chieviots and on the south bank of Boumont Water about 6 miles east of Kelso and Teviotdale. In 1890 remains could be seen and were said to resemble the bastle at Doddington, though built on a smaller scale.

Kirkharle Tower. F
Hodgson 2-I-249.

This tower was not mentioned in the early surveys of 1415 and 1541, but is first noted as such in 1722. The twenty-fifth year of Queen Elizabeth's reign finds 'a capital messuage' but that is all that is known of its early history. Capability Brown landscaped the grounds around the house when it had been made into a more comfortable mansion.

Kirkhaugh. G.38
Pevsner.

Kirkhaugh is situated on the east bank of the South Tyne and has within a short distance a number of pele-like structures of the sixteenth and seventeenth centuries. These require closer examination to determine their status. Underbank, just south of the Church of Holy Paraclete, is followed by Whitlow, ½ mile south. Low Row, ½ mile north, may be transitional when defence was not so important. Lastly is White Lea, which was remodelled *c.* 1682, shown by that date carved on a lintel.

Kirkheaton Manor House. F.63
***Northumberland County History* IV-386. Pevsner.**

At first glance you could not be blamed for thinking that this was a Georgianised tower with an early seventeenth-century manor house attached but the truth is just the opposite. The Georgian, eastern, part of the house was only built in the eighteenth century, perhaps by Dorothy Windsor, who rebuilt the church where a shield over the door is inscribed with 'H.D. Windsor building and endowing 1755'.

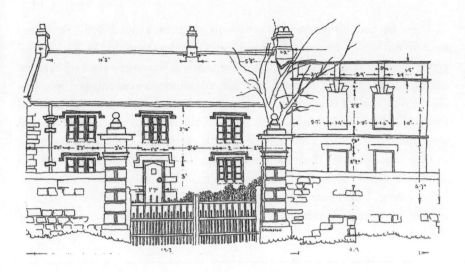

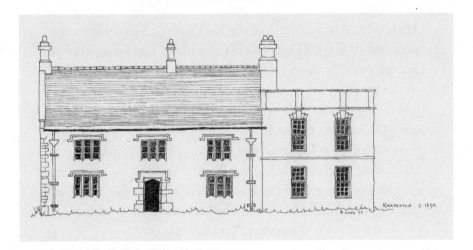

Kirkheaton: This collection of images shows the house, a neglected ruin, rise out of the ashes to become a fine house behind handsome gateposts.

The oldest part of the house had five rooms, one to each bay, all with low ceilings only 6ft 6in high. The roof was of stone slab fixed by sheen shanks. The 'better' rooms were in the Georgian addition. After a spell of thirty-two years when it was empty, it was restored in 1925 and the mullioned windows were enlarged by lowering the sills. The old roof was replaced by one of Westmorland slate. The back and east gable of the old house has walls 5ft 6in thick and there are traces of a newel stair pointing to an earlier house, either a bastle or strong house. On the north side of the village green are the scant remains of a pele. White House Farm could also contain within its fabric, with walls of 3ft 3in thick, remains of a further pele. A leaflet giving *A Short History*, now long out of print, is invaluable here.

Where are the gate posts and wall to the front of the house? Were they part of the 1925 restoration?

A Pele on Kielder Burn

Having lived and worked on the banks of the Kielder Burn for some thirty years, I knew of only one house that I suspected of having possible remains of a pele or bastle incorporated within its walls. I have since decided that this conclusion was wishful thinking on my part, so have not included it in this edition.

Keith Durham, in his book *The Border Reivers*, mentions a border standard, or at least the head of one, as being found in the wall-head of a pele on the Kielder Burn, reigniting the question of the existence of a pele in this remote area. The standard is the only known example and is housed in the Museum of Border Arms and Armour, Teviotdale.

Kirkley Tower. Ponteland. F
Northumberland County History XII-495. Hodgson 3-I-28.
The tower was in the list of 1415 but the site is not known and must have been near to the hall, much rebuilt, which is dated 1632.

Kirknewton Tower. C
Northumberland County History XI-150. Bates.
This tower is on the list of 1415 but is not mentioned again until 1516 in a border skirmish. In 1541 the Scots took the cottage that stood next to the tower and burnt it to the ground, almost burning the tower as well. In 1567, 200 men

took 400 head of cattle and 300 sheep, and in 1570, 2,000 horsemen fell upon Kirknewton and seized 400 head of cattle, horses, mares and household stuff and more than 200 prisoners 'besides the hurting of divers women and throwing of sucking children out of their clouts'. The tower still stood in 1584 but the last we hear of raids is in 1602 and then it was a false alarm.

Kirkwhelpington Vicar's Tower. F.27
Hodgson 2-I-189. Bates 46.
First mentioned in the list of 1541, it was small, being 27ft × 15ft internally. It stood on top of the bank above the Wansbeck and had walls 5ft thick. The east one was incorporated in the old vicarage and stood, in Hodgson's time, to the height of 20ft. See Bolt House.

Knowesgate. Kirkwhelpington. E.78
Bates. Pevsner.
A cottage at Catcherside has thick pele-like walls and a blocked byre doorway in a gable wall. This doorway has a round-arched lintel of a type in South Tynesdale. The remains of another pele are to be found at Ray Demesne, a little distance to the north-west with walls standing some 6ft high in places. Of further interest are the medieval earthworks at the Fawns recorded in the survey of 1541, when Sir John Fenwick had a tower or bastle here.

Kyloe Tower or Fortalice. B.9
Raine 194, 189. Bates. Pevsner.
Attached to farm buildings, a blocked door and parts of a vaulted basement remain to mark the site. The door was in the south-west corner and the stair was in the wall on the left. The walls were 8ft thick and there were corbels in the

Kirkley Tower was on the list of 1415, but its site is not known. It was replaced by the much rebuilt hall of 1632, which features this doorhead.

wall of the basement to divide it into two floors in case of need. In 1415 it was recorded as 'Castrum de Kaloule Vet'. Later, in the list of 1541, it was mentioned as belonging to David Grey. Tower and yard were of no great height but were very thick. There was a hall etc., in the yard for use in time of peace, and this was inhabited until 1633, when it was deserted for the comfort of a mansion. The yard seems to have been large in proportion to the tower.

Lambley Farm. G.39
Pevsner.

The house, like so many, has been remodelled and exhibits thick walls that may be medieval. Being close to the site of the Benedictine Priory, much material from there was used in the house. Other buildings on the east look pele-like but this whole area of the South Tyne has many houses now known as 'bastle derivatives', being houses of a later date yet built in the same tradition but not quite as stout as the earlier peles or bastles.

Langley Castle. G.11.
Hodgson 2-III-367, 3-I-27, 3-II-217. AA 2-X-38. Pevsner.

Like Haughton, Langley is a rectangular house with projecting towers at the angles. North of the south-east tower an entrance tower was added containing the stair and a vaulted room on each floor. The doorway on the ground floor had a portcullis and the groove, etc. can still be seen. On the first floor was the main entrance, through double doors in the main east wall. The south-west tower was full of latrines, all discharging into the former ditch. The castle must thus have been made for more people than the owners and family. There are corbelled-out bartizans on the buttresses but these are part of restorations by Cadwallader Bates (see below).

The first mention of a house at Langley was in 1292, when Henry de Bovindon, a carpenter, was paid 20 shillings for replacing the louvres on the roof of the Great Hall of the smoke-filled home of Thomas de Moulton. This may have been quite a fine house, but it was not fortified and the first we hear of a castle is in 1365 when Sir Thomas de Moulton died, leaving it to his son Anthony. Sir Thomas was an outstanding knight, being granted forty sacks of wool by Edward III for his services.

Most of our castles have enormously tall powerful keeps, as at Newcastle, Prudhoe and Norham, but there is a small group of elongated houses where the term 'keep' no longer applies and they become more correctly 'fortified houses'. The best example of this group is Langley, which had one large room on each floor of approximately 82ft × 25ft and four angle towers, a type heralded at Tarset in 1267. Another example still to be seen is at Haughton, which like Langley had started life as an unfortified 'Palas' but was converted to this type of fortified house in *c.* 1375. The large 'room' on each floor would have had screens and other partitions to divide it into more convenient spaces. Some indication may be had from the number of fireplaces of just how many sub-compartments each floor was capable of being broken into.

Langley is extremely impressive and very important in the history of British architecture, being one of a group not often found, and only saved from the hands of improvers by the fact that it was burnt out in *c.* 1405 and survived as an uninhabited shell until 1882. The disaster preserved as if in mothballs an almost perfect example of a late-medieval fortified house.

In 1835 John Grey of Dilston, then the agent of the Greenwich Hospital Estates, had the entrance tower reroofed to provide a home for a woodman and his family. He also repaired the walls, replacing fallen masonry and building up gaps.

This entrance tower was a fifth and additional one, a modification to the original plan, and was guarded by a portcullis, which was raised and lowered by a chain passing through the open mouth of a stone face. Another theory regarding this tower is that it did not originally open on to the ground floor, and that this was reached, as in many lesser houses, from the first floor by a trapdoor; this would account for the fact that today you trip over the foot of the spiral stair to enter the basement area. The tower may have been in reasonable order since the fire, as the castle was always used for receipt of rents and an office of some sort would have been required. Sir Reynold Carnaby found it the most secure part of the house when he took refuge in it in 1536 during the Pilgrimage of Grace. These uses point to it being the best preserved of all the towers and easy to maintain.

Cadwallader Bates, an outstanding historian, purchased the house in 1882 and set about its restoration, even living in a small room in the thickness of the east wall during the building. His home, Heddon House, Wylam, was quite close, but so involved was he that he had to be in the midst of the activity. The restoration took some twenty years of painstaking attention to detail.

The south-east of the four corner towers had a window more ornate than in any of the others and was thought to have been that of the original chapel. Mrs Bates had this restored, with Papel permission, as a memorial to her husband after his death in 1902, complete with original fireplace.

The south-west tower houses the 'Big Bell', formerly in St Nicholas cathedral in Newcastle but it is more often quoted because of its being devoted to latrines on an almost monumental scale. This lavish provision is a rare facility in houses of the

Langley Castle: This sketch by the author is of the main front of what is now a fine hotel. The famous tower housing the garderobes is still on view, with its location marked C on the plan below, taken from Parker's *Domestic Architecture* of 1853.

DOMESTIC ARCHITECTURE : FOURTEENTH CENTURY.

INTERIOR OF GARDEROBE TOWER,   AND SECTION OF THE SAME,
LANGLEY CASTLE, NORTHUMBERLAND.

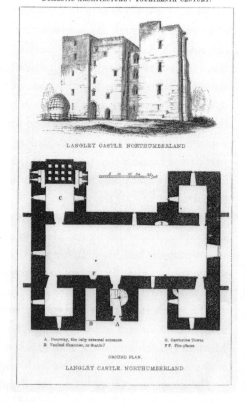

DOMESTIC ARCHITECTURE : FOURTEENTH CENTURY.

LANGLEY CASTLE NORTHUMBERLAND

A Doorway, the only external entrance   C. Garderobe Tower.
B Vaulted Chamber, or Stable?   FF. Fire-places

GROUND PLAN.
LANGLEY CASTLE. NORTHUMBERLAND.

period yet was common in monastic establishments. There are twelve garderobes, four on each floor, each one having a pointed arch to the recess in which were stone corbels to carry the seats. The shafts discharged into a pit below, through which a stream of water could be turned to flush it clean.

Even with this magnificent array, it was thought wise to have other lesser garderobes in other parts of the house. This lavish provision suggests that the house was intended, from its inception, to be well garrisoned, with more than just the family in residence. Provision of a bath of 'stues' was regarded as an act of hospitality to a travel-weary knight, and once again Langley was at the forefront, and hot water may even have been piped direct to the tub. Only a handful of the greatest of houses could offer this facility, and a fourteenth-century account describes the plumbing as having a 'square lead for heating water for the Tues'.

More recently the castle was used as a girls' school run by Miss Ella Hebron, then in 1972 it joined the ranks of stately homes catering for visitors in search of something out of the ordinary. It was then sold to Mr Robb of Hexham and is now a hotel of great character, set in beautiful countryside, with history in every acre.

Lanton. Two Towers. A
Northumberland County History XI-141.

Baxter Tower.
The first mention of any tower was in 1369 when a fortellet was known to have stood on the site of the manor – this was the Baxter Tower. In 1415 this tower was held by Henry Strother, but little else is known of it.

Tower of Ralph Reveley.
The other tower was mentioned in 1522 when it was intended to place in it ten men in wages under Ralph Reveley. The two towers seem to have merged into one in 1541 when Earl Rutland and William Strother were joint owners. It was cast down by James IV before the Battle of Flodden and the commissioners of 1541 estimated that it could be repaired for 100 marks, but was still in this state in 1584.

Leaplish. Kielder Water. E.79

The remains of a pele were incorporated in the farmhouse that was part of the Swinburn's Mounces Estate in the North Tyne. There is an account of the pulling down with axes and the burning of a pele here, which would tend to point to it having been made of wood prior to the stone one incorporated in the later house. The site is now under the waves of Kielder Water. Good photographs can be found in the Blankenburgs Collection held in the County Records Office.

Lemington Tower. Edlingham. D
Northumberland County History VII-176. Hodgson. Pevsner.

A tower, L-shaped in plan of fourteenth-century work, it was greater in size than Chipchase and Cocklaw Towers, measuring 53ft × 35ft, Chipchase being 516ft × 34ft and Cocklaw 50ft 6in × 35ft 8in. Much altered, it is now part of the hall of 1746 and has sham windows and ashlar facing on the south and east sides. There is a vaulted basement and the entrance is on the south in the projection. This projection has three remaining floors, while the main tower has two. There are now no signs of battlements, etc. but it stands on a strong site on top of Lemington Hill. In my elevation (below) the tower is that part of the house under the flagpole to the right.

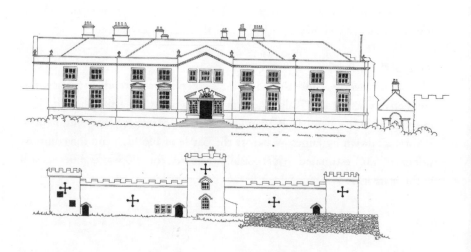

Lemington Tower: The tower is not incorporated in the folly on top of the hill but is lost in the mansion of 1746. Its location is indicated by the flagpole on the right of the elevation.

Lilburn Towers. D
Northumberland County History XIV-433. Bates. Pevsner.

The survey of 1509 names two towers that may have stood here, one being Lylborn, the other being Ilborn. The present-day Lilburn Tower is a fine mansion house of 1829 but in the grounds are the remains of an early tower now known as West Lilburn tower; the site of the second tower cannot be determined. See West Lilburn.

Linbrig Bastle. C.9
Bates. *Northumberland County History* XV-436.

The stone house of Linbridge has now vanished and its site is uncertain. In 1538 it was recorded as 'a great house now fallen', and in the survey of 1541 it is stated that it had in times past fallen at the hand of the Scots. Roger Horseley, the owner, moved the stones to a safer and stronger site. In 1903 a large pile of stones known as Ducket Knowe to the east of Linbridge marked the site, but this could also have been the dovecote of the Horseleys.

Little Bavington Tower. E
Northumberland County History IV-414.

Perhaps the present hall stands on the site of the tower mentioned as being at Little Bavington in 1415.

Little Harle Tower. (West Harle) F
Hodgson. Pevsner.

The remains of this tower are incorporated in a large Victorian house, and the tower has been very much modernised and is hardly recognisable. First mentioned in 1415, then again in 1541, it must be of the late fourteenth or early fifteenth century.

Little Haughton Tower. D
Northumberland County History II-404. Pevsner.

This was a medieval tower of about 25ft square, with walls 5ft thick with the usual vault and a newel stair in a corner. All that now remains is part of a tower, with a wing dated 1686 on one side of it and on the other a Georgian wing.

Little Ryal Bastle. Whittingham. D.41
Northumberland County History XIV-547.

The farmhouse of Little Ryal on rising ground by the Yetlington road has several blocked-up mullioned windows in its south gable and east side. A Tudor door-

way and a vaulted ground floor measuring about 57ft × 24ft remain, but there
are no signs of fortification. It is not mentioned in the list of 1541, and its style of
masonry suggests the second half of the sixteenth century at the earliest.

Little Ryle Pele or Bastle. D.41
Pevsner.

Here is a good example of a late bastle or pele surviving as the farmhouse that
is Little Ryle. It has a vaulted basement and both the basement and first-floor
entrances are in the same, long, side wall. Today, a modern staircase connects the
basement vault to the upper floor and there are early seventeenth-century mullioned windows, resulting in a comfortable house for its time.

Little Swinburn Tower. E
Northumberland County History IV-303. Hodgson. Pevsner.

The tower of Little Swinburn is first mentioned in the survey of 1541, was 40ft ×
27ft on the exterior and had a vaulted basement. The door was at the north end
of the east wall at ground-floor level. The ruins still show the doorway and the
lower part of the spiral stair.

Long Haughton. D
Tate I-222. Pevsner.

The tower of Saints Peter and Paul is of the early twelfth century and was used
as a place of refuge by parishoners. The top of the tower shown as being much
taller in old engravings was rebuilt *c.* 1840, then further 'restored' in 1873. Long
Haughton Hall is a pleasant-looking farmhouse with a pele-like blocked doorway in its east gable but the other walls are a bit on the thin side.

Longhorsley Tower. F
Bates. Pevsner. Hodgson 2-II-100–06.

This tower has the usual vaulted basement, which was 22ft × 18ft prior to being
divided by modern partitions. At the east end are two smaller vaults, one of
which now opens into a seventeenth-century wing. The stair in the south-east
corner and ends at the battlements in a small turret. The windows are all renew-
als, but look as if they had hoodmoulds. It is quite a late tower and was not in
any of the early surveys. Next to it stand the remains of a small park that is said
to have held fallow deer.

Low Buston. Warkworth. D.63
Pevsner.

Butleson House is dated 1604 and has some stout architecture but no real architectural details to point to what it started out as.

Low Fairnley Pele. Rothley. F.26
Pevsner.

At first glance this is a simple Northumbrian hill farm farmhouse with a wing of later date attached and breaking the rectangular plan of the original house. The later outshut was built by Sir William Blacket in 1723, shown by an inspiration of that date and the initials WB: B+. The original rectangular block is a late pele with its stone stairs to a first-floor entrance presenting in all a good example of a pele still occupied to this day.

Low Hirst. Strong House. Ashington. F.18
Hodgson. Pevsner.

Plans and elevations published in Long's *The Authentic Tudor and Stuart Dolls House*. See Hirst.

Lowick Tower and Castle. B
Northumberland County History XIV-85. Raine 83, 112, 278. Pevsner.

The village in 1328 and 1358 lay devastated by the Scots, and in 1360 the mill lay in ruins. Again in 1368, the hay crop was not gathered in as the land lay waste, but in 1388 there was comparative safety due to a forcelet (small tower) having been erected. The building was termed a tower in 1415 and was in need of repair in 1580. It would take, in 1584, an estimate of £50 to repair the tower, but since then no more was heard of it. The site may be at the north corner of Lowick Hall Farm, which was once called Bastle Corner. A little east of Lowick Old Steads are earthworks that may point to the site of a castle.

Low Leam. Corsenside. E.76
Ryder. Pevsner. Grundy.

The hillside above this farm has a number of most interesting remains, starting with the farm buildings on the north side of Low Leam farmhouse, which incorporate a good example of a pele with its byre door in the west gable. There are also corbels to carry a first-floor fireplace. The date 1602 and the initials W.C. are cut into a stone on the first floor.

Some 700yd north on the banks of Jointure Cleugh is a second pele of superior build but now ruinous. The byre doorway is in the south-east long wall with the

Low Hirst, Ashington: The detail of the tower is taken from my book *Authentic Tudor and Stuart Houses* and based on sketches by William Knowles.

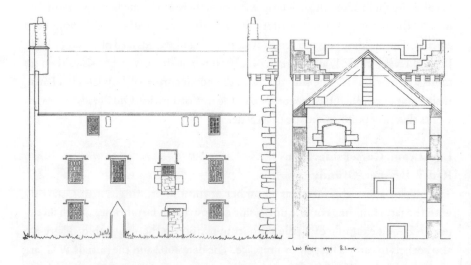

Low Hirst, Ashington: Elevation and section showing the house prior to demolition. Of note is that the blocked entrances to the ground floor and first floor are in the long front walls, as in the smaller peles and bastles.

Low Hirst, Ashington: A rear view of the house in 1886 by William Knowles, a Newcastle architect.

Two drawings of Low Hirst, Ashington, one showing how the battlements looked prior to demolition, the other, the house as built.

first-floor entrance above it. At least one window to the first floor had an iron grille, with another having had a single bar. These windows may have had harr-hung shutters. The west end of the basement has corbelling pointing to the position of a hearth. This house is now identified as Low Cleugh. West of Low Leam farmhouse on the Cleugh Burn and incorporated in sheep folds are the scant remains of a third pele, while not far away are the grassed-over foundations of at least two other buildings that would require excavation to determine their origins and status.

Low Old Shield. Greenhead. G.40
Pevsner. Ryder. Grundy.
About 1 mile west of Greenshead stands the farmhouse of Low Old Shield, which incorporates considerable remains of a pele or bastle. The walls are 4ft thick and there is in the east gable the usual basement doorway, now blocked. This doorway has a square head, not the usual round head found in this part of the county. Projecting from the wall is a stone spout but what its function was is open to conjecture. Most of the other details are the result of a seventeenth-century makeover.

Low Roses Bower. Wark. E.54
Ryder.
With a name like this it deserves to be a house of some comfort but all we see today are rather fragmentary remains of what may have been a pele on an impressive site perched on a crag overlooking the Warks Burn. See Roses Bower.

Low Stead. Wark. E.80
Ryder.
This old house stands on the north side of a small yard with the Pennine Way passing through it. Hard by on the west side is a precipitous drop to the Black Burn. The house consists of two peles being built end to end with the earlier, easterly one being 36¾ft × 23¼ft externally with the usual stout rubble walls, which are nearly 4ft thick. The later, westerly pele is of the same width but only 21ft long. I surveyed this group in 1951 prior to its sale and conversion into holiday cottages, when some detail was lost due to plastering and modern dry walling. Internally, few original features now survive other than vents and windows, now blocked, that can still be seen on the outside.

Low Trewitt Tower. North-West of Rothbury. D
Dixon 344. Hodgson 3-I-29, 3-II-212. Bates 17–44. *Northumberland County History* XV-403.
A fourteenth-century window in the west gable of Trewitt Farm is all that is left of the buildings of 1415, and foundations in a field nearby may also be of that date.

Meldon Tower and Barmkin. F.30
Hodgson 2-II-18. Pevsner.
Hodgson says there are signs of it 150yd south-east of the church, these being the walls of vaults, etc., 60ft × 15ft internally; a covered sewer running north from it; and also the remains of walls and buildings, on a hill south of the church, west of the tower. These could be the remains of a barmkin and other offices.

Melkridge Bastle/Pele. G.41
AA Nathaniel Lloyd. Pevsner.
I first came across this house in Lloyd's *History of the English House*, first published in 1931 by the Architectural Press, in which he dates it as *c.* 1642 and uses a photograph by Gibson of Hexham to illustrate it. The photograph shows the house with only minor alterations and no modern windows punched through its stout walls.

Probably the finest house of its kind in the county, with gunloops, lookout turrets with cable moulding, kneelers to the gables and the remains of a low parapet to the landing of the external stair, it was demolished in 1955. The Ancient Monuments Branch of the Ministry of Works surveyed the house in the previous year (1954) and my drawings are based on this and Gibson's photograph. The last recorded use of the house was as the village reading room. Why were we deprived of such a fine example of a pele/bastle, with even traces of internal plaster an unusual refinement? The floor plans and annotated drawings give details of dimensions and building materials required to build such a house.

Middleton Hall. Two Bastles. Ilderton. D.13
Northumberland County History **XIV-294.**
In 1541, 'The towneshippe of Mydleton Hall conteyneth II husbandlands plenyshed and hath in yt two stone houses or bastells, the one of thinherytaunce of Robt. Rotherforthe and thither off John Rotherforthe'. Little else is known of these two houses.

Middleton Tower. Bamburgh. B
Northumberland County History **VI-397.**
This tower was in the list of 1415, when it belonged to William Muschamp. Could the modern hall stand on the site?

Mindrum Tower. A
Bates.
This tower is shown on Dacre's Plat of 1584, when it was to be built to complete the line of defences.

MELKRIDGE BASTLE (.1642) ASTAIR VISION

Melkridge Bastle: Two views of Melkridge, one of the bastle in its ancient state, and the other showing the Victorian sash window to the first floor, designed to light the new village reading room.

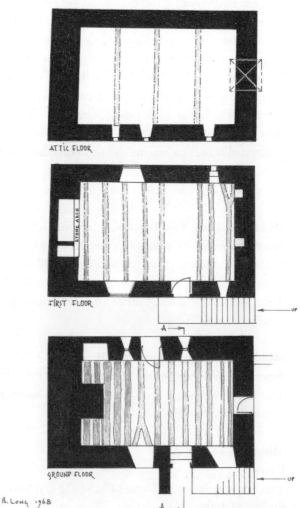

ATTIC FLOOR

FIRST FLOOR

GROUND FLOOR

Melkridge: Plans and a section showing gun loops in the basement wall and the line of the pyramidal roof of the lookout turret.

B. LONG 1968

Mitford Castle. F.21
AA 4–XIV–74. Pevsner. Hodgson 2–II–54.

Existing before 1138, the castle is one of many standing on the south banks of rivers, so using them as a first line of defence. The remains stand on a natural sandstone hill that has been scarped and heightened with refuse from the ditches so as to form a motte-and-bailey castle. The River Wansbeck flows past the north of the hill, with the Park Burn on the east and south. The west was protected by a moat running from the Park Burn to the Wansbeck.

A shell keep was built on the motte and traces of the buildings that lined the walls can still be seen. In the thirteenth century a small five-sided keep was built inside the shell keep, almost filling it. This is the only five-sided keep in England, and in building it, the walls of the shell keep were made to form an inner bailey. The vaulted basement is all that remains of this keep and consists of two chambers supported by a wall on the centre line. These vaults are entered by a stair in the thickness of the south wall. They had drains and each one has a small window.

The curtain walls of the outer bailey stand south of the keep, and have neither gatehouse, towers nor bastions left, but still retain marks from buildings that were built against them. In the south of the bailey, which has been quarried away, are the remains of a chapel and beyond the north wall was a barmkin, but all traces of walls have gone. The last occupants of the castle left it before 1327 and it has never been restored since. William Bertrams Oppidum at Mitford was mentioned in *Chronicles of the Reign of Stephen III* in 1138.

MITFORD CASTLE, NORTHUMBERLAND.

Mitford Castle and its shell keep stand on a hill used as a quarry and this engraving by T. Allom gives a view from the north.

Monk. Whitfield. G.42
Pevsner.
In 1547 this site was known as 'La Monke'. The house is superior in many ways and could be much older in origin. The south end of a range of stout buildings consists of an almost square structure with a corbelled-out dovecote on a gable, which may be the reworking of a lookout turret like that at Melkridge. Half a mile to the east is a strong house of *c.* 1610, which is now an outbuilding to Westside. The basement and first-floor doorways are both on the south side and have charming yet crude flat-pointed heads in square frames. The better than usual windows would point to this being one of the group known as 'bastle derivatives'.

Moor Houses. Allendale. G.30
Pevsner.
This is a good example of a traditional pele being extended and improved in the late seventeenth century. A nineteenth-century cottage completes the range, situated just over a mile north-east of Allendale Tower.

Morpeth Castles and Towers. F.20
Pevsner. Hodgson 2-II-384. Bates. Pevsner. Landmark Trust.
Morpeth Castle was taken in 1095 by William II, and Symeon of Durham was restored to it in 1138. There are considerable remains of a Norman motte-and-bailey, upon which is a gate tower such as at Bywell. The parapet is corbelled out and it has embattled angle turrets. This could be fourteenth century (1342–59) as William Greystock did work on the castle at that time but it looks more fifteenth century. In 1516 Margaret, sister of Henry VIII and widow of James III of Scotland, stayed in the castle for four months as she fled her enemies in Scotland and sought refuge with her brother. Much later, in 1644, a garrison of 500 Lowland Scots held it for parliament for twenty days against 2,700 royalists. Behind the tower, the bailey – enclosed by a curtain wall – is of much older workmanship. The bailey was 82yd north to south and 53yd east to west but nothing remains, above ground, of the buildings that once stood against them.

Morpeth Ha Hill. F.20
On the summit of Ha Hill many stones of Norman workmanship were found and with the scarping of the hill, these suggest a tower or castle on the site.

Morpeth Tower. F.20

This stood on the site of the old gaol that is behind the massive gatehouse of the police station, but no trace of it now remains. In 1310 it was known as a Turriolum, then in 1343 it was a Turellus and at another time the 'Turres De Morpath'.

The Town Belfry. F.20

The Belfry is in Oldgate, and is fifteenth century with later additions. This tower may well have been used for refuge as well as a signal or warning station.

Mortley Pele. Wark. E.81
Pevsner.

Just off the road from Wark to Stonehaugh are the ruinous remains of Mortley, which still retains its basement doorway and the slit vent at the other end.

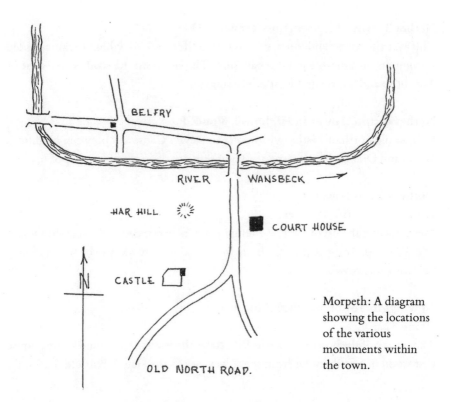

Morpeth: A diagram showing the locations of the various monuments within the town.

Mykle Swyneburne Tower or Castle. E.48

This house and 'Lytle Swynburne stood just to the west of the A68 (Dere Street) less than a mile north of the Colwell crossroads. Mentioned in various surveys, nothing now remains of the old castle and the mansion house that followed it has long since been replaced, leaving a house of many dates. See Great Swinburne.

Nafferton (Lonkins Hall) Tower or Castle. H
Northumberland County History XII-254. AA 4-XXXVIII-125.

A site just north of the bridge over Whittle Dene on the Newcastle to Corbridge road is known as Lonkins Hall. This tower or castle was never completed as it was being built without licence to crenellate and therefore adulterine. When it was dismantled the stones were used to build the bridge. There is evidence to show that this site was occupied at two distinct periods.

Nesbit Tower. A
Northumberland County History XIV-178.

In 1541 we read that 'the towre is longe synce for lack of reparacons decayed and fallen and no fortresse there now remayneth'. In 1415 it was mentioned for the first time and was only a 'pile', but nothing can now be seen of it.

Nether Trewhytt Tower (Low Trewitt). D

This was the tower and home of Edward Gallon in 1541 when it was recorded as being in 'measurable good reparc'ons'. The site is up the road north-west of Thropton and Snitter and west of Cartington.

Netherwitton. Tower in Highbush Wood. F

Half a mile north of Netherwitton on the Devil's Causeway between Highbush Wood and Dixon's Wood stand the scant remains of an irregular-shaped tower.

Netherwitton Tower. F
Hodgson 2-I-319. Pevsner.

Mentioned in the list of 1415, the remains are incorporated in the mansion house of *c.* 1700–10. At the rear of the house some old stonework is to be seen and may be part of the tower.

Newbiggin Tower and Barmkin. A.6
Raine 312.

The survey of the borders taken in 1541 states there was a tower and a stone house that stood in a field not far from the tower. See Groat Haugh Bastle.

Newbrough Tower House. G
Pevsner.

Among the farm buildings of the hall are the remains of what is known as Thornton Tower, a medieval tower house. Rectangular in plan, its west elevation is preserved under the shelter given by a later barn and shows a wall 20ft high made using massive squared stones.

Newburn Hall Tower. H
Northumberland County History **XIII-139. AA 2-XIV-22, 3-X-186.**

A fifteenth-century tower with a sixteenth-century dwelling house added was part of the steel works and stood just north of the railway. The basement was vaulted but the remains are now of little interest. Half a mile south stood a sixteenth-century manor house that was demolished in 1909.

Newcastle Castle. H.12
Pevsner. Guidebook. AA 4-II-1, 2-IV-45.

In AD 124 the Romans built the fort of Pons Aelius, and then the Saxons built Monkchester, near or perhaps on the same site, in AD 800. In 1080 Robert, son of William the Conqueror, saw the military advantage of the site and built a motte-and-bailey castle on it. The site was a very strong one with a steep hill down to the River Tyne to the south and a ravine with the Lort Burn running in it to the east and north. The west was then the only side with no natural protection, but was fortified by a deep dry moat. The stone keep now standing amid the railways was built for Henry II in 1172 by Mauricius Caementarius, who, twenty years later as Mauricius Ingeniator built the great keep at Dover.

Other remains are the Black Gate, the main entrance to the outer bailey and a small postern with fragments of wall in the inner bailey. The outer or north bailey was triangular in shape and had the gates on the west, the great hall on the east and the keep in between. The south or inner bailey formed a rectangular base for the triangle of the outer bailey and the keep could only be entered from the inner bailey. Part of the south wall of this bailey with a postern and remains of a small tower still stand on the edge of the 100ft drop to the Tyne.

The Black Gate dates from 1247 and corresponds to the gatehouse at Warkworth as they were both thirteenth-century additions of an 'improved' type. This gatehouse formed a barbican as it was built in front of an existing one and over the moat, with the object of flanking the west curtain. Another moat was dug in front of the gate and would have had to be crossed by a drawbridge, which was in turn protected by a barbican erected in front of the gatehouse in 1538. The keep, 62ft × 56ft with projections at the angles, still retains its fore-

THE   *SOUTH - EAST*   *PRO*

Newcastle: Part of the Bucks' view of the town, showing the castle in 1728.

building, an element not often surviving. At Newcastle this is very elaborate and contains a staircase up to the second and not the first floor, a feature that recurs at Dover only. The keep contains a chapel, under the forebuilding, and the great hall, camera and kitchen on the second floor. Also on this floor is the well room (as at Dover) and this meant that if the basement fell into enemy hands, the garrison still controlled its water supply. All the roof, including flag tower and battlements, are modern, and not reproductions of the originals. On the west side, the shutes from the garderobes are collected in a buttress, which has a vaulted chamber with a doorway on ground level for the purpose of clearing.

Newlands Tower. B
Northumberland County History I-365, 392.
This tower is on the list of 1415, but little is known of its situation, size or history.

Newstead Tower. D.7
Northumberland County History I-261.
The tower, which was attached to the 'court' there, is mentioned for the first time in the year 1405, and in 1415 it was in the hands of Sir Robert Ogle. The place was destroyed in 1532 and the Earl of Northumberland, writing to Henry VIII, said that Scots had 'brunte a towne of myne called Alenam ... also a woman ... also another towne called Newstede ... and hath shamefully murdered two younge spryngaldes'. This is almost the last we hear of this tower.

Newton Bastle. Rothbury. D.58
Dixon 467.
The Simonside Hills stand south of Rothbury and on their northern faces were three towers or peles: Great Tosson, Newton Bastle and Whitton. Newton could only boast a bastle house, while Tosson and Whitton still retain their strong towers. Dixon says the remains of Newton Bastle stood on a knoll overlooking a small stream. Up the hill from the Hamlet of Tosson are the fragmentary remains of a defensible house or pele that was pointed out to me by members of the Rothbury Local History Group.

Newton Hall Tower. Bywell. H
Northumberland County History VI-123.
The tower of Newton Hall appears to have been built in the fourteenth century and is of good ashlar work in courses, which average 12ft in thickness. On the north and west sides it stands just above 6ft high. The basement chamber was 31ft

long enclosed by a wall 9ft–10ft thick. The north-west buttress was occupied by a garderobe, the lower portions of the shaft of which still remains. There was a draw well 30ft deep, said to be in the centre of the floor. Equal in size to Chipchase and Cocklaw, but with diagonal buttresses, it resembles Edlingham more than these.

Newton Pele. D.62
AA 3–XIII–5.

In *c.* 1715 the remains of an ancient pile are recorded, but the site is not now known. See Newton Bastle.

Newton Tower. Edlingham. D.44
Northumberland County History VII–141.

The tower stood on a high hill, which was also the site of an ancient village, but there are now no visible remains. First mention of it was in *c.* 1334–35 and the next time was in 1415.

Newton Underwood Tower. F
Hodgson 2–II–72.

In Hodgson's time there were three arches standing and remains of 6ft walls and other foundations around it. They were known as 'old walls' but now very little remains to mark the site. The remains, even though they are poor, seem to represent something more than just a tower.

Ninebanks Tower. Hexham. G
Northumberland County History IV–111. Pevsner.

Part of one of the few houses in the hamlet, it has blocked Tudor windows and a Jacobean newel stair. It is very small and may have been the forebuilding attached to a larger tower. The upper storey was added at the same time as the wheel stair in the north-west corner. It is safe to say that a large sixteenth-century tower stood on the site and was entered by a ladder to a door well above ground level. The tower now standing was built to house this entrance and at a later date, the wheel stair and uppermost storeys were added, and the internal arrangements changed. That the tower was altered externally is shown by the string course, above which should be the battlements, but in their place is another floor. The string course rises by a step on approaching the south-west corner of the tower, inferring that a higher builder stood to the west. Most of the walls are thin, being only 2ft thick.

Nine Dargue. G.43
Pevsner.

A ruined pele with the typical, for the area, round-headed arch to the basement entrance.

Norham Castle. A.2
Raine 284. Pevsner. Guidebook.

The first castle was a Norman motte-and-bailey (of which the earthworks survive) built by Bishop Ranulph Flambard in 1121. In 1136 and 1138 the castle was taken by the Scots. Henry II regained Northumberland in 1157 and rebuilt the border castle in stone, and about this time Bishop Hugh of Puiset built the stone keep and fortified other parts of this castle.

The inner ward is more like a large shell keep with the kitchens, hall keep and other buildings all built against its walls. The keep was originally three storeys high and its roof line can still be seen. It was heightened to five storeys in *c.* 1423 and a new spiral staircase was built in the west wall to replace the original forebuilding. The dimensions of the keep are approximately 84ft × 60ft × 90ft high, a very large and impressive ruin. The motte or inner bailey is surrounded by a moat, which could be flooded, and the arrangements for this and for washing can be seen in the moat under the drawbridge.

Nine Dargue: The arched basement entrance is of a type found in the south of the county.

NINE DARGUE

The outer ward has two gates, one in the south wall and the other, the main gate, in the west wall. The towers and turrets of the curtain walls are of thirteenth-century work, being square at the back and round in the front, but in the sixteenth century they were altered so as to have pointed or V-shaped fronts. The east curtain is of the early twelfth century and has remains of a fifteenth-century aqueduct. The west gate stands in the north-west angle of the outer bailey and has a core of Norman workmanship, but was built over in the fifteenth century when a barbican with a drawbridge was added.

From the west the north curtain runs east above the river to the motte. This wall has three gun emplacements and is mainly of sixteenth-century work, but where it crosses the moat to reach the motte, the gates for flooding the moat can be seen. This gate, or rather the remains of it, is under the undercroft of a chapel, which stood across the moat and against the inside of the curtain. On the other side of the wall stood a tower protecting the water or sluice gates.

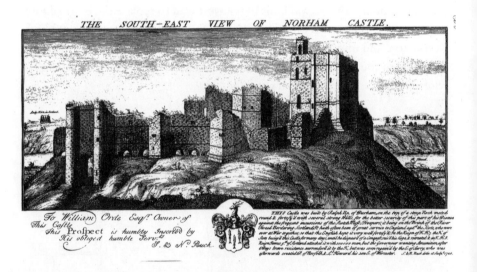

Norham Castle: 1728 engraving by the Buck brothers.

North Middleton Tower. F

The tower of North Middleton was in the list of 1415 when it belonged to Robti Ogyll Chir, but little else is known of it.

North Sunderland Tower. B
Northumberland County History I-318.
The tower was demolished *c.* 1790 when the church and vicarage was built. It was square and of solid masonry, the walls being 5ft thick. It consisted of two storeys, the lower of which was perfect, having an arched roof of stone with a large doorway to the north, and communicating with the upper storey by a hanging stair in the south-west angle of the building. Of this upper storey, portions of the walls were standing, but it was roofless and overgrown with weeds. A hammered cannonball was found by the sexton within 20yd of the tower site. While the tower was in course of demolition, several score of coins from the reign of Elizabeth to that of Anne were discovered. No trace of building work remains today.

North Togston Hall. D.48
Was this house defensible? A thick wall and a reset date stone of 1546 are now part of a later remodelling. See Togston.

Nunnykirk. Tower of the Grange of Newminster. F
Hodgson 2-I-330. Pevsner.
Built by an Abbot of Newminster, it was granted to Ralph Grey by the Crown after the Dissolution. Nothing now remains, but in building the present house, foundations and human bones were found. One mile west of the hall, at Combhill, the farm incorporates the remains of a pele, while at South Healey there are two more; one encased in the later house, the other showing as the remains of one wall some 100yd north-west.

Ogle Castle. F.38
Hodgson 11-I-379. Pevsner.
This house was once surrounded by a double moat and drawbridge and had towers on the walls that were square at the back but round at the front. Now remains of a fourteenth-century tower and a fifteenth- and sixteenth-century manor house can be seen, with evidence of an L-shaped plan. The licence to crenellate was granted in 1341.

Old Bewick Tower. D
Northumberland County History XIV-425.
First mentioned in 1514, it belonged to the Prior of Tynemouth and could hold a garrison of forty men. At the Dissolution it came into the king's hands, as did most of the property of the monasteries. In 1539 it was a stone tower kept entirely

for the defence of the inhabitants in time of war and in 1541 part of it had been covered with a lead roof, but the rest was out of repair. By 1584 it was an entire ruin but its repair was recommended. It was mentioned again in 1608 and was used as a prison in 1614. In 1676 it had a garth (barmkin) and dovecote. Some people in 1866 could remember the ruins, but the Edlingham to Chillingham road now runs over its foundations.

Otterburn Tower. E
Hodgson 2–I–107.

The site of this tower is now occupied by a hotel but some of the masonry of the west tower is medieval. In the survey of 1415 this tower is mentioned as belonging to Robert Umfreville.

Ottercops Farm. Elsdon. E.82
Pevsner.

Two miles south-east of Elsdon in the isolated farmstead of Ottercops are the remains of two peles with walls some 5ft thick. One house was recorded in 1604 while the other is a little later. What is unusual is that they are semi-detached, as at Low Stead and Hetherington.

The ancient tower of Otterburn is lost in the mass of masonry of an 1836 rebuild. The tower is now a hotel.

Overgrass Tower. Longframlington. D.50
Northumberland County History VII-405. Pevsner.
South-east of Newmoor Hall, the ruins are buried in trees and may be fourteenth or fifteenth century. It is rectangular in plan and some of the vaulting with ashlar and parts of the barmkin remain. The tower was not in the list of 1415 and very little is known of its history. Dimensions of the inside of the vault are 23ft 6in × 16ft, with walls about 6ft thick. There was a door at the east of the south side and a circular stair led up from the right of it. The remains of a garderobe shute can be seen north of the window in the west wall.

Paston Tower. A
Northumberland County History XI-171.
In 1415 'one Garrade Selbye Gent. Of late purchased this towne an in yt hath buylded a lytle tower without a barmkyn'. The remains are embedded in the modern house and consist of little more than the vaulted basement.

Peel Crag Pele or Tower. G.3
Nothing now remains of this building but it is said to have stood a little north of the cottage and on the line of the Roman wall. See Bradley Hall.

Penchford. E.83
Ryder.
On the north side of the Grasslees Burn and on the side of the road to the Raw are scant, pele-like remains.

Plenmeller, Haltwhistle. G.44
Pevsner.
The farmhouse of West Plenmeller, much rebuilt, exhibits in its east gable the blocked-up entrance to the basement of a pele-like structure.

Plessey Fortified Hall. F.36
Hodgson 2-II-302.
Of this old hall, nothing now remains, but Hodgson describes the remains of it as seen behind the seventeenth-century farm. The hall stood on the south bank of the River Blyth, with the Hall Dene protecting it on the west. There were remains of a fosse or moat on the south and this may have continued along the east side to the banks of the river, thus fortifying the house on all four sides. The hall was mentioned in deeds of 1242 and 1316. The present Plessey Hall stands about 2 miles upstream from Hartford Bridge and is not on the old site.

Ponteland Tower. F
Northumberland County History XII–446. Hodgson 3-I-30.
Pevsner.

Little is known of the vicar's pele or tower, a three-storeyed, heavily repaired ruin. It is now ivy-laden and stands in the rectory garden south of the Blackbird Inn.

Portgate Tower. G
Northumberland County History IV–211.

The new edition of *Camden's Britannia* states, 'there is at Portgate a square old tower still standing and great ruins of old buildings'. This tower, being of the same form as a multitude of others in the county, was thought to be of a late date. No remains are now standing and the site is unknown.

Prendwick Tower. D
Northumberland County History XIV–577.

Prendwick was raided by the Scots in 1538 and 1543. By way of defence, Thomas Alder built a 'lytle tower', which is mentioned in 1541 and 1584, but has now completely disappeared.

Pressen. A.30

Two miles south-east of Carham are the remains of a building that resembles that at Akeld, being 65ft × 26ft and having a vaulted basement. The ground-floor doorway is in one of the long side walls, with the first-floor entrance being in the west gable. Could this be the tower mentioned in 1541? A Norman motte-and-bailey castle was besieged here in 1138 but its location is not known (*Chronicles of the Reign of Stephen III*). See Carham Tower and Castle.

Preston Tower. D
Northumberland County History II–137. Pevsner.

This was a miniature of Langley Castle, with four corner turrets, all with tunnel vaulting. Preston was first mentioned in the survey of 1415. Originally a long building, the interior of the main body was 16ft 7in wide. The south front, south-east and south-west turrets and portions of side walls are all that now remain. The side walls were 6ft 9in thick and the height to the battlements was 49ft 9in. The pointed vaulting of the basement of the south-east tower rises to 7ft and from E–W is 8ft 9in × 4ft 7in N–S. There is a similar vault in the other turret but with the longer axis north to south. There are also vaults in some of the upper rooms of the turrets.

Prudhoe Castle. H.8
Northumberland County History **XII–72. AA 2–VI–116, 2–XIV–199.**
Pevsner 278. Bates 199.

The castle stands on a hill high above the south bank of the River Tyne. The site has been fortified since very early times and earthworks still remain outside the castle walls, but the castle was first mentioned as resisting two sieges in 1173 and 1174.

There is a small free-standing keep in an inner bailey and an outer bailey with the gatehouse and barbican. The keep is 41ft × 44ft and has a forebuilding with a staircase to the entrance on the east side. In the north-west corner the inner bailey still has a semicircular tower with an open back of thirteenth-century work. The base of a similar tower remains in the south-west corner. Of the dimension between the two baileys, little is known as a house now stands in its place. In the outer bailey a good garderobe remains and on the north side was the site of the hall. The gatehouse has a Norman passage but the upper floors are thirteenth century. A chapel on the first floor is said to have the earliest oriel window in the country. The barbican was added in the fourteenth century and has long side walls with an outer gatehouse and small doorways in the side walls. There was a double moat around all these works, between which stood a pele and barmkin.

Preston Tower: It had walls 6ft 9in thick and was a smaller version of houses like Langley, but only one stout gable remains, with a few offices behind.

Prudhoe Pele and Barmkin. H.8
Bates 214. *Northumberland County History* XII-72.

In 1326 it was ordered that a pele be built outside the gates of Prudhoe Castle. This was built between the two moats on the west side of the barbican, where a chapel and lodgings stood. The outer gatehouse of the castle barbican had projecting side walls, the east one projecting 11ft while the other – even longer – was pierced by the gateway to the pele yard. An old account says that the pele yard was entered by a large 'Gate Rowme', of which very little now remains.

Ratten Raw Pele. E.8
Ryder. Ramm et al. Grundy.

The scant remains of this pele stand on the Ratten Raw burn and in the farm of that name to the north of Otterburn. North-east of the farmhouse of Ratten Raw, which stands on the Banks of the River Rede just south of evistones, are the remains of two walls of a pele.

Engraved by Halpin from a Drawing by Richardson

PRUDHOE CASTLE.

Prudhoe Castle: An old engraving of the gatehouse at Prudhoe, with the ruins of the 'pele' in front of it.

Ratten Row. Haydon Bridge. G.24
Hodgson 2–III–384.
John Hodgson, the noted historian, points out that 'formerly a clyster of peles' stood at Ratten Row in the South Tyne parish of Hayden.

Raw Pele. Elsdon. E.14
Hodgson 2–I–99. Ramm et al. Ryder.
North-west of the road to Elsdon stands Raw Pele, which has a vaulted basement and is 30ft × 15ft. The upper floor is reached by an outer stair and has a high pitched roof, being typical of many such houses in the county (see p.250). Quite a number of peles in this area were very well built, having vaulted basements and not just the usual stone slabs resting on heavy oak beams.

Miss Margaret Crozier was a respectable old woman, who kept a small shop at the Raw. In 1792, William Winter, a man of powerful frame, but of desperate character, whose father and brother were hanged at Morpeth in 1788, returned from transportation for horse stealing and leagued himself with two cruel and profligate women, Jane and Eleanor Clark, who belonged to a gang of faws whose general place of rendezvous was at Hedley Fell, near Ryton, in the county of Durham … Supposing Miss Crozier to be rich, their first joint adventure should be to go and rob her … Early next morning, poor Crozier was found cruelly murdered, and her house robbed. All of them were condemned and hanged at the Westgate and Winter's body was hung in chains at Steng Cross, in sight of Margaret Crozier's house.

Hodgson, J., *A History of Northumberland* 2-I-99

Ray Demesne Bastle or Pele. F.68
Pevsner. OS Border Reivers Map.
This house is under the entry for Kirkwhelpington in Pevsner. Standing 2 miles north-west of the village are the remains of what was a small pele or bastle, with remains consisting of walls up to 6ft 6in high. There would have been a little room for stock in its basement and the now missing first-floor room would not have been the most comfortable, even for a small family.

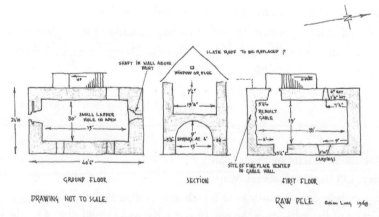

Raw Pele: Plans and a sketch of Raw Pele, the home of Margaret Crozier, who was murdered here in 1792 by William Winter. The top photograph is of the gibbet where his remains were hung.

Ray Pele. E.41
Hodgson 2-I-198. Pevsner.
Hodgson describes a cottage and a pele at Ray, but says they were in a ruinous state. He also mentions the earthworks and said that they could have been fish ponds. All that can now be seen are three banks and ditches of medieval work, not far from the line of the old railway at Ray Cottages.

Pevsner records 'another bastle' at Ray Demesne with ruined walls standing 6ft 6in high.

Redheugh. Tarset. E.84
Ramm et al. Ryder.
This is a large, substantial house with stout walls that are in the pele tradition but may be later, using stone from an earlier building in outbuildings to the south-east. A lintel with an illegible sixteenth-century date may suggest that even if there are doubts about the status of the house, there was a pele in the vicinity.

Refely (Reaveley). Site not known.
Bates. Hodgson 3-III-211. Wallis XIV-544.
A tower is shown on Christopher Dacre's Plat of 1584. It was one of a line of towers including Ryle, Coutwall, Screnwood, Ingram, Branton and Frawdon being part of 'decayed castles, towers and fortresses meet to be repaired, and other such new fortresses and enclosures as are meet to be newly made and enclosed'.

In 1587 the Armstrongs of Liddesdale made day raids on Prendwick, Ryle, Ingram and Reaveley and 'carried off 35 prisoners and large booty'. Located just downstream from Ingram and over the River Breamish from Ingram Mill, its actual site is not known. A reused lintel turned up shows the pivot hole for a harr-hung door and a raised door stop.

Ridge or Rig End. E.85
Ramm et al. Pevsner. Ryder.
The farmhouse of Rig End close to Falstone contains much old masonry, being a converted pele that was heightened to give an extra half floor, an attic, under a low-pitched roof. The basement entrance is in the long south wall with the first-floor entrance, now blocked, above. All the windows are later insertions. It has been suggested that there were three floors from the outset and that the once steeply pitched roof was lowered in the nineteenth century.

Ridley. Beltingham. G.27
Ramm et al. Pevsner.

Ivy Cottage sits on the roadside and incorporates much of an earlier pele. The gable end entrance to the ground floor is a little off centre and the large stone forming its head looks as if it has been reused, here suggesting an older house on the site. Part of the first-floor entrance can still be traced and each gable has corbels as if to carry a lookout turret or chimney as at Melkridge.

Ritton White House (Westryghton) Tower. F.11
Hodgson 2-I-322.

The survey of 1541 mentions a stone house and barmkins, which were in disrepair and late of the suppressed Monastery of Newminster. In 1547 there was a 'towre' at Westryghton, but no mention of its barmkin. Dacre's Plat of 1584 also shows the tower of West Ritton.

Rochester Pele. E.7
Ramm et al. Pevsner. Ryder.

A strong pele in the Roman fort of Rochester, but not made of Roman stones, and according to Hodgson, this pele stood until 1825. Another pele still stands in the fort and it is still occupied. This pele is quite small, being only 20ft × 10ft. The small hamlet sits within the Roman fort of Bremenium and many years ago I held WEA classes in one of the peles. Ryder gives a plan in his *Bastles and Towers*.

Rock Hall Tower. D
Northumberland County History II-122. **Pevsner.**

The nucleus of the present house is a T-shaped tower of which the walls are 4ft to 5ft thick. The stem and left arm of the T are fifteenth century and the right arm is sixteenth-century work. There must have been a tower or hall here since the twelfth century but the oldest part now visible is a doorway of *c.* 1340 and may be that of the oratory of Robert De Tughall. The people who lived in the great houses of the county were not always rich, as the will of John Swinhoe of Rock shows: '… my legacy. Item, to my mother and my sister, my wyffis clothis and my part of the corn …' John has little other than old clothes and his crop to leave, his property being so small. I put together a set of plans and a history of the house based on papers belonging to the owner, Mr Bosanquet, but I don't know who holds them now.

Roddam Tower. D
Hodgson 3-II-210.

Mentioned in the list of 1541, all trace of it has now vanished but it may have stood on Castle Hill, north of the present hall. As soon as conditions allowed it, we can assume that the owners of Roddam moved to a more comfortable site near the hall or Home Farm, where some medieval masonry was found.

Roses Bower. E.54. (Low Roses Bower)
Newcastle Journal, 15 July 1938.

The remains of a bastle house have been incorporated in a large byre and stand in the farmyard of Roses Bower.

Roseden (Ilderton). D.6

Just off the A697, a little north of Wooperton, is the hamlet of Roseden, where a tower was recorded in 1584 by Christopher Dacre on his Plat. He shows it as between Roddom and Ilderton.

Rothbury Castle and Tower. D.56
Dixon 371. *Northumberland County History* XV-343.

There was a prison at Rothbury in 1256 and Camden describes a 'brave castle', both of which stood on Haa Hill, 50yd south-east of the church. Part of the tower, which must have been on a Norman motte, was still inhabited in the mid-nineteenth century, and was only demolished in 1869 to extend the churchyard.

Rothbury Castle and church.

Rothley Tower (of Newminster). F.24
Hodgson 2-I-307. Pevsner.
The tower was built by John Buttler, Abbot of Newminster in 1467, and is in the list of 1541. Nothing now remains to be seen and the ruin on the hill is an eye-catcher from 1776.

Rudchester Tower. H.16
Brown II-66. Pevsner 284. *Northumberland County History* XII-198.
It is known that a hall was being built in 1285 but little or nothing of it now remains. The south end of the present hall incorporates the remains of a late tower house but this can only be identified by the great thickness of the walls at the east.

Rugley. Alnwick. Site not known.
Tate I-222.
Tate mentions in his *History of Alnwick* a small tower at Rugley, but its site is not known.

Ryal Tower. F.47
***Northumberland County History* XII-340.**
The site of this tower is uncertain but it must have stood on the hilltop with the church and small village. It was only mentioned once, in 1519, when it was given to John Fenwick by his father.

Saint Margarets. Alnwick. D
Tate I-222.
Tate mentions a small tower here but gives no other detail to guide us.

Scremerston Tower or Fortalice. B.2
Raine 240.
The tower or fortalice of Scremerston was first mentioned in 1402 and in 1541 was in need of repair. In 1561, together with a barmkin, it was in a good state of preservation. The site was north of the village and fell into disrepair after the accession of James VI to the throne of England.

Screnwood Tower and Barmkin. C.8
***Northumberland County History* XIV-579. Hodgson 3-II-211. Dixon.**
In 1895 Dixon wrote: 'We are informed that some years ago, the ruins of a large house with walls of great thickness, having pointed doorways and mullioned

windows besides the foundations were standing in the green fields east of the present Screnwood House.' It is probable that these were the remains of the tower and barmkin of the Horsleys. In 1514 a garrison of twenty was recommended for this tower and in 1541 the tower and barmkin were in good repair.

Seaton Delaval Tower or Castle. F
Northumberland County History IX-177. Pevsner. AA 2-XIV-27.
First mentioned in the list of 1415, the site is not known and no licence to crenellate exists. It is thought to have stood close to the present hall. Before 1628 there was more than one tower and the house had battlements, and in 1549 the beacon on the tower head formed one of a chain of signal fires to warn of invasion.

Seghill Tower. F
Northumberland County History IX-57. AA 3-VIII-15. Pevsner.
The remains are now built into an old inn, forming the cellars, and only the vaulted basement remains. The dimensions indicate that it was one of the largest towers in the county, measuring internally 44ft 6in × 16ft 6in, and it is said to have been three storeys high and to have had a lofty turret at one corner. Alas, this has now been demolished but the basement of seven bays points to more than simple isolated towers. All the remains were demolished *c*. 1990.

Settlingstones Tower. G
This tower is in the list of 1541, but no trace is now left.

Sewingshields Castle or Tower. E
Hodgson 2-III-386, 3-I-27, 3-II-216. Pevsner.
In 1592 it was an old tower in decay and now only the sites of the tower and the fish ponds are left, marked by mounds and ditches with a fence around. It was also mentioned in the surveys of 1415 and 1541.

Sharperton Pele. C.16
Northumberland County History XV-447.
Very little is known of the house but its remains may be incorporated in a ruined house at Sharperton. A Tudor doorway inscribed S.P. E.P. 1675. Roger Pots, and other stones marked A.P S.P 1667 and H.D. 1780 are memorials to former owners and alterations made by them. A very curious head and shoulders of a lady with a halo brought from a field wall was built into the wall of Sharperton sawmill and may be by the same hand as that at Raw Pele.

Shawdon Tower or Castle. D
Northumberland County History **XIV–557.**
The tower is mentioned in 1403 and must have been a place of importance as it was called a castrum in 1415 and was 'in measurable good reparacions' in 1541. There is little doubt that this stood in the grounds of the present hall.

Shield Hall/Tower. G
Northumberland County History **VI–368. Pevsner.**
Some 1½ miles north-west of Slayley, tucked away in farm buildings to the east of Shield Hall are the remains of a medieval hall house of the late thirteenth or

SHIELD HALL TOWER

B.LONG.

Shield Hall Tower: The remains are hidden amongst farm buildings. It was a rather fine house of the fourteenth century. At times it was compared with Aydon, but there is little left to allow such a bold step to be taken today.

early fourteenth century. The ground floor has a barrel vault and a mural stair rises from the ground-floor entrance to what may have been a solar. In the thickness of its north gable wall are a pair of pointed windows with window seats. A window at the south looks the same but is a nineteenth-century copy. The house has been compared with Aydon Castle but little remains to allow such a bold step.

Shilbottle Tower or Castle. D
Northumberland County History V–439. Pevsner.
Known as 'Pee House', Shilbottle Tower was formerly the vicarage adjoining the churchyard. It appears in the list of 1415 and has a vaulted ground floor, as is usual in the north. It is now much restored and the upper part is a reconstruction. It is thought that the tower may be part of a larger structure but the modern house is so built that it is impossible to verify this.

Shilburnhaugh Pele. E.26 and E.27
AA 3–XIII–14.
A list of *c.* 1715 mentioned an 'old pile' as belonging to 'one Robson'. Just over a mile to the north-west at Leaplish are what could be the remains of a pele. A document, if I remember correctly, of the time just prior to the uniting of the crowns tells us how some men from north of the border came and cut down the pele at Leaplish with axes. Even at such a late date some peles must have consisted of wood and earth.

Shilla Hill Pele. E.24
Northumberland County History XV–271.
This pele is 24ft N–S and 48ft E–W, with walls 4ft thick, except at the west where they were 8ft thick, and may have contained the stair. The door is in the east wall and is 2ft 3in wide with traces of unfinished decoration, also at the east end are remains of a later farmhouse and other enclosures, all overgrown and in very poor condition.

Shilling Pot. Falstone. E.29
The main road that climbs the hill from Falstone road end to Kielder Water Dam passes the overgrown foundations of a pele on the right. Also known as Yarrow Shillings Pot, the site would repay excavation.

Shitlehaugh Pele. E.10
Tomlinson 321. Ramm et al. Pevsner. Ryder. Hodgson 2-I-147.
This pele stands above the road north of Otterburn and was much the same as that of Iron House, being 30½ft × 10½ft and more like a very strong cottage than

the typical pele. The door is in one of the long sides and not in the end as at Iron House. Though not large, the house was superior in its build with the foundations of a porch and no door to the first floor above it. There may have been a projecting stair turret, which is unusual in such houses. Later work enlarged the house so as to make it suitable as the 'mansion of the Redes'.

Shoreswood Tower. A.4
Hodgson 3-II-190. AA 2-XIV-22.

Although mentioned in 1541, this tower was not in the survey of Norhamshire made in 1560 and therefore must no longer have been in existence, or at least have been in very poor condition.

Shortflat Tower or Fortalice. F
Hodgson 2-I-366. Pevsner.

The tower was built after 1296 and licence to crenellate was granted in 1305. The building was much altered in later years but it still retains a vaulted basement and battlements with rainspouts below them. In the late seventeenth century a house was attached.

The Sills Pele. E.6
Hodgson 2-I-147.

Hodgson describes a pele incorporated in the farmstead of Sills as having walls 5ft thick and interior dimensions of 33ft 7in × 16ft 9in and being in good condition. The site is north of Rochester on Dere Street.

Simonburn Castle or Tower and Barmkin. E.55
Northumberland County History XV-155. Pevsner. Wallis II-55.

The site is on a high spur between two streams and it could have been part of a motte-and-bailey castle, as the remains of a moat or ditch can be seen. All that now remains is the ruined vault of a tower, which has a turret that projected about 8ft from the north-west face. This tower was once repaired as an eye-catcher or park ornament.

Hall Barns
Northumberland County History *XV-192*.

In 1541 Hall Barns was called a bastle but no trace of it remains today.

Rectory

Northumberland County History *XV-192*. *Pevsner*.

The oldest part is a lintel dated 1666, which is part of the house that was built after the tower fell into disuse. Old documents describe it as a 'gate or castle', such as at Bywell, and a little tower.

Sinderhope Shield. Allendale. G.45
Pevsner.

This small, tower-like building was extended in the seventeenth century. What is interesting is the use of a local type of round-headed doorheads, but even better, the first floor still retains its sandstone flags carried by closely spaced timbers. See Ryder's reconstruction based on Nine Dargue, p.66 of Pevsner. At Hayrake, a pele has triangular doorheads. This house was built in two stages, extending its length considerably. South-west of Sinderhope is Rowntree Stob, a strange house using many traditional elements and built in the later half of the seventeenth century. Built into the hillside, the first floor was entered from that side without requiring the usual external stair. The basement still has, for this area, a round-headed doorway. Most importantly, the walls are too thin to offer any great defence, so as fine as it is, it is known as a bastle derivative.

Snabdough Farm (Greystead). Tarset. E.65
Pevsner. Ryder. B. Harbottle.

This house is in no way a typical pele or bastle, yet neither is it a small tower. I knew of it for many years, being introduced to it by V. Blankenburgs, the photographer, then later surveying it with Barbara Harbottle, the then County Archaeologist.

We found a pointed vault to the upper floor and bulging walls to the basement where a vault had been removed, making it a house unique on the borders. There was the usual gable end entrance to the basement, now a bit knocked about, and a 36ft-deep well in a later wing. The east gable in the attic has a blocked, spayed window with window seats either side. Partly obscured by the present ceiling of the first floor are the rear arches of the windows that once lit the large first-floor room, once again, superior workmanship for a typical hill farmer's home and if they were furnished with window seats as in the attic then this was comfort of which most bastle dwellers could only dream.

Northumberland is blessed with many fine eighteenth- and nineteenth-century farmhouses but Snabdough in its present state and at first glance, in the words of John Grundy, 'looks no more than an ordinary farmhouse and a pretty dull one at that'. This drab exterior hides one of the most unusual, exciting houses in the county, one that defies classification within existing groupings and is an outstanding one-off. It has been much improved by the removal of a cement render in recent years. There are good photographs in the Blankenburgs Photo Collection in the County Records Office.

Snitter Pele. C.18
Pevsner.

Many years ago, I held a WEA class in this tidy little village just west of Rothbury. There are the remains of a late pele incorporated in the Old School House exhibiting the lower treads of a spiral stair unusual in peles. A class report published by the students gave details of many of the houses, with drawings of front elevations in most cases.

South Charlton Tower. North of Alnwick. D
Bates.

In 1450 the 2nd Earl of Northumberland had built a tower at South Charlton for the safety of the village in time of war. This tower was built into the chapel but now neither chapel nor tower remain. Quite a number of church towers could be used as a place of refuge and among them were Ingram, Edlingham, Long Haughton and Ancroft.

The old school contains within its fabric the remains of a pele-like building still with the basement doorway in the easterly gable, the first-floor entrance being in the longer south wall. It is unusual that this house is so far east of the upland wastes where peles and stone houses were the norm.

Spartylea. Allendale. G.46
Pevsner.

About 2 miles south of Spartylea at Hope Head is what is regarded as the best-preserved pele in the area, with a nineteenth-century house being built on to one end. The existing roof timbers may be a little later than the stonework.

Stamfordham. Tower of the Vicar. F
Hodgson 3-I-29. Pevsner. AA.

The vicarage is a confusing building with at least parts of it being seventeenth century, if not older. Widdrington House retains walls 4ft 6in thick and the original first-floor entrance, now blocked, is to be found in what was the gable wall.

Stanton Tower. F
Hodgson 2-II-110. Pevsner.
Hodgson says that it was used as a shop, a poor house and a granary, and that 'one man lives and makes a living out of the walled garden'. The remains are now partly in ruins and consist of a rectangular tower house with a south projection and also, on the south side, remains of a garderobe. All the rest looks early seventeenth century or Tudor and the west front is early eighteenth-century work. In 1666, William Veitch was the son of a minister and brother of three others in the ministry and a Covenanter. There is a record that tells of his persecution under the Stuarts and how he 'got into a hole within the lining of a great window, which had been made on purpose for the whole room was lined about with wanscot'.

Starsley Pele. Falstone. E.28
AA 5-I-137–75.
This pele was excavated and measured prior to inundation under the waves of Kielder Water. The basement entrance had been enlarged and was in one of the long side walls. In the basement was a stout wall, breaking it into two rooms. This partition was not bonded with the back wall and there was no indication of slit vents. The house was just upstream from the much larger Hawkhope, being only 40ft 7in × 24ft 3in.

Starward Pele or Tower. G.14
Pevsner. Hodgson 2-III-373.
The pele or tower of Starward is built in a very strong position on a tongue of rock with its point to the north, the West Allen on the west and a smaller stream on the east. To the south, the ridge narrows to little more than 6ft. One angle of a gatehouse is left and the north wall of the main tower stands 10ft high. Fragments of a barmkin can also be traced. At the foot of the hill is Starward Manor, with evidence that it developed out of the existing peles.

Stokoe Crags Bastle/Pele. E.64
Blankenburgs Collection. Ryder. AA 4-L-249–58.
On the south side of the road up the North Tyne is a waterfall that tumbles off the edge of Stokoe Crags going by the name of Skitering Lin. A short walk up the hill from this point are the remains of what may be the much reused

remains of two peles/bastles but certainly one. My introduction to the site was by V. Blankenburgs, who photographed it while I made sketches of the layout; that was in 1969.

What remains of these buildings are aligned east to west along the slope of the hill. The building at the west end of the group was a pele/bastle of 34ft × 20ft 5in. A little unusual is the position of the ground-floor entrance, which is in the north end of the east wall. The doorhead has a socket to take a harr-hung door. The south wall has a rather fine window for a pele/bastle, having sockets for iron bars.

Adjoining this house are the remains of a second pele/bastle with a cross passage where the two join, and to continue the line, two further houses of later date, but as the whole range has been modified its chronology is uncertain. What is of interest are the many names used for the group over the years, from Stokoe Crags, Skitering Lin, Brown Hills – even Smalesmouth – and the name I knew it by, Barren Know.

Styford Hall. Riding Mill. H.19
Pevsner.

A little north-west of Styford Hall, high above the river, is a motte standing up to 20ft high with a ditch on three sides. The fourth, south side was defended by a sharp drop down to the River Tyne.

Sweethope Bastle or Pele. E.43
***Northumberland County History* IV-410. Bates 46.**

At Sweethope is a farmhouse on the site of the old pele, or bastle, as it was called in the survey of 1541.

Tarset Tower or Castle. E.35
***Northumberland County History* XV-243. Mackenzie. Sitwell. Pevsner.**

This position was fortified with a stone wall and ditch in 1267 as it stood on a road junction beside a ford over the Tyne. Licence to crenellate was granted in 1267.

Destroyed in 1525, it was never rebuilt but used as a quarry until only green mounds remained. During excavations in 1888 a passage was found going west past Tarset Hall Farm and a bronze key was found inside. Much the same plan as Haughton, it had an outer wall that extended all round and was broken round the outline of the corner turrets. There are remains of the ditch that enclosed two sides of an area of about 250ft square. The other two sides were defended by the steep bank of the river to the north and a shallower artificial bank on the west.

The tower stood in the east end of the earthworks running north to south. There is no evidence of a wall inside the ditch, although it may have been of wood and there must have been a bridge or gangway.

Highfield Pele.
In the Forest of Tarset is the old farm on Highfield and on it is a small moated mound, with traces of walls, rectangular in plan.

Tecket Bastle or Pele. E.56
Very little is known of this bastle, but a strong stone house is mentioned as being at Tecket in the survey of 1541.

Tharnham Tower. F
Bates.
The survey of 1541 mentions a tower situated at Tharnam, it following the entry for 'Lynne Brigge' but preceding that for 'Nether Trewhytt'. This would seem to imply that Tharnam lay between these but 'Lynne Brigge' is at the head of the River Coquet and 'Nether Trewhytt' some miles to the east and north of Thropton; the site is unknown to me but may be Harnam (F).

THIRLWALL CASTLE,
Northumberland.

This engraving of a ruinous Thirlwall Castle shows a farmworker's cottage built into what remains of a house with at least four floors.

Thirlwall Castle or Tower. G
Bates. Pevsner.

Mentioned in the survey of 1541 as a tower, it is difficult to date as it was built of Roman stones. Now in a ruinous condition, the walls are 8ft to 9ft thick, but there are no vaults remaining. The south wall has fallen, revealing that there was a large room to the north and a group of smaller ones in the south. The tower that now remains showed holes for the beams of four upper floors and is said to be of early fourteenth-century work.

Thornebie Tower. A.3
Bates.

The survey of 1541 tells us that within 1 mile of the River Tweed there was a little tower in good order here. Was this at Thornton, just north of Shoreswood?

Thornton (Newbrough) Tower. G
AA 3–XIII–15. Pevsner.

Not much is left to see but some walls were about 8ft high and some 20ft, but there are no details. Hodgson says that even with the ashlar gone from both the inside and outside of the walls, they were still 6ft thick and the tower was 42ft × 33ft.

Thornton (Thornbye) Tower. A.3
Raine 20–305. Pevsner.

There are some scant remains of this building standing up to 20ft high, but no details can be seen. The tower is mentioned in the survey of 1541 and again in 1560, when it and its barmkin, although in one piece, were in decay.

Throckrington Bastle. E.46
Northumberland County History IV–403.

The remains stand near the farm (to the north) and show bolt holes in the walls for a doorway. The mounds beside the tower are still known as the 'night folds'.

Thropton Tower and Bastle. D.55

Thropton Tower was in the lists of 1415 and 1541 and may have been part of the old hall demolished in 1811 to make room for the Roman Catholic presbytery and chapel.

Near the west end of the village stands a plain late bastle of massive rough construction, considerably modernised and still occupied. Thropton Bastle, known as 'the pele', stands towards the west end of the village. It is well preserved and still occupied. Interesting features are the rather high-vaulted basement and an original first-floor window with sockets for an iron grille, but best of all, the original doorways to the basement and first floor still exist in a gable wall. The attic may be an addition and while the present windows are of 1863, there is an original loophole in the southside.

Tiefort, Motte and Bailey.
Histoire Des Ducs De Normandie.

In 1216 Tiefort is mentioned in the *Histoire Des Ducs De Normandie* and has been translated as being either Styford, Tynemouth or Tweedmouth. A lot of research and enjoyable field walking is required here.

Tillmouth Tower and Barmkin. A.8
Raine.

This tower is on the list made in 1541, but it has now vanished. In 1560 the tower, with its barmkin around it, was in great decay.

Titlington Tower and Castle. D.32
Northumberland County History XIV-447. Hodgson 3-II-210.

In 1541 a little tower belonging to Kirkham Priory stood here but 'the imbat-tlements thereof were never fynyshed', and the roofs needed repair. There was also a motte and bailey and the mound of the motte is a short distance south of the hall, while the bailey is now the front lawn. At some uncertain date in the Middle Ages, the motte was lowered and a tower was set up on it. Its enclosure extended north-east about 75yd and the gateway is said to have been there. The fortress was removed in 1745 to make way for a new house, the remains of which are incorporated in the present house.

Todburn Steel, Slayley. H.20
Pevsner.

About 1½ miles north-east of the village of Todburn Steel, a farmhouse consists of peles with the westerly one retaining its gable end entrance to the ground floor, now blocked. The eastern house still retains its first-floor entrance, now partly blocked and having a window set in it.

Togstone Tower. D
Northumberland County History V-326.

Though not in the list of 1415, a tower stood here until 1820, when it was demol-ished, and nothing now remains.

Tosson. D
Ramm et al. Ryder. Pevsner.

What remains of Great Tosson Tower is the almost square ruin of an old tower with the facing stones surviving above the ground floor only. In 1541 it was listed as being the tower of the Lord Ogle's 'inherytaunce and not in good reparacions'. On rising ground south of the tower are the grassed-over remains of a building, having had walls 4ft 2in to 4ft 10in thick and known as Newtown, which would seem to be a pele or bastle.

Townfoot. Elsdon. E.18
Pevsner. Ryder.

Only the west end of what may have been a pele or bastle remains incorporated in a farmhouse of *c*. 1800. A possible slit vent, now blocked, is high up in a first-floor wall.

Tritlington Old Hall. F.65
Pevsner.

This house is built round a medieval tower, which had a new wing attached in 1595. A newel stair survives in parts in a rear turret.

Troughend Tower. E
Hodgson 2-I-133.

This tower existed from very early times, but now nothing remains to show its site, which was on or near Troughend Hall, west of Otterburn. An Elizabethan scribe once wrote of the Reeds of Troughend (pronounced Trowhen), 'A ruler and more lawless band there need not be yet if well tutored they might do Her Majestie good service.'

Tweedmouth, Two Towers. A.1
Raine 244–6–37.

A tower was built in 1202 by the Norman bishops in connection with the bridge, and King John tried twice to strengthen it, but William the Lion twice laid it level. The site is not known. The other of the two towers belonged to the hospital of Tweedmouth and stood at Spital. A motte-and-bailey built by Philip of Poitou in 1205 and destroyed by William the Lion of Scotland in 1209 is now lost and nothing appears to survive. See Tiefort.

Twizell Tower or Castle. A.10
Raine 313. AA 2-XIV-22.

The remains of this castle were incorporated in a later mansion, which is also in ruins. The original tower or castle was mentioned in the survey of 1415 and in that of 1541, when it had been in ruins for eleven years. The survey of Norham made in 1560 mentioned it as a little tower and a little barmkin 'much in decay'.

Gothic Revival and Twizell

The Gothic period (1190–1485) in Northumberland was a bloody affair with towers and castles sited for the security and defence of the county and its inhabitants. An area of hitherto little architectural significance sprang to considerable importance *c.* 1750, due to the economic boom that followed in the wake of new-found internal peace, with investments in farming, mining, shipping and other lucrative ventures.

J. Macaulay, in his book *The Gothic Revival*, said that there was, 'A bored and introverted society, secure in its social stations and protected by the privilege of wealth from the hardships brought on by the wars of time. The upper classes read of war and built warlike houses but seldom did a gentleman participate in war.'

In the late eighteenth century rather frivolous and fanciful 'Gothic' structures appeared in the parks attached to ancient seats of the gentry.

It was out of this melting pot that Twizell Castle's refurbishment was begun in 1770 by Sir Francis Blake. Now a ruin, this confection of a house engulfed the remains of the medieval house/castle and resulted in the finest house of its type in the borders. Old engravings, plans and elevations in the Butler Papers held by the County Records Office exist to show us what has been lost. My rough plan drawn in the field (see p.268) may help in the understanding of this ruin.

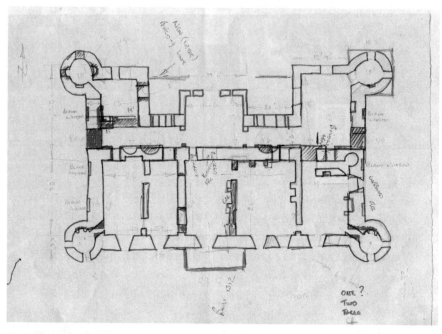

Twizell Castle plan.

TWIZELL BRIDGE AND CASTLE.

Printed and Published by T.Fordyce. Newcastle.

Twizell Castle from the bridge that for some time was the largest single-arched example in the world. Behind is the castle with four floors, not the five of legend.

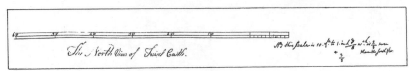

Twizell Castle: Two main elevations of Twizell, the finest Gothic Revival house in the county. The one overlooking the river (*top*) is subdued; the other (*bottom*) is a confection of Gothic detail.

Tynemouth Castle H.14
Northumberland County History VIII-148. Guidebook. Pevsner.

The castle stands on a very strong, rocky headland, with the sea on three sides. The west or landward side is defended by the castle proper, which has many Elizabethan military works in front of it. Since Saxon times a church and fortifications have stood on the site and remains of a Norman motte-and-bailey castle lie under the Elizabethan earthworks to the south of the gatehouse. Licence to crenellate was granted in 1296 and it was then that the headland was encircled by walls and towers. The gatehouse on the landward side is a gatehouse keep (as at Bywell, Dunstanburgh and Morpeth) with a barbican much the same as that at Alnwick. Strong high walls ran north and south from the gatehouse and east along the south and lowest side of the promontory. The other two sides still had walls and towers but not quite so strong.

The barbican was gained by passing two projecting towers, with a portcullis between them. The portcullis was hard against the entrance to a vaulted passage, which had guard rooms on either side and a pair of gates. An open passage follows with high walls on each side and a drawbridge pit between them, which was filled in in Elizabethan times. The road now passes under the gatehouse by a gate through a vaulted passage and another gate to a small inner barbican also with gates. Having gained the castle yard, a ramp up to the first-floor level and another drawbridge had to be crossed before the keep was gained. The keep had corbelled-out bartizans at its corners, but no trace of them remains today.

As mentioned above, the curtain walls were strongest on the south and west sides. The west wall is now nearly all Elizabethan, but the remains of the Whitley Tower, which projected beyond the walls and was destroyed when the earthworks were thrown up, can still be seen to the north-west. To the south of the gates were two towers, the West Tower and the East Mount Tower. In their place are more earthworks revetted in stone to carry artillery, as at Berwick on the town walls.

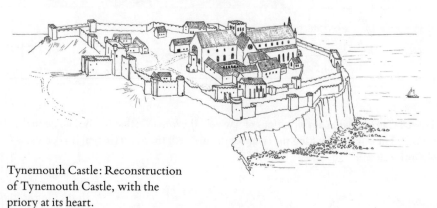

Tynemouth Castle: Reconstruction of Tynemouth Castle, with the priory at its heart.

To the south, remains of a gallery and a solid thirteenth-century tower still stand, but most of the south wall was destroyed in 1851. Much of the north and east walls have fallen into the sea. Bothwell, the husband of Mary, Queen of Scots, spent many weary days as a captive within the walls.

Wainhope Pele or Bastle. E.4
The site of this building is now in the Forest of Kielder.

Wallington Tower or Castle. F
Hodgson 2-I-265. Pevsner.
Of the castle, only some cellars remain, incorporated in the present house, a square of 120ft built around a courtyard in 1688. In the list of 1541, a tower and stone house are mentioned and Leland said that a Tudor house was added to the medieval fortress, much the same as Chipchase or Belsay.

Walltown Tower. G
Only fragments were left in Wallis's time, but the site is shown by mounds behind the present farmhouse. The stone from the tower was used for other work. A little to the east, the lines of the old houses of Walltown could be traced.

Walwick Tower. E
Camden III-234. AA 4-XVI-186.
The Gough edition of *Camden's Britannia* (1789) mentions the 'remains of a considerable castle' existing at Walwick, but little else is known of the supposed tower.

Warden. Hexham. G.52
Pevsner.
There are the remains of a motte-and-bailey castle just up the hill west of the church. The remains consist of ditches and artificially scarped natural slopes.

Wark Castle (on Tweed). A.16
Northumberland County History XI-44.
Built early in the twelfth century, it was captured by the Scots and later rebuilt by Henry II in 1153–56. The keep was an irregular polygon and measured 255ft × 165ft. It was a shell keep but three times the size of that at Alnwick.

The first mention of 'Carham which by the English is called Wark' was in 1126 by David, King of Scotland, when he seized it. Burnt to the ground in 1216, it was rebuilt and is Norman in plan. It shows work of almost every period up to the sixteenth century. The keep was four storeys high and in each were five great murder holes 'shot with great vaults of stone' (except one stage, which was of timber) so that great bombards could be shot from each of them.

The top floor was used for keeping ordnance and above it was a watch tower from which Norham and Berwick could be seen. Lower down, the Constable and forty footmen found accommodation, while a series of trapdoors in each floor allowed the hoisting up of ordnance. The gate to the outer bailey had iron gates in a vaulted passage, on to which was built a two-storey building to house 140 men; six men in each chamber on the upper floor, and horses beneath, twelve to a stable. The outer gate and the corner tower were three storeys high. Very little of this great castle remains, but its great motte-and-bailey with some fragments of masonry can still be seen.

Wark Castle. Simonburn. E.53
Northumberland County History XV-282. Pevsner. AA II-3-147

This was once a motte-and-bailey castle, but now only traces of the bailey remain as the motte was levelled to build the present farm, in which a Tudor doorhead is incorporated.

The original motte-and-bailey castle was 'rebuilt' in 1155–61 and withstood a Scottish army in 1174–75. It was taken and destroyed in 1336–38 but was mentioned in 1399–1400 and was in the list of 1415. Not a stone was standing in 1538 and in the survey of 1541 there was 'the apparence of a fortresse that hath bene in tyme past'. There was a strong, well-built tower or 'pele' in the village square and when it was demolished the stone was used to build some of the present houses there.

Warkworth Bridge Tower. D.46
Northumberland County History. Pevsner. *Warkworth and its Castle* by George Thompson, pp.60–61.

The tower stands on the town end of the ancient bridge built with the 20 marks left by John Cook of Newcastle in 1379. This is one of only a few fortified bridges in England but it is now much ruined above the arched passage over the original road. 'One side of the tower was the gatekeepers lodge later used as a temporary lock-up for disorderly persons.' The other side houses the stone stairway to the upper floors. George Clarkson, in his survey of 1567, writes:

> there is a little tower build in th' sayd bridge where a part of grytts ys hanged and nowe the sayd towre ys withowt roofs and cover and withowt amendments will in short tyme utterlye decay; yt shall be therefore verie requisite that th' tower be with all speade repared and the gaytts hanged uppe which shall be gret savefety and comoditye for th' towne.

Warkworth Castle. D.46

Northumberland County History V-18. Guidebook. Pevsner. Bates. AA
4-XV-115, 4-IX-194.

The castle stands in a loop of the river but only has it for protection on two sides, east and west. The south side has a ditch of great depth running along its length. To the north lies the town, protected by the river on three sides and the castle closing the loop at the south end. The castle is built on the mound of the motte-and-bailey and follows the lines of it on all but the east side, which is some 70ft short of the old wood and earthen fortifications. All that is left of the old twelfth-century walls are stretches in the east and west walls of the outer ward. The Great Gate, Grey Mare's Tail, Carrickfergus Tower and the rest of the curtain walls are mainly late twelfth to late thirteenth century.

The gatehouse consists of a long, vaulted passageway with guardrooms on either side that project in front of it in octagonal bays. The drawbridge has now gone but the recess for it can be seen above the entrance. Above the gate towers, as in other portions of the curtain, there are square holes to carry the timber supports for the brattishing. Behind the drawbridge was a gate, then a portcullis, an open passageway with arrow slits in its sides and an iron door at the court-yard end. At a later date, three-corbelled machicolations were erected above the passage entrance. In the bailey were the usual offices, with a collegiate church forming the boundary between the outer and inner ward. This church was never completed. The church, keep, kitchen and hall are all of late fourteenth century or early fifteenth century.

The keep standing on the motte lacks only roofs and windows to make it fully habitable, as part of it still is. Remains of an old arch suggest an older keep stood on the site. The keep is a square of about 65ft with its corners cut off and a projection on all four faces. At the entrance there was a portcullis and trapdoors just inside opening into a pit 16ft deep. The whole is very well planned and comfortable, being more of a palace than a keep. In the centre is a lightwell measuring 8ft × 10ft that served the double purpose of lighting parts of the castle and collecting rain water.

The basement has eight rooms or chambers, all vaulted. The south face of the keep was protected by the inner ward but the north, east and west were open to attack from the town side, making the fortification of the town very important. The Grey Mare's Tail, on the east curtain wall, a tower of the thirteenth century, is worth examination. As at Alnwick and Dunstanburgh, Warkworth has an underground dungeon, a rare feature in border castles. The original motte-and-bailey castle was in existence in 1158 and perhaps as early as 1138 but sorry to say, it was too weak for defence in 1173–74.

Warkworth Castle keep viewed from the gatehouse.

The number of windows in the keep at Warkworth indicates how comfortable it was.

Warkworth Bridge Tower: Bridge towers are a rarity, with only a few in the country. These views show it from the bridge (*top*) and from the town (*bottom*).

Warkworth Bridge Tower: A view over the river and bridge to the tower with the town beyond.

Warkworth Castle: The keep at Warkworth from the bailey.

Warton Bastles. D.54
Dixon 320.
There were several bastle houses at Warton, which were not mentioned in any of the old surveys, some of which were still in existence in 1717.

Waterhead Pele/Bastle. Tarset. E.86
I rediscovered this pele in 1987 under rampant vegetation in the garden of a nineteenth-century cottage. Incorporated in a field boundary are the remains of what was the south-east gable wall, its only architectural feature being a central slit vent. A trial trench could not locate the byre doorway but running under the wall where this would be expected was a drain. The walls are of massive rubble with the south-east gable wall being 5¼ft thick and the north-west end wall being 6½ft thick.

Weetslade Tower. F
At Weetslade there was a tower but it has now vanished and its site is unknown. Mentioned in the list of 1415, it was said to have been next to the sea, but the same is said of Horton, near Blyth.

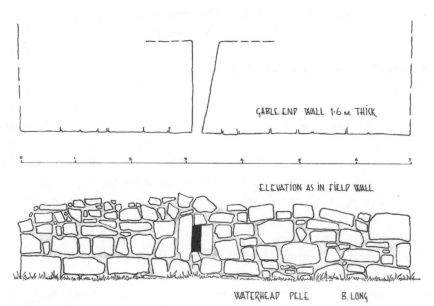

GABLE END WALL 1·6 M. THICK

ELEVATION AS IN FIELD WALL

WATERHEAD PELE   B. LONG

Waterhead Pele.

Weetwood Tower. D
Northumberland County History XIV–250.

There was a little tower 'in measurable good reparation' in 1541. It was again mentioned in 1587 and is now part of Weetwood Hall.

Welton Tower. H
Northumberland County History XII–210. Pevsner. AA 3–VIII–18.

The tower is early fifteenth century, made of Roman stones and ruined above the first floor. The dimensions are 24ft E–W × 20ft N–S, and the walls are 5ft thick. The original entrance on the east was very low and narrow and a stair ran north from it in the thickness of the wall. The basement is vaulted with two windows, of which one is now blocked up. The date on the door is 1614, but there are traces of an older thirteenth-century unfortified mansion behind the present remains and some fifteenth-century work in the north wall. Legend has it that Long Will of Welton Hall slept in the rafters of the kitchen and that his head touched one wall and his feet the one opposite, but to do that he would have had to be anything from 18ft to 25ft tall. So much for legend. It looks as if the tower was part of a much larger house of some considerable comfort.

West Ealingham. Bellingham. E.47
Pevsner.

The farm of West Ealingham is 2 miles south of Bellingham and some 300yd east and west are the remains of two peles. They both stand, in part, up to their eaves and both retain their ground-floor doorways in a gable end wall.

Wester Old Town. Allendale. G.47
Pevsner.

Near the confluence of the rivers East and West Allen are a group of pele-like houses in the hamlet of Old Town. A little south of these is Wester Old Town and another pele-like house with, as is common, the basement doorway in a gable wall that is 3ft 6in thick but all the other walls are only 2ft thick: too thin for defence or any great protection. At first glance these houses are peles but closer examination reveals them to be what are now known as bastle/pele derivatives.

West Lilburn, Two Towers. D
Northumberland County History XIV–433. Pevsner.

A tower held by John Carr is mentioned in 1415 and there are two towers in the list of 1514 capable of holding garrisons of forty. Two towers were again mentioned in 1524 in the letters and papers of Henry VIII.

By 1541 the western tower was in ruins as the roofs and floors had fallen in and only the walls were standing, while the east tower had lately been burnt. The repair of the towers was strongly advised, but only one tower remains and the position of the other is unknown. Early in the eighteenth century, a manor house was built and the castle or tower was abandoned and used as a quarry. It was 40ft from E–W and 33ft N–S, with walls 6ft thick, but there is no trace of a barmkin. Fragments of the north wall are standing and the springing of a ground-floor vault can be traced on the inside.

West Thornton Tower. F
Hodgson 2-I-311.

The farm of West Thornton stands on a high ridge. Formerly it had a chapel and a manor house within a barmkin and many hewn stones in the present buildings must have come from these. A field to the east had a strong wall around it in former times.

West Wharmley. Hexham. G.48

The impressive house and group of farm buildings stand on a small hill 3½ miles west of Hexham. This group has a wing to the east that may have been a pele, having a blocked pele-type doorway in a thick rubble wall.

West Whelpington. Kirkwhelpington. E.27
Hodgson 2-I-197. Tomlinson 237.

The village stood on an elevated plain, sloping gently to the east and defended on the other sides, more so on the south, by whinstone cliff.

Consisting of two rows of houses enclosing a large green in the centre, the houses measured about 23½ft × 21½ft inside, with a barmkin in front. Next to these was a small circle, probably the cockpit. The name of the house occurs in the parish register up to 1715, then it fell into ruins and nothing else is known of it.

Whalton Hall House. Whelton. F
Tomlinson 267. Pevsner.

There are scant remains of a pele incorporated in the present rectory and these were once 'the mansion of the vicarage'. More recent research informs us of a small tower with a basement containing two vaults and a mural stair. Attached to this are the remains of a 'hall', suggesting the tower was the solar of a hall house.

Whitefield Fortalice. G.18
Pevsner.

There is very little old stonework left at the back of the hall to mark the site of the fortalice of Whitefield.

Whitelees Pele. Elsdon (Harwood Forest). E.17
Pevsner. Ryder. Grundy.

The remains of this pele have been made into a barn or byre, and it stands about 2 miles to the east of Elsdon on the track to Eastnook. This is a strange building, being more of a defensible farmhouse than a pele or bastle and having living accommodation on the ground floor. The walls are of the usual thickness and the basement door is typical but there is a window with an iron grille in the south wall. The basement door is in the east gable but there is no trace of an external first-floor entrance. Compare this with similar houses at Smalesmouth and Stokoe Crags, both in Greystead parish in the North Tyne.

Whiteley Shield. G.49
Ramm et al. Pevsner.

On the outskirts of the hamlet of Carrshield, Whiteley Shield farmstead has, to the north of the house, the ruins of a pele 22ft × 32ft with now low walls 3ft thick. Against the east wall of this is another pele-like house standing to full height, having walls 2ft 10in to 3ft 4in thick. The basement door is in the east gable and the first-floor entrance is in the south front. The basement doorhead is cut from one massive stone and is triangular. The attic floor looks as if it were a later development.

Whitley Chapel. Hexham. G.50
Pevsner.

Four miles south of Hexham is the hamlet of Whitley Chapel, which has a number of houses of interest to us:

1. Holme House to the south is a well-preserved pele with the entrance to both floors in the long south wall. These have square heads to them.

2. Hesleywell is 3 miles south, and attached to the farm buildings is a pele with the basement door, and presumably the first-floor entrance, in the long south wall.

3. White Hall Farmhouse was remodelled in 1775, or so the date on a lintel says, but with mullioned windows, was it a pele?

4. Low Ardley Farmhouse incorporates an interesting square building with 6ft-thick walls, looking like the remains of a small tower.

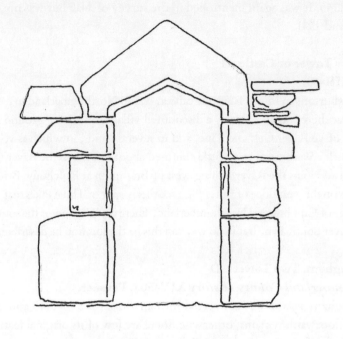

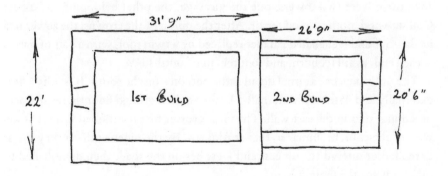

Whiteley Shield.

Whitley Tower. F.55
Northumberland County History XIII-395.

The site of this tower is not known, but licence to crenellate it was granted on 9 April 1345. It was again mentioned in the survey of 1415 but was not in those of 1538 and 1541.

Whitlow Tower or Castle. G
AA 3-XIII-10.

John Warburton, an Inland Revenue officer, was in Northumberland in *c.* 1715 and noted that there was at 'Whitely a discounted village, on arising ground near yee meeting of ye River Gelt and Tine, and in several hands, in which is ye ruins of an old castle'. Warburton was a little confused about this site as the River Gelt is in Cumbria and joins the River Irthing west of Brampton at Rulehome Bridge. The river rises on the west slope of Butt Hill, a southerly spur of Three Pikes that straddles the border of Cumbria and Northumberland. There is a Whitlow at the southern tip of the River South Tyne but in no way can this be the location he describes.

Whittingham, Two Towers. D
Northumberland County History XIV-503. Pevsner.

Whittingham Tower was converted into an almshouse in 1845 and only the ground-floor vault remains; otherwise, there are few of its original features left. It is doubtful if it existed before 1317, but in 1415 it belonged to William Herron. One hundred years later, it was suitable for a garrison of forty horsemen and in 1541 there were two towers, one the vicarage, the other belonging to Robert Collingwood, both in good repair. After the union of the crowns, the tower had its flat roof and crenellated parapet replaced by a twin roof, with a pair of gables at each end, as at Hebburn, and so it remained until 1845.

The only ancient external detail is the entrance on the south. It is 42ft × 46ft externally and 25ft × 19ft internally. In the vaulted ground floor there are traces of a mural stair in the east wall. The vicar's tower first mentioned in 1541 stood west of the church, similar to that at Alnham. By the nineteenth century it was extended or altered to run east and west beside the road, then demolished to make way for the present house.

Whitton Tower and Barmkin. Rothbury. D.59
AA 2-XIV-293, 2-XIII-13. Dixon 456. Pevsner. *Northumberland County History* XV-315.

Now part of a children's home, this was the residence of the Vicar of Rothbury and was vaulted in two, if not three, storeys. Of the fourteenth century, externally it is 46ft N–S and 33ft E–W. The doorway at the west of the north wall is pointed and made out of two stones. In the basement, with its 9ft walls, is a well of 3ft diameter and 15ft deep, and from the south-east corner of the first floor a spiral stair leads up to the roof.

The tower had a barmkin with a kitchen range and extensive outbuildings and was sunk into the hillside, so as to make it 60ft high on the north side and only 42ft on the south, where the ground rises. In the garden of Whitton Grange are the scant remains of a tower standing 9ft high in places. Traces of the basement vault can still be seen.

Widdrington Castle or Tower. F
Hodgson 2-II-211.

This castle has now vanished and it is said that its stone was made into workmen's homes. Licence to crenellate was granted in 1341 and Hodgson says that this was probably for a tower to the left of the entrance, he having seen some old prints. This tower had corbelled-out battlements and had round projecting turrets at each corner. In the old surveys it changed status from that of a tower to a castle. James I of England, VI of Scotland, stayed at Widdrington on his way to London to be crowned. The castle, or tower, was then held by Sir Robert Cary, who gave the news of the death of Elizabeth to James. Sir Robert also told the king of the death of his mother, Mary, Queen of Scots. In 1899 Tomlinson presented a paper on the French raid of 1691 by Jean Bart, who sacked the castle.

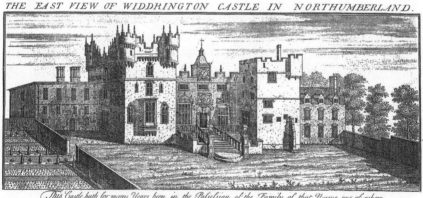

The east view of Widdrington Castle in 1728. Nothing remains of this house today.

Willimontswick Castle. G.12
Pevsner.

Now only two very narrow rectangular towers flanking and rising above the modern house remain. More contemporary masonry survives above the modern house, the top storey of which is projected out on three roll mouldings. The passage is tunnel vaulted and looks to be late fourteenth century.

Witton Castle or Tower. F.58
Hodgson 2–I–310.

John Hodgson mentions a castle built by Roger de Thornton the First. A tablet with the date 1483, he tells us, marked additions or repairs and stood just south of the gardens of the present house built by Robert Trollop. The tablet is incorporated in the present house.

Witton Shield Tower. F
Hodgson 2–I–321.

A mile and a quarter from Netherwitton in the farmstead of Witton Shield stands the remains of a late tower. This tower is three storeys high and was built in 1608. There used to be a Roman Catholic chapel in one of the upper rooms. It is similar to Stanton Old Hall and Doddington in having the entrance at the bottom of a projecting turret in the centre of the south wall. The top floor and chapel were removed in 1914. In the garden wall are what may be remains of an earlier house.

Woodhouse. Tarset. E.88
Ryder.

On the west bank of the Tarset Burn, south-west of Black Middings is a site marked by the Ordance Survey as a 'pele'. There is a rectangular plateau some 50ft above the stream. In the centre is a well-defined mound with a central hollow. Is this, as the OS suggests, a pele, or is it the site of an early timber pele?

Woodhouses Pele. Harbottle. C.20
Northumberland County History XV–490. **Pevsner. Bates. Dixon. Ryder.**
Sometimes claimed to be the unfinished 'strong pele' of Harecleugh, it was not completed until 1602. As usually happened in the district, a long narrow, one-storeyed thatched cottage was built at one end of the house in the eighteenth century. Both were 'in ruin' in 1866, but were restored in 1904. In plan it is the usual Tudor strong house, being well built. Measuring 30ft × 17ft, it is gabled and not embattled, but has a vaulted ground floor.

What is interesting is the use of galletting to the roughly coursed masonry; the usual gable end entrance to the vaulted basement and an internal stone stair in the south-east corner. An engraving in Dixon's *Upper Coquetdale* shows an external stair and a first-floor doorway. After much rebuilding in 1904, how much is original and how much is Edwardian Romanticism? From the outset this house had an attic floor, one of several features that lift it out of the run-of-the-mill peles and leave us with a building that looks most dramatic standing tall on the side of the hill.

Wooler Tower and Castle. C.5
Northumberland County History XI-329. Pevsner.
The remains are on the mound of a Norman motte-and-bailey castle and are of the late fifteenth century. Of the castle, all fortifications had disappeared as early as 1255, when Wooler was recorded as having 'a waste motte of no value'. Mentioned in a List of Holds in 1509, it is stated that Wooler would house twenty horsemen, and in 1522 it was proposed to place ten men in wages with Hector Gray in the tower.

In 1526 a 'new castel at Wooler' is mentioned and in 1541 it is 'a lytle towre standynge strongly whiche did much releyve' the inhabitants of Wooler and two or three other villages. It was then in need of repair. By 1580 it was in need of greater repairs and in 1584 in an even worse state, when it formed a link in the chain of forts on Dacre's Plat.

Only the rubble remains of it on the mound of the Norman castle can be seen today. Originally it was the castle of the Muschamps and later that of Isabel Ford (1255).

Wooley. Allendale. G.51
Pevsner.
Here is a group of buildings ranged round a triangular yard clearly intended for security or defence. A farmhouse to the east seems to have been a 'long house' of the sixteenth to seventeenth century, while on the north is a range including a pele-like structure. To the west is a small, square tower-like structure.

Wylam Tower or Sporting House. H
Pevsner. *Northumberland County History* VIII-101, XII-223.
A tower by the name of Monks House or Sporting House, because monks went there to disport themselves, was destroyed by the Scots in the early fourteenth century. The ruins were rebuilt in 1405 and the remains, a vault 60ft × 19ft, are incorporated in the present hall.

Yarrow (Shilling Pot) Pele. E.30
OS Map.
Nothing now remains of this pele, but it is known to have stood just north of the road beside the hamlet of Yarrow. See Shilling Pot.

Yeavering Tower. A
The tower of Yeavering was without a doubt a late sixteenth-century structure as it was not mentioned in the lists of 1415 or 1541, but it is shown on Dacre's Plat of 1584. The site of this tower is uncertain.

Appendix I

List of Maps

Appendix II

List of Illustrations

Bibliography

General Histories

Dixon, D.D., *Upper Coquetdale*, 1903
Headlam, C.M., *The Three Northern Counties of England*, 1939.
Her Majesty's Stationery Office, *Handbooks to Ancient Monuments*
Hodgson, J., *History of Northumberland*, 7 vols, 1820–58.
Mackenzie, E., *View of Northumberland*, 2 vols, 1825.
Northumberland County History, 15 vols, 1893–1939.
Parker, J.H., *Some Accounts of Domestic Architecture in England*, 1853.
Rayne, J., *History and Antiquities of North Durham*, 1852.
Scott, J., *Berwick upon Tweed: The History of the Town and Guild*, 1888.
Tate, G., *History of Alnwick*, 2 vols, 1866–69.
Tomlinson, W., *Comprehensive Guide to the County of Northumberland*, 1888.
Wallis, J., *History of Northumberland*, 2 vols, 1769.

More Precise References

Archaeologia Aeliana (AA), Publication of the Society of Antiquaries of Newcastle
upon Tyne (5 series, 1822–2022).
Armitage, E.S., *Early Norman Castles of the British Isles*.
Bates, C., *Border Holds of Northumberland*, 1891.
Brown, P., *The Friday Book of North Country Sketches*, 1934.
Brown, P., *The Second Friday Book of North Country Sketches*, 1935.
Graham, F., *The Castles of Northumberland*, 1967.
Grundy, J., *Historic Buildings of the Northumberland National Park*, 1987.
Lawrie, A.C. *Early Scottish Charters, Prior to AD 1153*, 1905
Ordnance Survey (OS) 25"-to-the-mile maps, 1841–1952. (This means the only
reference can be found on the relevant OS map.)

Pevsner, N., *Northumberland – The Buildings of England*, 2001.
Ramm, H.G., McDowall, R.W., Mercer, E., *Shielings and Bastles*, 1970.
Ryder, F., *Bastles and Towers in the Northumberland National Park*, 1990.
Sitwell, W., *The Border from a Soldier's Point of View*, 1927.

Note: Ryder's *Bastles and Towers in the Northumberland National Park* is drawn from his much larger survey covering the whole county and his contribution to the subject is to a large extent hidden under the reference 'Pevsner' in the gazetteer due to his participation in the revision of that work.

English Heritage Publications

Ashbee, J., Oswald, A., *Dunstanburgh Castle Guidebook*, English Heritage, 2007.
Cambridge, E., *Lindisfarne Priory and Holy Island Guidebook*, English Heritage, 2002.
Crow, J., *Housesteads Roman Fort Guidebook*, English Heritage, 2012.
Goodall, J., *Warkworth Castle and Hermitage Guidebook*, English Heritage, 2006.
McCombie, G., *Tynemouth Priory and Castle Guidebook*, English Heritage, 2013
Nelson, I.S., *Etal Castle Guidebook*, English Heritage, 2015.
Pattison, P., *Berwick Barracks and Fortifications Guidebook*, English Heritage, 2019.
Saunders, A., Dunn, P., *Norham Castle Guidebook*, English Heritage, 1998.
Summerson, H., *Aydon Castle Guidebook*, English Heritage, 2016.
White, R., *Belsay Hall, Castle and Gardens Guidebook*, English Heritage, 2016.
West, S., *Prudhoe Castle Guidebook*, English Heritage, 2014.

Independent Publications

Hexham Moot Hall and Prison, guidebook.
Shrimpton, C., *Alnwick Castle: Great Houses of Britain*, Heritage House Group, 2004.
Watson-Armstrong, C., Waters, L., *Bamburgh Castle, Souvenir Guidebook*, 2021.

Other informative publications are produced by churches, WEA study groups and local history societies.

Figure 14: Map showing the areas covered by the general histories of the county of Northumberland.

Acknowledgements

It is with gratitude that I acknowledge the valuable assistance of the authors, past and present, of the aforementioned works and the following for allowing use of material in their care or possession. While every effort has been made to obtain permission from the copyright holders for all materials used in this book, the publishers would be pleased to hear from anyone who has not been appropriately acknowledged and to make the correction in any further reprint:

Warner Group Publications, for the drawing of a fisherman's cottage and photographs of Gatehouse Pele/Bastle.

The Guild of Master Craftsmen publications for drawings, plans and elevations of Low Hirst, Hole Head Pele or Bastle, and the photo of the entrance to a house in Jersey.

Northumberland County Record Office for the plan and elevation of Twizell Castle, the plan and elevations of Ford Castle, the photographs from the Blankenburgs Collection of Hawkhope Pele or Bastle and Hebburn Bastle, and the photograph of Melkridge Pele or Bastle by Gibson of Hexham.

Mr George Taylor for access to Elsdon Tower, 1967.

Mr Swinburn Brown for access to Capheaton Hall, 1974.

The Public Records Office for the photograph of an old drawing of Haughton Castle, Christopher Dacre's Plat of 1584, and the survey of Melkridge Pele/Bastle, 1954.

Strutt and Parker, estate agents, for the elevation of Coupland Castle.

Northumberland Estates Office for permission to use the drawing of Shell Keep, Alnwick.

Photopro Co. Ltd, Whitley Bay, for the postcard of the Blackbird Inn, Ponteland.

Airviews Ltd, Manchester Airport, for the photo of Peel Castle, Isle of Man.

English Heritage and the Gillian Dickson Charitable Trust for support in the use of the photo of the murals depicted in Belsay Castle.

Index to Introductory Chapters

FINIS.

WI° I: I ·1602
TAM

WOODHOUSES